MW00577910

Hardship Duty

*Women's Experiences with Sexual
Harassment, Sexual Assault, and
Discrimination in the U.S. Military*

STEPHANIE BONNES

OXFORD
UNIVERSITY PRESS

Oxford University Press is a department of the University of Oxford. It furthers
the University's objective of excellence in research, scholarship, and education
by publishing worldwide. Oxford is a registered trade mark of Oxford University
Press in the UK and certain other countries.

Published in the United States of America by Oxford University Press
198 Madison Avenue, New York, NY 10016, United States of America.

CIP data is on file at the Library of Congress

ISBN 978-0-19-763624-4

DOI: 10.1093/oso/9780197636244.001.0001

Printed by Integrated Books International, United States of America

I dedicate this book to U.S. servicewomen.

To past and current U.S. servicewomen: May you read the words here and feel as though I told your story.

To future U.S. servicewomen: If you read this book, I hope you do not recognize the organization described in these pages.

To Chargy: For three decades I've benefited and enjoyed being witness to the light that you shine so brightly. Our friendship has deeply shaped who I am and who I hope to be. This book is for you.

CONTENTS

ACKNOWLEDGMENTS

In the middle of writing the first full draft of this book, I had a miscarriage. I was disappointed as I saw a future that I had hoped for vanish. I was still grieving and processing when two months later, shortly after my daughter's second birthday, we were in quarantine due to COVID-19. I remember the stress of those early days: How can I make sure my family stays physically safe? How can I ensure we have enough supplies while also minimizing potential exposure? How can I maintain social connections with friends and family? How will I balance childcare, work, and maintaining a household? Then my university cut salaries and benefits. The university administration hosted a weekly call where we were told to find other jobs. I was mourning the loss of my pregnancy and then, suddenly, the future of my career was also in flux. I thought to myself, what is the point? When I started to feel hopeless about all of these fears and questions about the future, I asked myself why I pursued research in the first place. That is the moment where I refocused all of my work time toward re-reading the transcripts from the interviews I conducted for this project. I prioritized spending time listening to the interviews as well. I knew that I had to tell these stories. Thank you to the servicewomen who trusted me with their experiences and shared hours of their time with me. Your courage pushed me out of my own fears, stressors, and anxieties and got me back to work revising this manuscript. I learned so much from you all and have respect for your strength, honesty, emotions, and experiences. Without the women who trusted me with their stories, there would be no book, and I am deeply thankful for their participation. A special thank you to my three Marines who helped me understand and connect with this project in unique ways.

I am forever indebted to Chargy, who is my life-long best friend. Thank you for letting me not only get a glimpse into a chapter of your life, but also to become an expert on it, to drag you into conversations about things that happened long ago as if they only occurred yesterday. I have no idea what it is like to have a friend who studies you, but from my end it is truly an incredible experience. I have a rare glimpse into one period of your life, and now this is a large part of our friendship. You are strong, intelligent, and adaptive, and these things have carried you far. You are also loyal, adventurous, funny, supportive, and caring, and these things have carried me far. I have relied on you in many ways throughout the last three decades. You are a supporter of women and try to make each community you are a part of better and more equitable. I thank you for all you did for your Marines while serving and for what you did for servicewomen who came after you to ensure equality when it came to combat careers. Of course, this project would not exist without you, but more importantly I wouldn't be who I am without you. As my constant companion through childhood, adolescence, young adulthood, and now motherhood, our lives are interwoven and connected in so many ways and through almost every single life phase. I hope the same for our girls as we teach them the importance of carrying the banner. I love you. I am honored and humbled you wanted to be my neighbor, and I thank you for always choosing our friendship.

Jeff, I thank you for your friendship, patience, and support. You know far more about the issues in these pages than I do, and I appreciate you being my guide and waiting for me to catch up. You have done so much to help, advocate for, and represent victims of sexual violence in the military and beyond. Thank you for offering your insights to me, inviting me to your work, traveling with me, and making me laugh. I think many of the times I have laughed the hardest was with you and members of Pizarro (+). It was so amazing to write a paper with you, and I can honestly say even though we've come a long way from getting twentieth place in Science Olympiad, I'm still down to identify, and watch out for, birds with you any time.

Thank you to BEF for promoting my work and scholarship and for helping me so much in the early days of this project. It has been amazing to gain a deep understanding for all you experienced in the military and I am so proud of you. Thank you for all the years of support and friendship as well and for always treating me like a little sister.

There would not be a book without Claire Renzetti. She had the vision that my research should be a book before I even finished my dissertation. It meant the world to me to be a young academic presenting at a conference and having a scholar like Claire approach me about writing a book. She gave me the confidence to try it and the pathway and opportunity to actually do it, and I am grateful for her mentorship and support.

I thank Dana Bliss for guidance throughout this process. Thank you to Mary Funchion for assistance with submission and for always answering my questions. I also thank the anonymous reviewers of this manuscript for their suggestions and questions that improved this book. Some of the arguments I have made in this book are drawn from articles I wrote that appear in *American Sociological Review*, *Gender & Society*, and *Violence Against Women*. I thank the editors and reviewers at these journals for suggestions that improved those pieces. A special thank you to Rachel Harris for volunteering her talents and time to design my book cover. I cried when I saw the options she made for me and am so happy with the cover!

I learned so much from my academic mentors and friends. I thank Janet Jacobs for her words of wisdom, her insights into nuance, and her friendship that kept me grounded in graduate school. I thank Joanne Belknap for teaching me how to research sexual violence in ways that center those who share their stories. She mentored, encouraged, and supported me in all aspects of my life, from comments on drafts of my work, including the book proposal, to knitting sweaters for my daughters. I thank Adriana Núñez for her love, support, and intellectual engagement in graduate school. Thank you to Beth Whalley, who knows just how to respond when I reach out to discuss sexual violence, trauma, academia, or reality TV. Thank you to Jennifer Pace, who is a kind friend and a great co-PI, and amazing at data analysis. I appreciate Jen taking on the admin of our grants while I worked on this book and for all her support along the way. Thank you to Sanyu Mojola for expanding my thinking on femininity and masculinity and for offering feedback on my work. Sending a draft to Sanyu always makes me nervous, but she responds with careful attention and comments that make me excited to do the work that will make the piece indisputably better. Thank you to Mike Messner for being in touch with me about issues related to gender and the military and for encouraging my work in this area.

A large portion of this book was reorganized and rewritten at La Carreta in San Juan, Puerto Rico, with my friend and graduate school companion, Andrew. I benefit from all your insights into gender and masculinity and your ability to be honest and vulnerable. I have relied on your kindness and friendship for the last ten years and I await to hear "what level friends we are" after you read this.

I am one of the luckiest people to have been nurtured by and able to learn from an accomplished group of people that I happened to meet at the age of fourteen. While group text messages and less frequent in-person visits have replaced the daily interactions of School Road, my Friends from Friends have continued to push me to think, reflect, center, and learn throughout the process of writing this book.

Abby: You've been my emotional, intellectual, and social co-analyst in life. I think it is rare to turn to the same person for questions about serious issues, career challenges, hot takes on reality television shows, parenting advice, or to debrief inside jokes from high school. It is so easy to pick up the phone, call you, and feel immediately better and validated. I think this comfort stems from all the time we spent together in the early years of our friendship. I thank you, Caroline, and John for opening your home, advice, and love to me in high school. Additionally, your excitement and support for me as I became a mother was so beautiful and appreciated. I think back fondly on my last days of pregnancy with Eloise because you were there with me. Your friendship has filled me with happiness and emotional support in ways that allowed me to focus on this book, even when it was hard. You just get me, and I love you.

Erin and Meredith: I get emotional when I think about our friendship. To have grown up with you and then to become a parent alongside of you has been a joy in my life I am constantly thankful for. You held me up as I completed my dissertation, moved across the country, and had a baby in the same year. Knowing that one of you was up all hours of the night when I was (either nursing or writing) made me feel less alone. You validate me in my career and remind me that the book is important while at the same time encouraging me as a parent and loving me as a friend. When you two surprised me in the summer of 2021 to complete our trio of surprises, I knew we were about to start the cycle all over again. I look forward to seeing how it plays out and for all of the trips with Emmy in between. Thank you to Judy and Jim for hosting me so many nights in my adolescence and young adulthood and all of their kindness along the way. Chi and Merry, I truly thank you for loving and supporting me for twenty years.

David: you always provide the healthy dose of skepticism I need to see nuance in an argument. Your sarcasm and dark humor in times of melancholy were predictably uplifting as I wrote this book during a pandemic and amid great political and social stress in our country. Thanks also for your careful reading of my first rough draft of this book. Your notes were what propelled me to submit the first complete draft. And you get major friend points for being the only one who has read a draft of this book in its entirety (so far . . . I hope). Also, every major piece of writing I have done since my high school senior thesis has had a soundtrack, and the music that accompanied me on the book journey was Pop 32. I thank you for creating it. You never know what you can accomplish with a pop mix by your side, so please keep them coming. I also appreciate Jana and Farogh for their support over the years and for loving me like a daughter.

Shawn and Matt: Thanks for engaging me in critical thought about issues in our country and providing lightness and levity in the form of ceiling fan chats and Catan. Please read *this* book even if you never get to the others I have asked you to read.

A special thanks to Ryan, Karyn, and Sloanie. The three of you helped us not only survive quarantine but to thrive in it. The friendship we created in the midst of childcare and shutdown chaos has enriched my life. Together we navigated boundaries, obtained supplies, acted as caregivers to each other's children, and socialized as a unit for five months. You three are a big part of how I was able to have the mental space to write a first draft of this book in 2020. So glad we passed down the friendship to the newest little girls in the squad. I look forward to our continued trips to Maine, Florida, and maybe even the long-awaited camping trip.

I thank Eric Carmichael for the intellectual insights he shares with me. His ability to unpack social and political issues through multiple lenses forces me to reflect, see, and analyze in nuanced ways. Eric, we may live in the dark place, but you are a source of lightness in this world.

Thank you to all of the wonderful women who helped take care of my children while I worked on this book. Thank you to Lindsay Smith, Deirdre Morris, Amanda Wigham, Samantha Hathaway, and Erin Boyle for nurturing and encouraging Eloise in preschool. I appreciate Jillian Haversat, Jamie-Lee Maenza, Megan Cordeau, Sarah Anderson, and Kelsey Welch for loving and snuggling Sylvia. A special thanks to Leidy Baquero, who spent much of Sylvia's babyhood with her and with us learning what made her happy and how to soothe her to sleep. Knowing that my children were well taken care of and loved by you all provided me with the mental space and physical energy I needed to complete this project.

I thank my friends whose company strengthens me. Any time spent with Anna, Eric, Muffin, Matt, Mo, Joe, Phil, Jackie, Kyle, Vincent, Beth, Kate, and Gomey are filled with laughter and love that refuels me to write. Memories of TLOMAH, Muffinfests, Saco, Lion's Rock, Sun Lion Villa, and nights at the Rat make me smile. I also thank Brian and Samantha for enriching our lives by being our friends and neighbors.

I love my family and thank Aunt Clare, Aunt Debbie, Uncle Bill, as well as cousins Angie, Tine, Kayley, Sean, Patty, and Pat. Thanks for all the memories from time spent in Pennsylvania, New Jersey, Brigantine, the Keys, Europe, Boulder, and Connecticut. Tine, I thank you for being there during every life phase, jumping off the dock with me, scratching my back, and supporting me during my journey as a mother. I admire how you keep family close. Sean, I admire your loyalty and thank you for making me laugh, hugging me tightly, and always joining me on the first bus. A special thank you to Angie who visited me right after my miscarriage and after a major academic rejection that hurt. Angie, you have the energy and spirit that lifts others up and I thank you for using it on me in these moments. I thank Hope and Tyrone for loving us and for having "grandparent vacations" and camping trips with the girls. Thanks to my siblings-in-law Elizabeth, Heather, and Matt for their support over the years.

Thank you to my Mom, Donna Sweeney, for giving birth to me and sacrificing so much of her young life to raise me. Thank you for encouraging me to love reading by doing silly voices and playing library with me as a kid. Thank you for loving Eloise and Sylvia and for making sure they get special experiences with you, Nana, and Joey in Sea Isle. I thank my siblings, Adrianna, Joey, and Sarah, who are in the midst of navigating young adulthood and bear the weight of solving the issues in the next generation. I love you and good luck.

Thanks to my Dad, Pete Bonnes, who was the first person to encourage me to be a critical thinker, challenge assumptions, and consider perspective. Since that moment when I told you I could run faster than a plane and you said, "Can you run faster than a car?" you have been encouraging me to understand different viewpoints. In high school, you would not allow me to simply do the pool table angle geometry problems I had for homework without also encouraging me to consider friction to "get the real answer." Through you I saw that problems were not so simple to solve, but that they could be worked out. I also learned that sometimes the questions being asked can be problematic or limiting. This encouraged me to ask questions about questions, and ultimately to ask my own questions and design research projects to answer them. Thank you also for growing with me and nurturing my non-academic interests and hobbies. You taught me to love fishing and I like to think I pushed you to enjoy travel, and together with Marina, Sarah, and Drew we have combined these two things. I love the adventures we have been on as a family, including cleaver cab, tea in London, determining we *could* both eat and fish in Panama, not getting passed in Belize, and now beach days with the girls. Thank you to my stepmom, Marina, for supporting me, for encouraging me, and for knowing exactly what I need, whether it is Wawa coffee, a new chair, a venting session, or a good laugh. I always look forward to our chats around the island. I cannot thank Dad and Marina enough for all they do for our girls, and especially for that one time they watched them during daylight savings while Drew and I went on vacation (sorry!!).

To Andrew Stinson. My partner, intellectual companion, emotional support system, best friend, officemate, and editor. You are worlds more eloquent than I am, and I wish I could convey how thankful I am for how you have improved this manuscript. You carefully read my chapters, word by word, to push me on the claims I was making, and even on the phrases I was using. You checked the tone, the content, and the substantive arguments. You were invested in the book, and you are a huge part of this even happening. You have an unmatched upbeat attitude and optimism amidst times of great stress. This serves as an important reminder that the feeling that we can't do anything to help is a tool of domination. I was able to use your optimism to breathe new life into these pages. I am sorry if I over-rely on you for this and I promise to let you engage in cynicism from time to time in the future. You have co-created with me a life that I did not know was possible. A life where I love being in our home together. Where I get teary-eyed watching you carry the girls down the stairs, one in each arm, as they laugh and shout silly things at you because I know those moments are fleeting. But I do not worry since I know such moments will be replaced by new little traditions because you create magic out of daily life and the seemingly mundane. A life where we know loss, grief, and pain are inevitable, but you know how to nurture and center me in ways that let me mourn and grow at the same time, like back in that bathroom in Sint Maarten. A life where I also love our trips and know that we will have an adventure whether it is seeing Victoria Falls, Twin Coves, or a coelacanth. A life where you will still play me in Civilization even if I win five times in a row. A life that you keep musical. A life where after seventeen years together I still stare into your eyes and ask, "How am I this lucky?" Andrew Stinson, without you there would be no us. Without us there would be no book, just a woman who had heard too many frustrating, sad, and traumatic stories to make sense out of. You give me the space to grieve, love, and flourish, which allows me to write and more importantly to live the life I want to live.

Eloise, you like to say "we made each other" and you are 100% correct. I grew you for months and you made me a mom and in doing so you taught me so much about myself. Being your mother is one of the most amazing, thrilling, and memorable endeavors of my life. You have a gentle curiosity about the world, an amazing memory, a sense of adventure, and a caring spirit that you work on and cultivate in your friendships and with your sister. I thank you for being interested in the fact that I am writing a book and asking about it often and for being my constant companion throughout this whole process. Watching you learn and grow has reminded me how much I love learning and how important it is to share knowledge.

Sylvia, my Sylvie Sue, you were born two months before I received a contract from OUP to write this book. I can honestly say I spent my time wisely by prioritizing you in your newbornhood and babyhood. I spent mornings snuggling you while you slept, nursing you, and listening to all of your little grunts and sounds. You cried a lot in the beginning and close cuddles were the only thing that calmed you. Even now, at two, you love to snuggle, and I am glad I held you close all those months. I needed that intimacy with you before I was prepared to take on the intensive focus required to write the final version of this book. You have a true excitement for the world and approach new activities with an eager energy and intensity that I try to match each day.

Eloise and Sylvia, I want the world to be a better place for you two and I thank you for reminding me of my role in this task. I love you so much.

Introduction

I still remember the empathy and confusion I felt after speaking with Kay, a young woman so full of hopeful energy that she joined the Navy two days before graduating college. I recall struggling to reconcile the strength and optimism that she described upon entering the military with her weary and disgusted departure only three years later. Our conversation was fast-paced, she was confident and candid in her responses, and I could tell there was a lot she wanted to share with me. But her upbeat attitude and occasional laughter did not mask the severity and litany of harassment experiences that she revealed from her short time in the military. I remember wondering, "What is going on that someone so eager to serve and willing to challenge themselves mentally and physically ends up leaving the service and burning her uniform, never looking back?" In her own words:

> I was running around base. And one of the guys I know from my command pulled up next to me in his car. I didn't know him really well, but he was always nice, kinda quiet . . . He said, "You need a ride?" I was like, "Yeah." So, he gave me a ride and we ended up not going to my barracks. I was like, "Where are we going?" He took me to this pier over on the other side of base. And he attacked me in his car. Turned his car off and he just attacked me. It was nighttime. It was dark. And he attacked me. . . . He tried to rape me. I ended up running out the car and just getting away from him and catching the

little shuttle and going back to my barracks and crying. I remember I was like, "Forget this." I had this number from my therapist, and I said, "I'm very depressed. I want to hurt myself." They took me to a mental hospital, and I was there for like a week with crazy people— like, crazy people who were detoxing from drugs . . . When I got out, they put me back into my regular command. Nobody knew what happened, supposedly. I reported what happened when I got back to my command . . . And he [her attacker] actually came to the window [where she worked] one day and he just like stood there. And he said, "How are you doing?" And I . . . just wanted to burn his face off . . . Come to find out, I reported it, they investigated it, and it was his word against mine and of course because I was technically "crazy," they didn't believe me . . . Then when I went to get out of the Navy, I got this code that said I have a personality disorder. (Navy, enlisted, Black)

This is not what Kay envisioned when she joined the military. Shortly after her boyfriend broke up with her, Kay enlisted for a fresh start and to "get my life on track and kinda heal. For some reason, I thought putting myself through this really stringent, hard environment in boot camp would help me." She was so excited to start her military career that she did not consider going to Officer Candidate School (OCS) despite having a college degree. She feared OCS might slow down the process and push back her start date. She was eager, impatient even, to be in the Navy. However, this bright anticipation for the future that encouraged her to enlist contrasts starkly with her outlook upon leaving the Navy. Kay explained that at the end of her service, "I burned my uniform—like, when I got my separation papers, I burned my uniform. And I was like, 'Peace' . . . I, like, did not look back." What were the experiences that lead to this drastic change in how Kay viewed the military? Why was it so important for her to be rid of the physical representation of her membership? Kay's disdain for the organization can be traced through her experiences with pervasive sexual harassment, an intrusive sexual advance from a man who outranked her, an attempted sexual assault, and inadequate efforts from military leadership or the military bureaucracy to address or resolve these issues. Kay, like many women that I spoke with who were sexually assaulted while serving in the military, viewed the institution as complicit in her victimization.

When Kay got to her first duty station, she "was very happy and excited. I felt like I could really do my four years and do well. And travel and see the world." These feelings quickly receded: "When I got there, I was sexually harassed from the minute I walked through the office." After four months of inescapable sexual harassment, Kay had "completely let myself go physically to protect myself from the things people would say to me." This did not alleviate the harassment. When an older noncommissioned officer, a master chief close to retirement, tried to kiss her at work, she reported it to another noncommissioned officer. He told her that he would "take care of it." A few days later he approached Kay and said, " 'I think you have it wrong. I think you have it wrong. Just stay out of his way and he'll stay out of your way, and, you know, do your job . . . you're doing a great job.' That was the last I heard of it." Nothing happened. She was not asked to report it to anyone else. He was not formally reprimanded. A few months later, she had to attend the master chief's retirement ceremony, where "I had to sit there and watch him as he marched by me. And he smirked at me." This incident led Kay to lose trust in the man she reported to, a man she described as "a pretty decent guy." It also shows how servicemembers can use their own positions of responsibility or power to silence victims of sexual harassment, thereby allowing harassment to continue unchecked.

Kay's experiences of harassment from other servicemen continued daily. She endured comments about her body, men asking her for dates, and sexual comments about women in general. Yet, there was no response or intervention from military peers or leaders. In particular, the lack of action in response to her reporting the master chief took a toll on her mental health. She said, "I was a mess. I was a mess. I was so depressed." A short time later, a man assaulted her in a car, which is described above. Kay clearly was suffering from the experience of an attempted rape, and her vocalized suicide ideation and depression were reactions to the assault. The military's response to place her in an institution is standard procedure to prevent suicide when a servicemember says they are going to hurt themselves. However, her institutionalization in the aftermath of the attempted rape was used to question her creditability as a witness and to dismiss her sexual assault case rather than as evidence that she had experienced trauma. Furthermore, her institutionalization resulted in her receiving a mark on her record that she had a personality disorder. In the military, a personality disorder is considered a pre-existing condition, meaning that the military could sever some post-service benefits that Kay would have otherwise received, including medical and mental health support. This made Kay feel as though the Navy used her victimization against her. She left the military with the perspective that the organization protects harassers and abusers and silences, marginalizes, and even punishes victims.

When I first heard stories like Kay's, I found myself wondering: How did this happen? Kay served at a time when the military had sexual harassment education, sexual assault education and prevention strategies, multiple reporting streams, and victim-friendly policies to assist with processing and to encourage reporting. Did these programs and policies simply fail in this instance? Or was this a broader phenomenon?

As I listened and heard more stories of pervasive sexual harassment, of sexual assault victims being prevented from reporting or being informally and formally punished for reporting, I tried to reconcile this with the long list of victim-friendly policies and victim support resources the military advertised. I already knew that the frequency of sexual harassment and assault in the military was high, and estimates indicated that servicewomen experienced sexual violence from their supervisors and peers at higher rates than women in the civilian workforce. For example, Bostock and Daley (2007) found that the lifetime prevalence rate of rape among active-duty women in the Air Force was 28%, compared to a lifetime prevalence rate of 17.6% among a sample of the national population (Tjaden and Thoennes 2000). Antecol and Cobb-Clark (2001) found that 70.9% of active-duty women experienced some form of sexual harassment in the year they were surveyed. Similarly, in examining 558 servicewomen who served in the military during the Vietnam War through the early 2000s, Sadler et al. (2003) found that 79% had experienced sexual harassment,

54% had experienced unwanted sexual contact, and 30% had experienced one or more completed or attempted rapes. In 2021, the Department of Defense found the estimated prevalence of unwanted sexual contact almost doubled since 2016 (Department of Defense 2021a). Notably, the Department of Defense estimates that the rate of reporting actually decreased during this time, with an estimated one in five victims reporting in 2021 compared to an estimated one in three victims reporting in 2016 and 2018. This might be due, in part, to a decline in confidence in the military's ability to appropriately respond to sexual assault, which is at a ten-year low. In 2021, only 34% of women stated that they trust the military to protect their privacy if they are sexually assaulted compared to 64% of women in 2018 (Department of Defense 2021a).

Armed with this information, I started this project by questioning how sexual harassment and assault remain highly prevalent in an organization that has longstanding and evolving policies, prevention strategies, and education programs that address sexual violence, as well as victim services and legal assistance. I wanted to understand the processes and mechanisms that sustain sexual violence vulnerability, and what institutional and interpersonal factors might be contributing to harassment in the military. I also had broader questions. I wondered how organizational values and meanings around gender, masculinity, and femininity shape harassment and violence vulnerability as well as other workplace experiences.

Long before I started researching women in the military, I heard about military sexual harassment and assault in the news. The Navy Tailhook incident of 1991 spotlighted both the vulnerability of servicewomen to sexual assault from servicemen and the poor institutional response and failure of the Department of Defense's bureaucracy to address sexual violence. The Tailhook Association, an organization representing Navy and Marine Corps aviators, held conventions attended by aviators, servicemembers associated with aviation, admirals, and their aides. At the 1991 Las Vegas meeting, a woman asked about the potential for women to fly fighter jets during a panel and her question was met with laughter and jeering from the servicemen in the room. The admiral who answered the question did not reprimand this behavior. This example of servicemen dismissing women's equality in the military as a joke and a lack of response from leadership would be played out on a much larger scale as the convention progressed.

A flier advertising a party to be held during the convention read "A-6 Tailhookers All-Weather Attack. We Stay up Longer and Deliver Bigger Loads. Please join the intruders for an evening of imbibing, chicanery, and debauchery: Las Vegas Hilton Suite 307" (PBS.org 2019). This flier highlights how the Tailhook convention's notoriety for drinking, partying, and rowdy behavior (Department of Defense 1992) was steeped in masculinity and misogyny. The party culminated in what was known as "the gauntlet," where servicemen lined the halls of the third floor of the hotel to block access to doorways and then assaulted, groped, and ripped clothing from eighty-three women (both civilian and servicewomen) and seven men who walked by. One woman, Paula Coughlin, reported her assaults to her boss, Admiral John Snyder, who dismissed her experience by stating, "That's what you get when you go to a hotel party with a bunch of drunk aviators" (Lancaster 1992).

Some claimed that the Las Vegas convention meeting of Tailhook was a unique event because its participants, mostly Navy and Marine Corps pilots whose elite positions represent the military's values of heroism, dangerous work, and warrior status, were brought together shortly after the U.S.-led defeat of an Iraqi invasion in Kuwait (Caproni and Finley 1994). However, the institutional misogyny that permeated the organization was so apparent that even the initial Naval Investigative Services (NIS) report, which downplayed the assaults, could not provide cover for the events at Tailhook (Dean et al. 1997; Whitley and Page 2015). Among the failings of the Navy's initial investigation was excluding interviews with top Naval officers in attendance at the convention, including the Secretary of the Navy. Further, the commander of the NIS made several sexist remarks, questioned whether women belonged in the Navy, and "made comments to the effect that a lot of female Navy pilots are go-go dancers, topless dancers, or hookers" (Department of Defense 1992). As the investigations continued, it became clear that the military did not intend to hold perpetrators accountable. A Department of Defense review of this initial report states: "The gauntlet was a loosely formed group of men who lined the corridor outside the hospitality suites, generally in the later hours of each of the three nights of the convention, and 'touched' women who passed down the corridor. The 'touching' ranged from consensual pats on the breasts and buttocks to violent grabbing, groping and other clearly assaultive behavior." Even in a document that was critical of the initial investigation, the gauntlet is still not portrayed as the planned, organized series of sexual assaults that it was but rather a seemingly isolated event that included consensual and nonconsensual acts.

In the wake of poor institutional response, Coughlin went on national television to bring attention to the issue, which resulted in media, congressional, and civilian pressure to examine sexual violence in the military. A Pentagon investigation found the initial Navy investigation problematic and attempted to address its shortcomings. As a result, the Secretary of the Navy was forced to resign, and some organizational changes were made, including the closure of officer drinking clubs and required gender sensitivity training. Simultaneously, there was an extreme backlash against exposing Tailhook and against Coughlin herself. In the end, while 140 men faced punishment, and some were demoted, no one was prosecuted for what happened in Las Vegas. Coughlin quit the Navy.

The events at Tailhook reveal how a culture of military warrior masculinity can lead to systematic and ritualized sexual violence. The inaction of the military administration demonstrates how gendered values can be embedded in an institution. When the organization prioritizes masculinity and denigrates femininity, the bureaucracy works against victims and protects perpetrators rather than confronting them and checking their behavior. In the process, victims of sexual harassment and assault are ostracized and get pushed out of the workplace altogether.

This book will show that even though the Tailhook incident resulted in external pressure on the military to reform and an institutional promise to explore its problem with sexual violence, the military has not followed through with this transformation. The military has taken several steps to make changes at the structural level but has not fully addressed its gendered and misogynistic culture nor made changes that shift how servicemembers interact with one another. For example, the military has adopted multiple policies, programs, orders, and even laws aimed at preventing sexual assault and enhancing equality in the organization since 1992. In 2005, the Department of Defense created the Sexual Assault Prevention and Response (SAPR) Office to spearhead institutional efforts to decrease sexual assault in the military. This office clarified and improved reporting streams. It also offered more services to victims, such as the right to request an expedited transfer, the ability to report and track retaliation for reporting sexual assaults, and guaranteed access to a victim advocate. This office also encourages a coordinated response to sexual assault, where all parties who interact with a victim (such as lawyers, victim advocates, and medical staff) are required to meet monthly to discuss each victim's case. In 2022, President Biden signed an Executive Order requiring the Department of Defense to codify sexual harassment as part of the Uniform Code of Military Justice. None of these policies existed at the time of the Tailhook assaults.

Policy changes to address discrimination in the military include the repeal of "Don't Ask, Don't Tell" (DADT) in 2011, which formally ended the policy that prevented gay servicemembers from openly discussing their sexuality at risk of being discharged. The combat exclusion policy was repealed in 2013, opening combat positions to women and forcing formerly gender-segregated units to integrate across the Department of Defense. The military made these changes in an attempt to make the military more inclusive and to curtail discrimination, harassment, and sexual assault.

Kay served almost twenty years after Coughlin at a time when most of these policies, trainings, and programs around gender equality and sexual assault prevention were in effect, and yet there are similarities between their two experiences in the Navy. Almost all the women I spoke with started their service between 2005 and 2015—and harassment, assault, and institutional non-response or negative response to these issues remain at the heart of their stories.

Every few years another major sexual assault issue in the military is uncovered, is widely discussed in the media, and is met with promises to prevent future assaults. Every branch in the military has been implicated in major incidents of sexual harassment and violence: the 1996 Army Aberdeen sexual assaults, the 2009–2012 Air Force Basic Training sexual assaults, the 2017 Marines United Facebook incident (Callahan 2009; O'Neill 1998), and the 2019 Navy "rape list" case. In 2020, Army Specialist Vanessa Guillén was murdered on a Texas military base after telling her family that she was being sexually harassed and that she was too afraid to report. The issue of military sexual harassment and assault is ongoing and, according to the 2021 Department of Defense Sexual Assault Prevention and Response Report, the problem is escalating.

In this book, I will show how sexism and misogyny adapt to institutional and policy changes, creating slightly different organizational arrangements with the same negative effects for women. I show how structural factors such as spatial arrangements, bureaucratic procedures, and the organizational values of trust, loyalty, and family combine with overarching meanings around military masculinity to create gendered experiences that result in discrimination and sexual violence vulnerability for servicewomen. I trace the specific ways that the military as an institution creates sexual violence vulnerability that can render many of the organization's victim-friendly policies ineffective. I show how these policies may even function as tools of further harassment. Sexism and misogyny are embedded in the military as an institution, and yet its narratives are gender-neutral, reinforcing a façade of inclusion for all. Military bureaucracy still operates in ways that perpetuate inequality and enable harassers, leaving victims with few choices. Many women I spoke with give up hope of institutional change and, like Coughlin did decades ago, end up leaving the military because of sexual harassment, assault, and misogyny. While the ritual of the "gauntlet" may have ended in 1991, ritualized sexual harassment has certainly persisted: It is entrenched in institutional narratives, values, and expectations, embedded in military spaces, and nestled in military bureaucratic policies.

INTRODUCING THE PARTICIPANTS

In this book I use the words, voices, and perspectives of fifty U.S. servicewomen whom I interviewed over a period of five years (2014–2019). I recruited participants using convenience sampling; women were referred to the study by email, listservs, and social media. One benefit of convenience sampling was that I avoided formally engaging with the military hierarchy and bureaucratic structures, which could have complicated my ability to protect participants' anonymity. At first, three initial contacts served as key informants and gatekeepers and introduced me to their networks of servicemembers. I sought participants across military branches, across ranks (officers and enlisted servicewomen), and from different classes and races (see Table A1 in the appendix for demographics). Throughout *Hardship Duty*, I refer to participants by pseudonyms and specify the branch, race, and whether the servicewoman was an officer or enlisted after she is quoted. At the time of their interview, twenty-five women were active duty, four were in the reserves, and twenty-one had left the military. Among women who were out of the military, most (n = 18) had been active duty within five years of the interview.

The sample was designed to engage servicewomen's military experiences that reflect current military policies, issues, and practices. The early 2000s to 2010s brought many policy changes that impacted servicewomen's lives and careers, including the development of the SAPR program, the repeal of DADT, and the repeal of the ban on women in combat. I wanted women's voices to be the center and heart of this book; therefore, the questions I asked in interviews were intentionally broad and aimed at encouraging women to discuss issues and experiences that were important to them (see the appendix for more details on sample design, data collection, approaches, and analysis). Though I was interested in issues of sexual harassment and abuse, and despite considerable media attention on military sexual violence before, during, and after data collection for this project, I planned not to ask about harassment and assault until the end of each interview. Only in three interviews did the topic of sexual harassment not come up until I asked about it near the end of the interview.

Instances of harassment were discussed by 94% of the sample (forty-seven women), with forty-three women experiencing sexual harassment, forty-five experiencing gender harassment, twenty-six experiencing bureaucratic harassment (Bonnes 2017), and nineteen being sexually assaulted (see Table A2 in the appendix).[1] Most women were victims of multiple forms of harassment or assault across their service and these experiences came up frequently, often when I asked about servicemembers' most prominent memories of their military service or about frustrating experiences at work. Harassment was central to women's discussions of military training, deployments, military social events, and what it was like to live on base. Harassment was embedded in women's memories of pregnancy, dating, and socializing while they were in the military. It was cited as an explanation for leaving the military, even for women who thought they would spend twenty years in service and make a career out of the military. It seemed that harassment, whether servicewomen were labeling their experiences as such or not, pervaded many of their daily interactions and made a memorable impact on their military careers. In these pages, I examine the many ways in which the military as an organization facilitates sexual harassment and violence as well as how servicewomen understand, respond to, and cope with these experiences.

SEXUAL VIOLENCE IN THE WORKPLACE

Sexual harassment and assault are not new; neither is it new that victims share their stories. What *is* new is the platform victims have been given and society's *somewhat* receptive response to victim experiences in the #MeToo era. #MeToo has exposed rampant sexual violence in the film industry, in the tech industry, in sports, in politics, and in other masculine-defined work environments like policing, firefighting, and the finance industry. The media has focused on cases of men such as Bill Cosby, R. Kelly, Matt Lauer, Larry Nassar, Charlie Rose, Kevin Spacey, and Harvey Weinstein who used their positions of power to exploit, harass, and sexually harm women and girls and, in some cases, men and boys. The media has focused less on how these individuals were made powerful and protected by institutions that both enabled them to harass and assault and gave them the tools through which they could cause harm. The focus has been on "bad apples" and not on how these apples are produced by "rotten trees" (Ray 2020). This book takes a different approach by exploring the intersection between bureaucracy, institutional values, geography, a gendered institutional environment, and harassment in the context of the U.S. military. In doing so I demonstrate how the sexism and misogyny that is built into this institution not only creates, sustains, and emboldens the "bad apples" but can also plague most of the apples in the bunch.

These troubling dynamics and institutional devaluation of femininity and prioritization of masculinity are found in many other workplaces. Broadly speaking, this research aims to highlight the problematic values, attitudes, interactions, and cultural dimensions that can facilitate harassment and assault in various workplaces. The book takes as a case one setting, the U.S. military, where masculinity and unequal gender dynamics are intensified by other organizational features. Two key features of the military that amplify issues occurring in other workplaces are (1) the military's status as a near-total institution and 2) the military's femmephobic culture that denigrates femininity and encourages warrior masculinity.

A Total Institution

One of the features of the military that exacerbates conditions found in other workplaces is its dual status as a near-total institution and a transient workplace. In his work *Asylums* (1961, xiii), Goffman defines total institutions as "A place of residence and work where a large number of like-situated individuals, cut off from the wider society for an appreciable period of time, together lead an enclosed, formally administered round of life." He argues that in total institutions, "all aspects of life are conducted in the same place under the same single authority." Callahan (2009) argues that at the U.S. Air Force Academy, cadets go through a series of depersonalization processes by having their heads shaved, replacing civilian clothing with a uniform, and being hazed. Similar rituals across military branches are found at basic military training, boot camp, officer training school, and OCS. For example, upon entering OCS, Marines start an intensive training program, are restricted from wearing civilian clothing, are told how to wear their hair, and are regulated in how they interact with other candidates, military personnel, and their own friends and family. Introduction into military institutions often involves physical and mental stress, lack of sleep, surveillance and inspection of daily activities, and the regulation of appearance and behavior. Additionally, new military personnel are introduced to the military hierarchy and indoctrinated with core military values (Rohall et al. 2006). The military hierarchy is reinforced through tight regulation and control of the work and daily life of military members. For example, the military regulates how servicemembers should dress, behave, and speak in both military and civilian spaces (Bryant 1979; Department of the Navy 2018). Most branches of the military (Army, Navy, and Marine Corps) require a uniform but also have a "civilian attire policy"[2] that dictates how servicemembers should dress in nonmilitary spaces and specifies clothing that is prohibited, such as frayed garments, and the expected length of skirts, dresses, and shorts (Department of the Navy 2018). Bryant (1979) argues that dictating clothing (by enforcing a uniform) represents the broader control that the military has over the other aspects of servicemembers' lives. Indeed, there are many other rules and regulations relating to both the military and civilian life of servicemembers.

The military can be described as "part residential community, part formal organization" (Goffman 1961, 12), especially when considering military bases. The Air Force describes this as a benefit, stating on its website that "Air Force bases are basically self-contained cities with everything you need to live and raise your family." While this can be convenient, it also means that social, residential, and work life occur in the same geographic space. This means that servicemembers could be subject to military rules and regulations at work, while socializing, exercising, dining at a restaurant, or even at home and are more easily surveilled in the confined area of military bases. This is similar to people in other confined spaces, such as students at boarding schools or on university campuses, workers on boats and ships, and even firefighters who work and sleep at their place of work. Yet, unlike other total institutions, the military's blending of work, personal, and social life is underscored by the transient nature of the institution. While servicemembers spend prolonged periods of time with one another at work, on-base living quarters, and on-base spaces like restaurants, gyms, and shops, they are also accustomed to frequent moves and changes to their social circle. The military's blending of social, personal, and work life on bases and its transient nature has implications for sexual vulnerability, as perpetrators of violence can have persistent access to potential victims against the backdrop of frequent transfers. The fact that people move often in the military sometimes makes it difficult for victims to come forward or continue with a case against their perpetrators. Some victims told me that they knew their harasser would be gone in a few months and so they did not report, knowing it would be better when he was transferred. Perpetrators might know this, too. They know that either they can move onto a new base and potentially to new victims, or that their victims might move on before a case is opened or resolved. In this way, the military context provides an environment where perpetrators can easily monitor and have access to victims while also providing a built-in mechanism to avoid detection or consequences.

The military's blend of work and personal life is amplified by the fact that unlike other confined work/student spaces, it also controls the legal, medical, and policing response to its servicemembers. The military is also its own bureaucratic organization, with hierarchal power structures and a complex division of labor, rules, and regulations (Chappell and Lanza-Kaduce 2010; Weber 1947). It has its own education system, legal system, police, lawyers, courts, and medical system that operate separately from civilian systems (Turchik and Wilson 2010). These policies and regulations are reinforced by a strict division of labor and chain of command, as well as group punishments (Chappell and Lanza-Kaduce 2010). For these reasons, several scholars have classified the military as a total institution or a near-total institution (Callahan 2009; Hale 2008; Hinojosa 2010). This is not to say that the military is immune from outside influence. Congress has often forced the military to change or update policies. In 2013, Congress passed legislation to end the statute of limitations on rape cases and to prohibit commanders from overturning jury convictions in sexual assault cases, and made retaliation for reporting sexual assault crimes legally punishable. Additionally, lawsuits have also played a role in changes made by the Department of Defense. In fact, it was a lawsuit by four women against the Department of Defense over the ban on women in combat that shaped Leon Panetta's decision to lift the ban in 2013. However, military employment is experienced by servicemembers as a closed environment. In this book, I show that sexual harassment and abuse occur at multiple sites in servicewomen's military lives, including at work, on base in non-workspaces, in recreational spaces, and even in their places of residence (particularly for those who live on base). This means that sexual harassment and violence can be more prevalent in the military compared to other workplaces, as perpetrators live, work, and socialize in many, if not all, of the same spaces as victims. The closed environment also has implications for how women experience and respond to harassment. Finally, the fact that sexual abuse is handled within the institution, and that a court-martial has historically been convened by one's own unit, means that the risks and fear of retaliation for reporting are also heightened. The military's status as a total institution helps explain how the organization itself creates sexual violence vulnerability.

Warrior Masculinity in a Femmephobic Organization

Sexism in the military is sometimes blatant but more often it is enigmatic, seeping into institutional narratives, interactions, geography, and bureaucratic features. Gendered organization theory argues that "gender is present in the processes, practices, images and ideologies, and distributions of power in the various sectors of social life" (Acker 1992, 567). Gender is not limited to the individual level but has interactional, collective, and institutional components (Martin 2004; Risman 2004).

The military has a gendered context that encourages a "warrior masculinity," which rewards servicemembers who display aggression, control,
dominance, physical strength, and violence (Bayard de Volo and Hall 2015;
Bonnes 2020, 2022; Callahan 2009; Enloe 2000; Hale 2008; Higate 2002;
Hinojosa 2010). The ideal servicemember is also constructed in direct opposition to femininity and to women, and actively denigrating femininity
is often a part of enacting the warrior masculine identity (Allsep 2013).
"Warrior masculinity" is a dominant military identity and is related to
Connell's (1987, 1995, 2005) concept of "hegemonic masculinity." Connell
(2005) defines hegemonic masculinity as a set of behaviors, practices, and
processes that privileges a specific kind of masculinity in a given context and legitimates unequal gender relations between men and women.
Hegemonic masculinity is constructed in relation to all femininities and
non-hegemonic masculinities to reveal a gendered hierarchy (Connell
1987, 2005; Connell and Messerschmidt 2005; Messerschmidt 2018;
Pyke 1996).

Connell (2005, 238) explains that hegemonic masculinities are those
that are given the most "patriarchal dividends." Patriarchal dividends refer
to societal benefits, such as wealth, power, prestige, and ability to have
one's masculine identity confirmed by others, that derive from the "overall
subordination of women." Those with the most social privilege (heterosexual, wealthy, white cis-men) are best positioned to achieve hegemonic
masculinity (Connell and Messerschmidt 2005). Hegemonic masculinity
is difficult to achieve for most men, and men's access to full "patriarchal
dividends" is constrained by other social locations such as race, sexuality,
class, and age because these identities intersect with gender in ways that
create a hierarchy of privilege within masculinity (Collins 2004; Connell
2005). Men engage in masculinity displays and masculine identity work
to claim their space in the hierarchy and attempt to access patriarchal
dividends. Hegemonic masculinity is also context specific, and in the military context warrior masculinity is especially valued and rewarded.

In conceptualizing hegemonic masculinity, Connell (1987) outlined the
concept of *emphasized femininity*, which can be understood as forms and
displays of femininity that complement and are compliant with hegemonic

masculinity. In accommodating the interests of men in a given context, emphasized femininity helps legitimate the unequal gender order and the subordination of women to men. Emphasized femininity often aligns with the ideal version of womanhood in a given context and is the version of femininity women are expected to perform, revealing a hierarchy of femininities (Collins 2004; Hoskin 2017; Schippers 2007). Emphasized femininity (or what Hoskin [2017] calls "patriarchal femininity") is not static but usually converges with existing power structures such as race and class, thereby privileging heterosexual, able-bodied, White, affluent cis-women (Collins 2004; Hoskin 2017). When women embody emphasized femininity, they usually receive interactional benefits (e.g., status, popularity, or protection from harassment) for acquiescing to men's dominance and the existing gender order (Collins 2004; Hamilton et al. 2019; Hoskin 2017; Schippers 2007). When women embody masculinity or forms of femininity that deviate from emphasized femininity, they are often punished through harassment, discrimination, ostracization, or violence (Collins 2004; Hoskin 2017, 2019, 2020; Schippers 2007).

Hoskin (2017, 2019) argues that "femmephobia," or the systemic devaluation of femininity, maintains the unequal gender order by imposing and policing boundaries around femininity and "proper womanhood." Femininity that does not complement hegemonic masculinity is challenged, reprimanded, and contained by a variety of interactional strategies, such as coercive language and feminizing insults and jokes (Hoskin 2019). Schippers (2007) argues that when women enact masculinity, they question the unequal gender order and threaten men's exclusive access to hegemonic practices and benefits. Therefore, women who invoke characteristics associated with hegemonic masculinity are cast into "pariah femininities," and their masculinity displays are feminized to maintain men's dominance over women (Schippers 2007). For example, when women display aggression, they might be labeled "bitches"; when women express interest in sex, they might be labeled "sluts"; and when they express sexual desire for women, they might be labeled "dykes" (Archer 2012; Brownson 2014; Schippers 2007). It is well established that women who embody pariah femininities suffer consequences, such as ostracization, harassment, and abuse, that reinforce the subordination of femininity to masculinity. However, in the military context, the organizational devaluation of femininity can also produce negative consequences for women who embody what would be considered "proper womanhood" in many other contexts—that is, "emphasized femininity" (Bonnes 2022)—because any association with femininity is problematic.

The military is a space dominated by men, which has been associated with an increased risk of harassment (Kanter 1977; MacKinnon 1979). Women make up 17.2% of active-duty personnel across the armed forces: 21.1% of the Air Force, 20.4% of the Navy, 15.5% of the Army, and 8.9% of the Marine Corps (Department of Defense 2020). Among active-duty top officer positions (paygrades O7 to O10), only 10% in the Air Force, 7.5% in the Army, 6.9% in the Navy, and 3.3% in the Marine Corps are women. In hyper-masculine settings, men might derive some of their identity through the notion that the work they do is masculine and thus different from and better than women's work (Bayard de Volo and Hall 2015; Schrock and Schwalbe 2009). Femininity and workplace competency are often constructed in opposition to one another, and women in masculine occupations are frequently ostracized (Byron and Roscigno 2014; Denissen and Saguy 2014; Ridgeway 1997; Ridgeway and Correll 2004). When women enter traditionally masculine spaces, some men respond by increasing their displays of masculinity (Prokos and Padavic 2002). Men might point out flaws of women in the workplace, show disdain for femininity, and make claims that women do not belong to accentuate perceived differences between men and women and to reassert the space as masculine (Ainsworth et al. 2014; Bayard de Volo and Hall 2015). This can explain why the integration of women into the military has historically been met with resistance, including claims that women will weaken the military (Bayard de Volo and Hall 2015; Winslow and Dunn 2002). For instance, the last all-men class in the Air Force Academy (Class of 1979) call themselves the "LCWB"—officially "loyalty, courage, wisdom, bravery" but unofficially the "Last Class with Balls" (Bayard de Volo and Hall 2015). The LCWB moniker demonstrates pride in an all-men class that is seen as more masculine, and therefore better than, the mixed-gender classes that would follow. Resistance to gender integration continues in the military today in 2023, with the Marine Corps failing to fully integrate boot camp despite being legally required to do so. Women's presence in the military, and now in combat occupational specialties, challenges the idea of the "masculine warrior" (Hale 2012; Martin and Jurik 2007; Prokos and Padavic 2002; Woodward and Winter 2004).

Femmephobia has usually been conceptualized to explore interactions between individuals, to explain who gets targeted with harassment, discrimination, ostracization, and stigmatizing slurs (Hoskin 2017, 2019). This book extends the concept of femmephobia to examine organizations. I reveal the layers of this femmephobic context to show how the organizational and cultural denigration of femininity contribute to rampant sexual harassment and assault in the organization. Military policies, even those designed to create equality or discourage sexual violence, adapt to the femmephobic context and can be tools of harassment. I also examine how women navigate this gendered context and how femmephobia constrains women's responses to harassment they experience while serving.

CHAPTER OVERVIEW

In Chapter 2, I explore how the gendered context of the military denigrates femininity and prioritizes and values aggressive masculinity. In military training servicemembers are taught core values, resocialized, and encouraged to adopt an aggressive warrior masculinity. The warrior identity is constructed in opposition to femininity. I show that in this context, women are often automatically associated with femininity even when they try to distance themselves from it and when they try to embody masculinity. Men ostracize, harass, and label women with stigmatized identities like "bitch" and "slut." Men also impose gendered and sexualized meanings on women's life-course events to further limit women's organizational inclusion. These events, such as pregnancy and engagement or marriage to a heterosexual partner, serve as "femininity anchors" (Bonnes 2022) that tether women to femininity within a hyper-masculine environment.

I describe women's elevated sexual and nonsexual harassment episodes related to these life-course events and argue that "femininity anchors" present serious interactional and individual consequences for women. While an emphasized feminine identity that complies with hegemonic masculinity is often rewarded in other contexts, in the military's femmephobic culture association with this form of femininity is especially denigrated. Overall, this chapter shows how the military's femmephobic context shapes how individuals interact in the organization, determines power dynamics in the organization, results in rampant sexual harassment and sexual violence for women, and explains episodes of elevated harassment servicewomen experience.

In Chapter 3, I show how masculinity and femmephobia are built into the military's spatial arrangements. Femmephobic, hyper-sexual, and hyper-masculine décor are built into physical structures and geography of military spaces, which normalizes messages of inequality. Military spaces are also dominated by men, making women stand out and more easily monitored by individuals wishing to cause harm. Further, men in leadership positions can use their power to protect masculine privilege and to downplay the seriousness of sexual harassment and assault in military spaces. Men in leadership positions can also exploit their position in the hierarchy to harass, assault, and harm others. These conditions make enlisted women particularly vulnerable because they are often required to live on base in addition to working there. I argue that the military's blend of work, social, and personal life creates a sense of omnipresence of harassment for women. While military structures exist to reprimand, fire, or even court-marital those engaging in sexual harassment and assault, women are at times prohibited from accessing these channels or triggering these processes. Further, when women try to challenge these dynamics, they are often ignored, ostracized, or harassed for doing so, preserving men's power and domination over military spaces.

In Chapter 4, I examine the centrality of bureaucracy in servicewomen's harassment experiences. This chapter explains how military policies addressing harassment and assault in themselves are not sufficient to combat the issue. I show how the femmephobic and hyper-masculine culture of the military seeps into the military's administrative polices and define "bureaucratic harassment" (Bonnes 2017) as the purposeful manipulation of legitimate administrative policies and procedures, perpetrated by individuals who hold institutional power over others, to undermine colleagues' professional experiences and careers. I then discuss the tactics used to accomplish bureaucratic harassment and demonstrate how it is used to achieve sexual and racial harassment or to prevent reporting of sexual violence. This form of harassment can be used to limit individual women and women as groups and is enabled by military features such as discretion, power, and hierarchy interacting with gendered workplace assumptions. I show how bureaucratic harassment can also be used to continue the effects of banned policies like excluding women from combat. It also renders ineffective the policies designed to help victims of sexual harm. Finally, the policies themselves are used as tools of harassment and ostracization.

In Chapter 5, I explain how during recruitment and training the military promotes itself as a family where servicemembers protect and look out for each other. While this attracts many people, it makes the military especially appealing for young people seeking to escape neglect, abuse, and sexual violence at home. Although the organization encourages the idea that the military is family, this narrative operates in highly gendered ways. The idea of the military family is supported by institutional goals around trust, loyalty, protection, and caregiving. While all servicemembers are encouraged to espouse and practice these values, women often do not receive protection and caregiving in the same way as men. Servicewomen come to learn through interacting with other servicemembers, especially servicemen, that the military family is actually a brotherhood that excludes women. I explore how the same values of caregiving, trust, and loyalty can be exploited in ways that make women vulnerable to sexual harassment and assault. These values of institutional support and protection are especially inaccessible for sexual assault victims, who are instead vilified for reporting. This chapter shows how the interactional level creates severe consequences for women who use reporting streams or try to access victim-friendly policies created by the military. I then argue that due to these factors, servicewomen who have been sexually violated feel betrayed by both their attacker and the military as an institution. Even for women who report and go to court-martial, the military's legal response can retraumatize victims. I outline how this leads sexual assault victims to reject the idea that the military is a family and to see the organization as complicit in their victimization.

In Chapter 6, I turn to exploring how the femmephobic and hyper-masculine culture affects how servicewomen respond to harassment. The military's emphasis on embodying a warrior portrays military identities in opposition to victim identities. I demonstrate how many servicewomen do not confront harassers or use official reporting channels but rather develop individual strategies to manage harassment (i.e., seeking transfers and avoiding known harassers) to eschew the stigmatized victim label. In addition to the immediate challenge of determining how to respond to their experiences with sexual harassment, servicewomen are also left trying to understand and make sense of these jarring incidents. Some women reframe the motives of those who harass them. Other women claim that enduring harassment is a marker of strength or a test of their commitment to the brotherhood. I show how the power of the femmephobic context and culture creates powerful interactional-level barriers for servicewomen to confront or report harassment. I then argue that women with combat experience have enough "masculinity insurance" (Anderson 2002) to wield in interaction with servicemembers who are disrespecting them and do confront harassers. Their status as a warrior gained through combat deployments means that admitting to being a victim of sexual harassment does not threaten their status as military insiders. They mobilize this power to confront and report harassers. I show that while women make choices in how to resist harassment, these choices are constrained by the prioritization of masculinity at the institutional and interactional level.

Overall, this book shows why sexual abuse persists in an organization that has adopted policies, programs, and strategies to both prevent sexual violence and to assist victims. I trace how the femmephobic and hyper-masculine context encourages the denigration of women, seeps into the geography and spatial arrangements of the military, is entrenched in the military's bureaucracy, and is embedded in institutional promises of family and values of caregiving, trust, and loyalty. I show how misogyny and femmephobia have adapted to institutional change and policies designed to address sexual harassment and assault and highlight the prominence of the cultural and interactional level in maintaining sexual violence vulnerability in the organization. In the conclusion, I make recommendations on how the military can address its femmephobic context and begin to intervene at the interactional level to make military spaces sexually safer.

At the moment, being in the military for women comes with a persistent battle to be treated like an insider, constant sexual harassment, and threats of sexual violence. For these reasons, I have titled this book *Hardship Duty* to reveal that women are placed in conditions that fulfill the military's justification for Hardship Duty pay as a part of their normal everyday service. The military does not define servicewomen navigating a masculine, misogynistic, and sexually dangerous work and living space as "arduous" or even problematic but I argue that pervasive harassment and sexual violence vulnerability in military spaces constitutes "extraordinary arduous living conditions, excessive physical hardship, and/or unhealthful conditions" (Department of Defense 2023). This book opens the doors to a normally closed institution and gives voice to those who are marginalized and often silenced within it.

Bitches, Sluts, and Femininity Anchors

The Denigration of Femininity and Harassment

Olivia had always been interested in the military.[1] She was athletic and enjoyed pushing her body to accomplish physical challenges. After college, she found herself in the midst of a recession, in debt, and without an athletic team to challenge her. Within a few months she signed up for Marine Corps Officer Candidate School (OCS). She chose the Marine Corps because "it's the toughest one" and she wanted to join the branch that had been described to her as the "ultimate physical challenge." OCS was strenuous for her, especially in the middle of winter. Candidates get very little sleep and have only five to ten minutes to eat their meals, which likely contributes to the program's high attrition rate. Olivia was told upon arrival that "the female failure rate is 70% and likely only forty from the 128 females who started will finish." Though the environment was competitive, Olivia described some of the women in her platoon as encouraging and motivating, helping her to be among those who passed and were commissioned as an officer. She was honored to receive her first salute from a gunnery sergeant she respected. She adopted the mantra "The fewer, the prouder," a gendered spin on the Marine Corps slogan "the few, the proud," representing the fact that, at the time, women made up only around 6% of the Marine Corps.[2] After holiday leave she entered The

Hardship Duty. Stephanie Bonnes, Oxford University Press. © Oxford University Press 2024.
DOI: 10.1093/oso/9780197636244.003.0002

Basic School (TBS), proud to be a Marine and excited about the traditions and service ahead of her.

The Basic School is a six-month Marine Corps training required for all officers. In the years since she completed TBS, Olivia has described it as "some of the worst months of my life. It was so depressing." It was here where the gendered dynamics of the Marine Corps, such as the promotion of aggressive masculinity and the denigration of femininity, became inescapable for her. Olivia learned that it was not enough to keep up academically, physically, or on the rifle range. Masculinity was prioritized but was often devalued when women attempted to embody it, a phenomenon known as "pariah femininity" (Schippers 2007). TBS was where Olivia, and many women like her, encountered gendered labels and insults that would be hurled at them throughout their military careers. For Marine Corps officers like Olivia, TBS was often where women were first told they can be "bitches, sluts, or dykes" and were coached to "try to be the bitch," alluding to a hierarchy within stigmatized feminine identities. I spoke with women in all branches who experienced these gendered labels, usually when they got out of training and into their first regular unit.

Women explained that they were often labeled one of these identities when trying to embody or embrace traditional displays of masculinity. Deborah explains:

> If I do my job and I have a really strong personality, I'm a bitch. If a guy does his job with my exact personality, he's just assertive—and there's that double standard . . . I don't know when that will change or how that will change, but I think that's a constant and I dealt with . . . I thought if there was a profession out there that would embrace strong assertive women it was going to be the military and that has been the one aspect where the military has mildly let me down. (Air Force, officer, White)

Prior to joining the military, women like Deborah and Olivia thought that an organization that valorized bravery, aggression, assertiveness, athleticism, leadership, strength, and courage would reward anyone who displayed those traits regardless of gender. Other women, like Vivian, sought out the military because they perceived themselves as masculine before they joined and hoped this would help them fit in. Vivian described herself as "a tomboy . . . I never fit in. I was not a typical girl; girls never liked me, I never had girl friends, and I was not into girly things. That's why I joined. I thought I would really like the challenge; how tough it was." She thought the Marine Corps would be a place where "my personality was finally, like, . . . acceptable." What Vivian and others found was that when they were assertive, aggressive, tough, strong, or athletic, they were usually not valued but ignored, mocked, used as motivation for servicemen to do better (i.e., are you going to let a female[3] beat you?), stigmatized, or even harassed. Women came to learn that it was really masculinity tied to men's bodies that was rewarded, desired, and valued. On the other hand, femininity was met with disdain, harassment, and even violence. These are the gender dynamics that permeated many interactions Olivia had at TBS. Eventually, this gendered context shifted how Olivia saw herself, other Marines, and civilians.

Olivia sees herself as someone who is guided by principles of equality, community, and service. When she discussed the sports she played, it was clear she valued teamwork. She was encouraged by her peers, and she motivated them as well. Even before her time in the military she believed in the equality of women and men and would bemoan women who tried to tear one another down. After a couple of weeks at TBS there was a noticeable change in how Olivia spoke about and viewed other women. For example, she told me that "Females are slower, so it makes sense that they [male Marines] get pissed off." Another time, in response to my surprise at a story she told me, she said, "Oh, yeah, all of the males say 'pussy,' but it doesn't mean anything. Like, they are joking, and they don't mean it to be about females. It's just like . . . no one is offended." In addition to comments like these that denigrate women and prop up masculinity, Olivia began to view other women as competition. In one instance, she seemed to celebrate when a "female Marine" who she noted had studied harder than her was rejected from her top Military Occupational Specialty (MOS)[4] choices. It seemed that she sought validation from the men around her, was especially proud of moments when she outperformed men, was validated when men praised her, and worked hard to be seen as a "'*guy's* girl' and not a '*girly* girl.'" It was shocking how quickly this change took place. What I did not realize then was that the military deeply and actively devalues femininity, forcing servicewomen into impossible situations. While living and training at TBS, Olivia was fully immersed in a military environment and was only free from this context for a portion of some weekends. With so few women in the Marine Corps, the intense training of TBS and the military's hyper-masculine norms and values can lead women to feel like they are pitted against each other. Because women were systematically devalued, Olivia felt like she was constantly competing with other women to be the *one* to stand out. To do so, Olivia was trying hard, as many do, not be seen as feminine. Even though she had earned her eagle, globe, and anchor like other Marines, for the rest of her service she would carry the extra weight and stigma that came along with the label "female Marine." While she still valued service, she learned that being a part of the military community meant accepting gender inequality and trying to carve out a space for herself within the gendered hierarchy.

Several years later, when Olivia made the decision to leave the military, she reflected on her experience at TBS: "That is one of the main reasons that I don't want to stay in [the Marine Corps]. Pretty much every guy makes fun of girls—I hate it. I can't even tell you how many times I've been made uncomfortable by men in the Marines . . . Seriously. I feel like even I changed at TBS, and it took me about a year to find myself again." I appreciated these comments as I had been confused by the changes I saw in her when she was at TBS. What I did not realize at the time is that I had been witnessing her way of *coping* with the misogyny she encountered every day when men demeaned her and mocked women during lectures, training, and hikes. It was so bad that she was afraid to speak in class, since men made often laughed at any woman who raised her hand. The noticeable shift in how Olivia spoke about men, training, and the military when she was *in* TBS compared to how she spoke about these things years later is demonstrative of the intensity of military training, the pervasiveness of masculinity, and how women must endure harassment to try to fit in. Olivia's survival adaptation to the inescapable context of training in an extremely masculine environment was to frame men's derogatory comments, sexist actions, and misogyny as jokes or other non-harmful banter. She also increased her criticism of other women, viewing them as competition rather than as sisters, teammates, and supporters. These were adaptive strategies to succeed in a misogynistic and femmephobic (Hoskin 2019) context. It took several years for Olivia to verbally express that the actions of the men around her were harmful and part of the military's pervasive culture of sexism, rather than jokes or the actions of a few "bad apples." While she felt like an outsider in TBS, she held out hope that she could carve out space for herself or be one of the few women to stand out. Over the years as she rose in the ranks, this hope receded as she recognized the behavior she saw in TBS as omnipresent, often regardless of rank, status, or military experience. The military's cultivation of an aggressive warrior masculinity, especially during training, is a central feature of the way servicemen and servicewomen come to see the military as a brotherhood and as a space that denigrates femininity. In this chapter, I explain how this hyper-masculine organization that disparages femininity and encourages a warrior masculinity makes women vulnerable to sexual harassment, nonsexual harassment, and violence. The women I interviewed were harassed both for being perceived as too feminine and for trying "too hard to be masculine," for the way men perceived their intimate relationships, for being pregnant, and for simply being women in the military.

THE BROTHERHOOD

When asked why she joined the Air Force, Iyana thought for a minute and said: "I think because I didn't join a sorority, or I didn't do those clubs in school, that was kinda like my . . . my . . . my brotherhood, . . . if you will." It is telling that Iyana paused to think about the right word to use and deliberately chose "brotherhood," a masculine term, to describe the Air Force. Similarly, when asked why she enlisted in the Marine Corps over other branches, Carol stated that "the camaraderie that we have, it's very much the brotherhood of the Marine Corps, and from what I've seen it's even stronger in the Marine Corps than other branches of service." The connection between men, masculinity, and the military is reinforced in broader U.S. culture. If I were to ask most Americans to imagine a Marine, they would likely describe a man in fatigues in a combat zone. The idea that the military is a brotherhood is depicted in TV shows like *Band of Brothers* and movies like *American Sniper*, *Full Metal Jacket*, or *The Hurt Locker* that focus on the combat experiences of men. In fact, research has found that very few women have central stories in military films. When women are featured in movies about the military, they are usually portrayed as nurses, or are depicted in ways that mark them as military outsiders (Furia and Bielby 2009). Women are also often under-represented in military promotional and recruitment materials. For example, the webpage to request more information about joining the Marine Corps features four men in dress blues staring off into the distance, and while different races are represented, women are not. The military actively recruits women, but the images they project predominantly represent men and masculinity. Just as masculinity is embedded in the military's outward image, gender is also inherent in the military's values, practices, operations, and processes.

The military is a gendered organization (Acker 2006) where violence and aggression are encouraged, pushing people to display warrior masculinity (Bayard de Volo and Hall 2015; Bonnes 2020, 2022; Callahan 2009; Enloe 2000; Hale 2008; Higate 2002; Hinojosa 2010). The military is also a "femmephobic" organization that systematically devalues and denigrates femininity (Hoskin 2017, 2019), and this begins in training. Military training is a grueling and exhausting collective experience. Diane, whose family history of military service sparked her interest in joining, highlights this intense experience when describing Marine Corps training:

And the first phase is all about breaking you down, killing the civilian in you, taking away your identity, so that's all about recruit training. It takes away your identity. It takes away everything that you are and then second phase starts coming as they start training you. They begin to start building you up in a way that they want you to be built up. And then in third phase, they actually teach you on how to think and act like a Marine. (Marine Corps, enlisted, White)

Diane explains that this training included messages like "Be polite, be professional, but always have a plan to kill every person you meet."[5] She also explained that training was hyper-focused on cultivating an aggressive warrior identity, which she worked hard to embody. She said, "When I got out of boot camp, I was proud to be a Marine. I was motivated, but the schoolhouse . . .[6] the schoolhouse showed me what I was really involved in." Diane's boot camp was gender segregated and she said men learned in their boot camp to distrust women Marines: "The male Marines actually get taught in boot camp . . . they get taught to hate us . . . not to trust female Marines." She mentioned that gender-segregated training and the different standards for men and women to complete boot camp led to men learning that women "are not real Marines. They [women] don't go through what you've gone through." This was reinforced by drill instructors who denigrated women. Diane's friend told her that his drill instructor said: "The only fit female Marine is one on her knees." The messages that men receive in initial training are to not only denigrate women and femininity but also to distrust women in the Marine Corps. While men and women are rebuilt to subscribe to military values, Diane said that men in Marine Corps bootcamp are "rebuilt to hate women." Once women move into mixed-gender settings, such as in TBS like Olivia or in job-related training like Diane, they experience a hyper-masculine context that is dominated by men and where there is an investment in denigrating women. In this context, harassment is commonplace.

The ideal servicemember is associated with an aggressive masculinity that is constructed in opposition to femininity and encourages the devaluation of women (Allsep 2013). Men and women are quickly exposed to the military's culture of aggressive warrior masculinity, they internalize the institutional hierarchy that devalues femininity, and they employ adaptive survival strategies to succeed in this environment. Men and women are competing to stand out and gain status as a superior servicemember.

A common way for men to assert masculinity is to denigrate femininity, especially within a femmephobic context that already associates femininity with weakness. For example, servicemembers often direct feminine insults at men who cannot keep up physically, labeling them "girls" or "pussies" to challenge their masculinity (Barrett 1996; Bayard de Volo and Hall 2015). The derogatory use of feminine terms for men who underachieve both affirms the masculinity of those who perform well and maintains the subordination of femininity to masculinity (Barrett 1996; Hoskin 2019). Angela, a woman enlisted in the Navy, said: "The idea of a woman is that we are weaker, and it's a way to put down men." Therefore, a dichotomy is set up between men and women in the military, where men become synonymous with strength, success, and military insiders, and women are constructed as weak military outsiders.

Within this environment, women may try to suppress or denigrate femininity themselves in an attempt to fit in with the masculine military space (Basham 2009; Crowley and Sandhoff 2017; Sasson-Levy 2003; Steidl and Brookshire 2018). Many of the women I spoke with tried to embody masculinity by denigrating other women, posturing against others they perceived as "non-masculine," emphasizing their physical strength, and embodying stoicism. At times, these behaviors were successfully perceived as masculine. At other times, these behaviors were seen as problematic because they were traits associated with masculinity but displayed by women. The effectiveness of women's gender strategies depends on if their displays are validated. Identity theorists argue that power in the social structure produces the power to control social interactions, including resisting or confirming the identity work of others (Cast 2003; Stets and Burke 2005). In the military context, men have easier access to traditional markers of masculinity and are thus better positioned to confirm, deny, or redefine the gender or sexuality of others. Men can treat women as "honorary men" (Höpfl 2003; Kanter 1977; King 2016; Miller and Brunson 2000) by confirming their masculinity displays, they can cast women into pariah femininities by labeling them "sluts" or "bitches" (Schippers 2007), or they can simply deny their masculinity identity work altogether.

Reflecting on the military environment where denigrating femininity is normalized and expected, many of the women I spoke with described gendered harassment experiences. Marie was the only woman I spoke with whose military career ended at a service academy. I included Marie in the book because she was "medically discharged" from the Air Force Academy (in other words, kicked out) due to a medical condition she contracted from a senior cadet who raped her. Marie explained that men would blame women for unit or training issues at the academy. Describing one upperclassman she interacted with, she said, "It sounds so mundane— but he has this funny way of saying female. He said it so it's two words, like 'feee male.' Look, the 'feee males' are bringing us down again." The Air Force cadet training manual bans the use of profane or insulting language, and gendered insults like "bitch" would likely violate this policy. However, by emphasizing female in a disparaging way, this cadet was able to demean individual women as well as show broad disdain for femininity, without being detected for a violation of cadet policy. His message is that women are weaker than men, not fit for military life, and deserving of contempt. His words and taunts also serve to justify his violence, as he also actively harmed women during training exercises. Marie explained, "The same guy used to kick sand in women's eyes, and call us names, and, you know, took every chance he could to single out women." In this way, he used femmephobia, or the devaluation of femininity, to justify violence against women. Women's presence in the military, and now in combat occupational specialties, challenges the assumption of the "masculine warrior" (Hale 2012; Martin and Jurik 2007; Prokos and Padavic 2002; Woodward and Winter 2004). Some men respond with increased harassment and violence, and they are enabled to do so by the power the military gives them through their rank and position. Women come to understand and expect this, as many told me that displaying femininity would result in harassment. Therefore, women tried to hide what they thought others might consider feminine.

Meredith joined the Army to "see the world" and because she had a family history of military service. Once she joined, she consciously downplayed femininity by not wearing makeup and dressing "masculine" when wearing civilian clothing. She coached other women on these strategies and told one woman who she thought "wore too much makeup" and "short skirts" when in civilian clothing that "you can't be doing this." She told this woman, and me, that her strategy was to "be one of the guys." She explained that she often endured physical pain in silence to demonstrate strength to men in her unit:

> Because being the female in the job that I held, I was always being watched. I was always being looked at. I remember this one time I got hit in the face with, uh . . . I was running a fuel truck. And it had a fuel nozzle about this big [gestures] . . . solid metal. And it was cold, cold, cold. It was like January. And I'm rolling the hose up and it came off the hook . . . the hammer came off the hook and it spun around, and it hit me right in the jaw. It felt like somebody punched me. And it was cold. And I remember looking around first to see if anyone was around before I cried. Because crying . . . because they pounded it into your head, don't cry . . . never show your weakness. Don't . . . you know? So, you had to learn how to be stoic and not show emotions. (Army, enlisted, White)

Enduring physical pain is problematically seen as a signal of strength (Barrett 1996; Hockey 2003; Sasson-Levy 2011) and the need to demonstrate strength in front of servicemen can be seen as way to gain acceptance. Servicewomen learn to constantly regulate their behavior to try to distance themselves from femininity. However, they still tend to be labeled a "bitch" or "slut" at some point during their military careers, and these displays do not protect them from sexual harassment or assault. Meredith, who worked hard to be perceived as masculine, to distance herself from femininity so much so that she "used to laugh and say my perfume was 'eau de diesel,'" was groped by a soldier in what was clearly a planned assault. She was at work "and all a sudden the guys all swarmed around me. I'm like, I don't know what's going on," and then one of the soldiers told a joke where the punchline was him grabbing both of her breasts with his hands. Despite her masculinity displays, the fact that she had breasts made her a target. In such an environment, it is clear why women distance themselves from anything they think might be seen as feminine as they try to guard against harassment and assault.

Margaret joined the Marine Corps after working as a civilian on a military base. While she didn't describe the transition to military life as hard, she did say that she missed being able to be feminine when she was a Marine. She explained that "You couldn't be feminine" and "if you were or showed a tiny bit of that side, it wouldn't be good." What she meant was that displays of femininity would be met with insults and harassment. This assessment was supported by the experiences of other women I spoke with. Women learned during military training, from organizational rules, and through interactions with other servicemembers that femininity was not welcome and is often met with hostility. This sentiment relates to traditionally feminine displays such as wearing makeup but also extends to other actions or displays that servicemembers *may perceive* as feminine. In the rest of this chapter, I show how in a femmephobic context that operates on a strict gender binary, women become synonymous with femininity regardless of how they act, what they wear (or do not wear), or how they try to display gender.

FEMININITY ANCHORS AND ELEVATED HARASSMENT

Most of the servicewomen I spoke with (forty-seven out of fifty) discussed harassment during their military careers (see Table A2 in the appendix). This harassment came in sexual and nonsexual forms. Sexual harassment included inappropriate sexual comments, unwanted sexual attention, obscene gestures, seductive behavior, and sexual bribery and coercion. Nonsexual harassment included behaviors that did not seek sexual cooperation or submission but were used to denigrate and demean based on sex or gender, enforce stereotypical understandings of gender, and punish perceived violations of gender. Nonsexual gender harassment included demeaning terms used to refer to women, masculinity and femininity slurs, and sexist insults.

In the context of pervasive harassment, women also noted moments of elevated harassment throughout their service. Of the forty-seven women who experienced harassment, twenty-seven used expressions where they identified increased or elevated harassment. When women used phrases like "worse," "particularly bad," "really bad," "the most terrible," "extreme," "severe," "increased," or "escalated" to describe a harassment episode, I categorized it as elevated harassment. I also considered an experience or episode to be elevated harassment if participants described it as an increase in the severity or frequency of harassment. Often, elevated harassment was associated with life-course events that men perceived as representing femininity, especially moments when women were viewed as representing emphasized femininity (Connell 1987), or forms of femininity that often align with the ideal version of womanhood. More than half of the women who discussed elevated harassment (59%) experienced elevated sexual harassment that was related to an event like dating a man, getting engaged to a man, or marrying a man, and 29% of them described elevated nonsexual harassment directly related to their pregnancies. Men interpret servicewomen's heterosexual relationships and pregnant bodies as signaling and displaying emphasized femininity, which anchors women to this identity. Although an emphasized feminine identity brings status in the civilian world, it is a direct affront to the hyper-masculine military space because women who display femininity can no longer be seen as bodies doing masculinity. In response, servicemen engage in increased objectification and sexual harassment of servicewomen when women are revealed to be in relationships with men, and increased nonsexual harassment when women are pregnant. Therefore, heterosexual dating, engagement, and pregnancy operate as "femininity anchors" (Bonnes 2022) that tether women to emphasized femininity (Connell 1987).

Heterosexuality and Elevated Sexual Harassment and Assault

Many women experienced incidents of elevated harassment because of gendered and sexualized meanings around women's intimate heterosexual relationships. Lyla joined the Navy because "I wasn't ready for college, but I didn't want to stay in my small town . . . It seemed like there were mostly dead-end jobs and so going in the military would give me an exciting job and I'd get to travel." Right after Lyla told me about her transition to military life, I asked her to describe her three most prominent military memories. In response, Lyla described a serviceman who made sexual comments and propositioned her for sex at multiple points during her career. She explained how she experienced an increase in *severity* of sexual harassment from this noncommissioned officer (NCO) after she got engaged:

> Because I wouldn't have sex with—I called him—the darling of the command. . . . Because I wouldn't have sex with [name] or play around with [name], it was very difficult for me at work. And I can remember, I was out in the . . . we had a section party. . . . His family was there . . . wife and kids, and everybody else brought their family. And I think probably my fiancé was . . . he wasn't there with me. Anyway, [name] took his clothes off. And I was in the water. I could tread water; I could swim pretty well. But I didn't know what was in the water. So, I was kinda nervous out there. It was dark. It was dusk. And he was standing in the water with his trunks off and, basically, blocking my ability to go back onto the beach. (Navy, enlisted, White)

Lyla explained that after she got engaged, the NCO's behavior increased in severity and moved from sexual comments to actions. She continued: "So I just had to stay out there and tread water and I kept hoping that somebody on the shore would call for him to come back, or his wife would need him or something . . . that somebody would see what was going on. Eventually, he got tired of trying to cajole me back on the shore." Although he relented and stopped pursuing Lyla in the water, he approached her later that day and asked her to walk with him alone in the woods. Lyla declined because she assumed he would sexually assault her:

Things weren't going so well for me at work. And things weren't going so well for me at work, in part, because I had met and fallen in love with an Air Force guy. And so, there were only ninety Navy people on the base. And so, for me to pick an Air Force guy was something. And then because of that I . . . was sexually harassed.

Lyla shared that after her relationship became known in the unit, servicemen who had not previously targeted her made comments about her sex life and denigrated her choice of intimate partner, and one propositioned her for sex. That is to say, after her heterosexual cross-service relationship was revealed, she became objectified and then harassed by more men in her unit. This example points to the ways that gendered and sexualized meanings can be layered over other organizational meanings, as it hints to inter-branch rivalries where men in the Navy might have been particularly irritated that Lyla chose a man in the Air Force over them. When they respond with harassment, it shows how servicemen feel authorized to police women's personal and intimate lives. These men claim harassment is justified because the servicewomen are with men who are outsiders in some way (i.e., not in the Navy). However, their negative actions are directed toward women who are their peers and subordinates, with the effect of making women feel like outsiders.

Women who dated servicemen of their same rank, unit, and branch were also the targets of elevated harassment or assault. Janet enlisted in the Army to escape her negative home life. When I asked her to describe her most prominent military memories she replied, "I wish that I could speak more highly of my experience in the military." She described several instances of sexual violence, including a time she was sexually assaulted by a military peer shortly after she started dating another soldier. She initially described her attacker as a friend but clarified that she was closer to his wife (who was not a servicemember). She was staying at the couple's house and her colleague walked into the room:

And, basically, he just, like, propositions me for sex. And I was like, "No, a million times, no." I was like, "I've got a boyfriend, you've got a wife, I'm friends with her. There's a baby in the bed. There's a million reasons that this is not going to happen. No." So he was just kind of like, "Okay." And he left and walked out of the room, and it was kind of not a big deal. I don't know how much time passed because I fell back to sleep. And he came back into the room, and he was wearing a t-shirt. Just a t-shirt. . . . And the first thing that he did was he grabbed my hand and put it on his erect penis. . . . So, I took my hand away, and then he put his hand into my underwear. And so, I pulled his hand back out of my underwear, and I didn't want to wake up the baby. Yeah, I didn't want him to, like, wake up and see some man standing over him with an erect penis. Yeah, I just didn't want that to happen. So, while I'm talking to him, like pleading with him to please just leave, he's like touching my breasts. (Army, enlisted, biracial)

Eventually, the baby woke up and the soldier stopped assaulting her and "booked it out of the room probably before his wife got in there." Janet shared that this soldier had never harassed her nor expressed sexual interest in her prior to the assault, which occurred shortly after she started dating her boyfriend.

Rosa-Maria described a similar situation when she started dating a man of her same rank in her unit, meaning no military rules prohibited their relationship. Soon after they started dating, her boyfriend was sent away for a two-month training. The day her boyfriend left, their NCO, who knew about the relationship, sexually assaulted Rosa-Maria:

R-M: This NCO cornered me and grabbed and kissed me. I was completely caught off guard. I mean, it was right in front of his home, with his wife inside. The rest of the platoon was heading inside. I must have been talking to my ex [her boyfriend at the time] on the phone and that is why I was outside and got caught up in that.

Me: Did the NCO harass you prior to this moment?

R-M: No. I had no issues with him. Like I said, I was completely caught off guard. Other guys, yes; never had an issue with this one until that night. I feel like . . . the way it happened that he was waiting for my boyfriend to be away or something. It was weird. (Marine Corps, enlisted, Latina)

Rosa-Maria described at least four instances of sexual assault during her four-year military career. She also explained that the reason she joined the Marine Corps and not the Navy as she had planned was because she was sexually assaulted at the hotel the night before she went to the Navy's Military Entrance Processing Station (MEPS).[7] When she explained her *worst* moment with sexual abuse, it was the incident outlined above. Rosa-Maria was "caught off guard" because this man had not harassed her prior to this moment, and she believed her NCO was angry about her relationship or punishing her for talking to her boyfriend outside the party. Hart (2021) argues that individuals navigate unwanted sexual attention and strategize ways to minimize sexual harassment in the workplace by being vigilant and monitoring interactions with potentially problematic people. Rosa-Maria had categorized several other men as sexually dangerous, but she had considered her NCO a safe person to interact with *until* she got into a relationship with another serviceman. When assessing the landscape at work for sexual danger, servicewomen may be surprised by the shifting and elevated harassment that occurs when their relationships with men are revealed.

In contrast to these experiences, Rita, who enlisted in the Marine Corps after being impressed at a military graduation ceremony for her friend, explained how servicemembers reacted when she started dating a woman in her unit: "They were surprised because we were such good friends. Well, even we were surprised because we were such good friends. But they were happy for us." Rita explained that the biggest obstacle related to her relationship and work was that her wife was planning on becoming an officer and she would remain enlisted, inviting a potential violation of the military's fraternization policy. They circumvented this issue by getting married before Rita's wife applied to be an officer. The lesbian women in my sample were also harassed throughout their military careers and some were sexually assaulted, but they did not report *elevated* harassment when their relationships, engagements, and marriages to women were revealed to other servicemembers. In contrast, 32% of the heterosexual women I interviewed described heightened harassment when they started dating, got engaged to, or married men.

Heterosexual relationships create flashpoints of harassment because servicemen attach feminized meanings to these life-course events, and the presence of femininity is a threat to the gender order in hypermasculine contexts. Butler (1990) theorizes that heterosexuality creates and sustains the gender binary by emphasizing an attraction based on difference—that is, masculinity versus femininity. In the military context, expressing sexual desire for men is interpreted as feminine and unacceptable. Collins (2000, 87) argues that the dominant gender ideology suggests a "woman's true worth should occur through heterosexual marriage." In this way, gender and sexuality are mutually dependent: Through heterosexual relationships, women are assumed to be feminine, anchored to emphasized femininity, and thus perceived as sexual objects unfit for the military (Butler 1990; Collins 2000; Ken and Helmuth 2021; Messerschmidt 2018; Schippers 2007). In a competitive environment where servicemembers are seeking to project masculinity and the heterosexual conquest of women is one way of doing so, servicewomen's heterosexual relationships may remind servicemen of their own failure to sexually conquer them (Archer 2012; Hennen 2001; Higate 2007; Sasson-Levy 2003). Intensifying harassment against these servicewomen would be a way for servicemen to reassert their own masculinity. Against the intrusion of femininity, men use sexual objectification and harassment to re-establish the gender order and regulate the gendered boundaries of inclusion in the military workplace.

Slut Discourse and Femmephobia

The military's interactional culture sends messages that promote masculinity and devalue femininity. The "slut label" is an example of a pariah femininity (Schippers 2007), where women perform an aspect of hegemonic masculinity, and it is perceived negatively because it is being done by a woman. In this case, sexually active heterosexual men would be celebrated and rewarded but sexually active heterosexual women would be considered problematic. Slut discourse is commonly understood as a way for men and women to hold women accountable for violating expectations of sexuality and femininity (Armstrong et al. 2014; Payne 2010). The "slut label" allows servicemen and servicewomen to police boundaries around military inclusion. Even the perception that a woman might hook up with a serviceman can lead to the slut label. Margaret summed this up as "We were told, and the culture is, that any contact with male Marines makes you a slut." Lisa, who joined the Air Force after college, experienced consequences of this perception when she was talking to a serviceman:

> Okay, so there was one time I was sitting outside . . . with this guy and talking . . . And then this female senior leader saw and she came up to me and she started berating me and yelling at me and like, "People are going to think you're a slut." (Air Force, officer, White)

The speculation that a woman and a man talking indicates a sexual relationship reveals how sensitive the military environment is to heterosexual relationships. The leader here did not directly call Lisa a "slut" but aggressively warned her that others would label her as such if she continued to interact with men one on one in public. Gendered and feminine meanings are placed on *perceptions* of women's heterosexuality and policed by all servicemembers.

Vivian described how other servicemembers spoke about a woman who was removed from OCS for talking to a man (who was also in OCS) in a car:

> I recall one of the other females saying: "She didn't want to *be* a Marine; she wanted to *marry* a Marine." But the perception was that she wasn't one of us or that . . . she wasn't like us. To risk your career, and I think anyone who risks their job and life dreams just to have sex probably had some promiscuity issues or issues with sex in general. (Marine Corps, officer, White)

Both the woman and the man Vivian spoke about were kicked out of OCS after the incident. Even though these individuals had only been caught *talking*, it was assumed they had a *sexual* relationship. OCS has strict rules about women and men speaking to one another while in training, spending time with one another, and, according to Vivian, "even looking at one another." These rules assume that heterosexual encounters are distractions in the military workplace. In this case, even though the behavior and consequence were the same for both parties, the reactions of other servicewomen had gendered implications. Vivian told me that even though her colleagues thought the serviceman was "dumb" and had made "a stupid mistake," he was not portrayed as an outsider to the Marine Corps. This incident shows that despite the military's strict romance rules, heterosexual interactions are considered normal for servicemen but problematic for servicewomen.

Melanie, who enlisted in the Army following a family history of military service, reflected on the "problem" of women displaying heterosexuality when discussing servicemen who pressure women for dates:

> Yes, I think, you know, some of the instances where the guys come on to the girls, and it's unfortunate because there are so many women who just want to go to work and do their job and serve their country, but there are those few out there who are there to serve the men they work with. (Army, enlisted, White)

Melanie's complaint about servicewomen who date servicemen came up in a conversation about her toxic work climate: "I'm just, like, overwhelmed. You can't go into a dining facility without getting stared down. You can't walk around the gym without getting stared down. It's like I don't want to go out because I don't want to feel like a piece of meat." While describing an over-sexualized workplace where men pressure women for sex and dates, she blamed some *women* for responding to their advances, which, as a display of emphasized femininity, would be seen as compliant with hegemonic masculinity in many contexts. This type of response legitimates the unequal gender order present in the military's femmephobic organizational culture. Melanie's comments also demonstrate how slut discourse (Armstrong et al. 2014) is a part of military masculinity.

In certain contexts, like college campuses, women can avoid stigma and escape the "slut label" when they enter monogamous relationships with men (Armstrong et al. 2014), because doing so shows an acquiescence to hegemonic masculinity and displays emphasized femininity. However, in the military context, the slut label is used *in response to* the presence of emphasized femininity. For example, when Melanie discussed women who date servicemen, she portrayed them as different from women who "just want to go to work and do their job and serve their country," thereby casting them as military outsiders. As a discursive practice, the "slut label" allows servicemembers to control the boundaries of military inclusion and prop up a hyper-masculine culture that facilitates harassment and abuse.

Not only are women who marry servicemen portrayed as disingenuous servicemembers, but their relationships and marriages are seen as duplicitous. Women who marry servicemen, especially women who do so and then subsequently leave the military, are viewed as problematic because other servicemembers retroactively define their motives for joining the military as centered around men and marriage—the "wrong," "feminine," reasons to join. Sexual attraction between servicemembers is also rejected because it interrupts the notion that servicemembers are brothers. When women date or marry servicemen, it is often used against them as evidence they did not choose the military for the right reasons, and as proof they cannot succeed in the military, thereby legitimating men's power and dominance in the organization. This is an assumption that women must work against while serving. For example, Margaret explained that:

> It's hard to overcome that [stereotypes about women] until the guys realize that there are women out there who are not looking to have sex. Who are not looking to get married. Who are just there to do their job, and that's someone you can rely on and depend on. (Marine Corps, enlisted, White)

Margaret's discussion of how to gain the respect of servicemen implies that servicewomen who get married or have sex are unreliable. In an organization where trust and loyalty are constantly portrayed as necessary for military functionality and effectiveness (Harrison 2003; Verweij 2007), being labeled unreliable makes one incompatible with core military values. Margaret sums this up when she shared "I can't be very flirtatious. I can't be showing weakness" conflating heterosexual flirting with weakness demonstrates how women are often aware that heterosexual relationships can anchor them to unwanted identities.

Further, slut discourse is also used to question women's career success. Allison, who joined the military mostly for financial reasons, shared a joke that her recruiter told her before she joined the Marine Corps:

> So, a joke that my recruiter told me was, you know, military people get rank and it's painted as stripes on their uniform? Well, the joke . . . it goes, what's the difference between a zebra and a WM [woman Marine]? A zebra didn't have to lay on its back to get its stripes. (Marine Corps, enlisted, White)

This joke assumes that women can only rise in the ranks through sexual activity because they are not hard-working, smart, or physically fit enough to be promoted any other way. "WM," an abbreviation for "woman Marine," was then corrupted by men Marines into "woman mattress" or "walking mattress"[8] as a way to assert men's domination and to relegate women as perpetually objectified outsiders. Allison commented that by the time she joined the moniker WM was not used any more, but her recruiter still told her the joke with the outdated term so he could also explain the evolution of WM. The idea that the only purpose for a woman in the Marine Corps is to sleep with men Marines is reinforced through interactions with military peers, commanders, and those in charge of servicewomen's careers. For example, Samantha was an enlisted Marine who later commissioned as an officer. When inquiring about this process from the Marine Corps Commissioning Program (MCP) she explains:

I was verbatim told that "you are only here as a body warmer or a bed warmer." He went into stories about how women went in as prostitutes for the military, like a long time ago or whatever. And then he said, "Now you are just *in* the military." Going to MCP to see that attitude was very disheartening. (Marine Corps, enlisted/ officer, White)

The MCP office oversees the enlisted-to-officer transition process. Rather than directly call Samantha a "slut," the serviceman in this office discouraged her from pursuing an officer track by reinforcing the slut label and sexually objectifying women in general. In doing so, he used the power of his position in that office to protect the space as masculine.

Servicewomen also rely on the slut insult to distance themselves from this particularly stigmatized identity. Women are aware that at any moment they could be labeled a slut and they try to escape this label by stigmatizing other women. Margaret recalls a time where a higher-ranking woman in her unit pulled all the other women aside:

She was talking about—her roommate from when she first got in the Marine Corps. . . . She would carry around a book bag with a pillow in it . . . to sleep over at, you know, other guys' rooms. And she's like, "Don't be that" and she would immediately tell us, "It reflects upon everyone. It reflects upon me." (Marine Corps, enlisted, White)

This woman used the slut construct to set an example of how she expected her servicemembers not to act. At the same time, she validates the denigration of femininity inherent in the slut label. Mallory, who joined the Army for financial reasons, stated:

You gain respect just by working. If you don't flirt with the higher-ups and everything, and you don't flirt with every guy you see. You don't build that sluttish reputation; as long as you work hard, you pass your PT [Army Physical Fitness] test, you don't complain, you don't talk about your personal life. As long as you go in acting like you're hardcore at least, people won't want to mess with you. (Army, enlisted, Black)

In Mallory's opinion, women who flirt are not only deserving of the slut label but should also be viewed as the direct opposite of women who are hard-working. While at first Mallory claims women can gain respect by working, at the end of her quote she describes the benefit of hard work as simply "not being messed with." Therefore, harassment is so normalized that servicewomen conflate not being harassed with respect. Further, not being "messed with" is conditional on avoiding stigmatized femininities.

In the military context, stigmatized femininities are difficult to avoid as any display of heterosexuality for women can result in being labeled a slut. The slut label opens the door to also being labeled lazy, stupid, or physically unfit for the military. Even Mallory, who described herself in opposition to women who flirt, was labeled a "slut" during her service:

> Well, the other girls just decided to start this rumor that me and him were having sex while we did combatives[9], which obviously was not true. I talked to my drill sergeant . . . There's nothing I could've got in trouble for, and that's why they were giving me a hard time and stuff about it because they were just making this big rumor that I was sleeping around with one of the guys. Honestly, I never talked to him. He was in a separate platoon. I saw him maybe three times during the training.

Here, Mallory attempts to explain how the other servicewomen misunderstood her interactions with a serviceman to distance herself from the slut label. However, as shown previously, she also applies the slut label to others and calls out what she perceives as problematic behavior. This shows the difficulty for women in avoiding stigmatized femininities. Servicewomen are hyper-visible in the military and are constantly being tested by those around them. The femmephobic context ensures that other servicemembers (both men and women) can place servicewomen in a stigmatized identity. The use of stigmatized identity labels, either in opposition to one's own actions or to label and ostracize other women, negatively impacts all women. Importantly, not every servicemember engages in problematic labeling, and not every display of heterosexuality will result in the stigma. However, the fear of being labeled a "slut" at any moment is an omnipresent fear that forces women to monitor and surveil their own behavior in an attempt to avoid this form of gendered humiliation.

The slut label and corresponding ostracization and harassment also intersects with racism. This is evident in a military cadence that was shared with me by Marie, who explained that even though the song was officially banned she was still forced to sing it at the Air Force Academy: "I wish that all ladies were holes in the road, and I was a dump truck and I would fill them with my load. Hey mama-rita, I love my mamacita." The cadence's use of the slut label mocks women's presence in military spaces and portrays them as incompatible with military service outside of their ability to service men's bodies. The cadence goes on to condone violence against women by portraying women as disposable sex objects: "I wish all the girls were statues of Venus and I was a sculptor I'd break them with my . . . [penis is implied here but not said aloud]. Hey mama-rita, I love my mamacita." The line "hey mama-rita" is a play on margarita, invoking the notion that women of color are objects that exist for men's pleasure and consumption. The racial element to the cadence points to the hyper-sexualization and devaluation of Latina women in particular (García-López 2008), portraying them as objects to consume and then violently dispose of after they are used.

In summary, the presence of femininity is disruptive and threatening to the idea of military warrior masculinity. For servicewomen who are trying to demonstrate military masculinity, the femmephobic context that relies on a strict gender binary ensures that relationships with men are viewed as a display of femininity, which is met with disdain. Similarly, pregnancy serves to anchor women to femininity and results in increased harassment.

Pregnancy and Elevated Nonsexual Harassment

Women who were pregnant in the military shared many stories of nonsexual harassment during their pregnancies, including sexist insults, comments denigrating the pregnancy, pressure to terminate the pregnancy, and being prevented from accessing policies aimed to assist pregnant and postpartum women. Servicemen interpret pregnant bodies as feminine and incompatible with military service. Pregnancy anchors women to femininity, and men respond with increased nonsexual harassment in an effort to polarize notions of the ideal mother versus the ideal worker (Byron and Roscigno 2014; Glass and Fodor 2011; Ridgeway and Correll 2004). Women explained that pregnancy in general, and *their* pregnancies in particular, were viewed as detrimental to military work. Many servicewomen, even those who had never been pregnant, explained there is a perception that women intentionally get pregnant to avoid military obligations. Rebecca routinely heard throughout her service: "If the Marine Corps wanted you to have a baby, they would have issued you one."[10] She mused that "pregnancy and harassment seem to go hand in hand in the military, especially the Marine Corps." Although this joke pokes fun at the strict organizational discipline of the Marine Corps, the point is that servicewomen are not supposed to get pregnant.

Military policies exempt pregnant women from annual testing and deployments, require them to take leave after birth, and advise that postpartum women do not have to meet the same physical fitness standards as others in the unit. These accommodations are necessary and important protections, but they are also public markers of pregnant and postpartum women's altered status within military units. Rather than seeing these accommodations as necessary for the health and success of pregnant and postpartum servicewomen, some see them as allowing women to evade institutional obligations. These perceptions lead men to elevate nonsexual harassment against pregnant women, sending the message that pregnant women are organizational outsiders.

For example, Rebecca described instances of increased nonsexual harassment from multiple men when she was pregnant in the Marine Corps.

She stated, "The pregnancy did not go over well." Rebecca worked an over-night shift at an armory, and despite being tired due to her pregnancy, she never asked to change this demanding schedule. Like many servicewomen, Rebecca already felt out of place in her unit because it was dominated by men. After her pregnancy, she said that servicemen enhanced their efforts to ostracize her, and they often directly invoked the pregnancy to question her work abilities:

> They were faster at loading magazines than I was . . . It always seemed like I got new rounds, and the new rounds, they stick to-gether, whereas if you have used rounds, they just go in real fast. I don't know if they were setting me up or not, that would be specu-lation . . . They had a speed loader, I didn't. Anyway, they left without me. And the sergeant for the other crew said: "Just because you're pregnant and just because you are female doesn't give you an excuse to be late." I said, "I wasn't late. I was told to be here at 11 and I got here at 11." I don't know what was said. I'm sure something was said. It was just that feeling like you're not fitting in. And then when I got preg-nant it felt like that even more so. (Marine Corps, enlisted, White)

Rebecca also described what she said was her worst military experi-ence, which occurred during her second pregnancy. This time she worked day shifts because she had an accommodating commander:

> So, I stayed behind, which was not usually the case, I was usually with a male Marine on my crew, and this time I was by myself. It would have been around lunchtime. So, they all left, and I had an M16 sitting at the picnic table, which wasn't unusual. . . . I was facing down the road so I can see oncoming cars. . . . I had the newspaper out; I'm eating my lunch. It's a hot day. . . . All of a sudden, I feel something in the middle of my back and "don't move." And my heart is just racing and I'm absolutely sweating. . . . I want to say he said to me, "let this be a lesson to you." And I'm thinking I'm either going to be raped or something bad is going to happen to me. . . . When

he said "don't move," I put my hand down next to me and my rifle wasn't there anymore. It was gone, it was . . . in my back. And I stood up, he must have told me to stand up. He came around the side of me and slammed my rifle down, the buttstock down. And he just was standing there, I don't remember the words he said to me. But he gave me my rifle back. And he just stood there. He wanted me to give him the greeting of the day and salute him. And so I did. That was probably the worst thing that happened to me in the Marine Corps. I thought for sure I was dead. That rifle was loaded. I know it was loaded because I'm the one that loaded it.

When Rebecca described this incident, she said, "I don't know if it was the pregnancy. I just know this was the worst moment of my Marine Corps experience. I thought I was going to be raped or die. He wanted to teach me some sort of lesson." The lesson could have been about proper weapon care or staying attentive, but Rebecca interpreted this as a gendered experience that produced gendered fears. A serviceman saw a visibly pregnant, junior-ranking servicewoman sitting alone for lunch and decided to sneak up on her, steal her gun, and threaten her with a loaded weapon. She recognized she was vulnerable to sexual violence or even death at this moment. She later remarked that this pregnancy "caused a lot of trouble" and invited jealousy from those in her unit who desired day shifts. Her new schedule could have been perceived as preferential treatment rather than a necessary accommodation for her pregnancy.

Like Rebecca, most of the women who were pregnant during their service stated that their most extreme memories of harassment occurred during pregnancy and postpartum periods. Black, Latina, and White servicewomen all described episodes of elevated harassment when they were pregnant. However, there were racialized differences in how pregnancy harassment manifested. Only the two pregnant Black women in my sample were explicitly told to terminate their pregnancies. For example, Kay believed a Navy doctor told her to have an abortion to protect the career of her boyfriend (whom she mentioned was also Black):

I got pregnant and he [her boyfriend] was going places. He was like the golden boy at the school. Everybody liked him. He had it in his mind he wanted to apply to go to the Naval Academy, and he was working on getting his application together to go. But we were like in love . . . puppy love or whatever. And I remember going to the doctor on base and telling him I was pregnant. And he's like, "Well, you shouldn't have the baby . . . you should terminate the pregnancy." And I was like, "What?" And he was like, "Yeah, you could terminate the pregnancy." You know, "I can arrange that." He said that my boyfriend, he was going to the Naval Academy. He said something like, "If you do this, you'll hinder him. He can't have any dependents." (Navy, enlisted, Black)

Kay was advised to terminate her pregnancy based on a doctor's perception of her boyfriend's potential military career. She was not sure if the doctor even knew her boyfriend directly, simply telling me that "everybody knew him" and there was a collective investment in him getting into the Naval Academy.[11] The doctor's advice suggests Kay's career, life, and future were viewed as an obstacle to the unit's mission of advancing one serviceman's career. Kay's experience speaks to broader patterns of institutional control of Black fertility, particularly the perception that the fertility of unmarried Black women is dangerous and needs to be controlled (Collins 2000; Davis 1981). She summed this up well when she told me, "They feel like they own your body."

The specific ways servicemen harass women reveal a hierarchy of femininities based on race. Kay was seen as a threat to the institution for distracting her boyfriend from his military career and was advised to terminate her pregnancy. Here, the combination of negative views of pregnancy in general, and Black women's fertility specifically, created a response where a military health professional advocated for abortion. Pressuring Black women to get an abortion can be understood as an attempt to control their fertility and ensure they will remain in service to the military as deployable members. Whereas pregnancy for White women triggers episodes of harassment targeting their inclusion in the military space, pregnancy for Black women also triggers harassment that targets their bodies and their ability to reproduce. This demonstrates how racist assumptions can be embedded in assumptions about femininity and in harassment experiences.

Individuals in an institutional culture that denigrates femininity may interpret policies designed to support pregnant people as proof of their outsider status rather than as necessary accommodations. For example, pregnant servicewomen are exempt from deployment. Deployment is an important marker of military insiderness and an expression of self-sacrifice for the organization (Shields et al. 2017). Servicemembers train to deploy, plan to deploy, and can be separated from the military if they cannot deploy. Servicemembers who cannot deploy often fall into the following categories: physically unfit, mentally unfit, or pregnant, all of which are seen as problematic. Margaret expressed this sentiment, saying, "Being in the Marine Corps and not deploying is like training for the Olympics and never playing." Another Marine explained, "We're 6% women, and if you become pregnant, there's a stigma to that which sucks but it's there."[12] Allison described the stereotype that women intentionally get pregnant to avoid deployment:

> And it's [pregnancy] seen as a way to scam out of deployments where you can't get in trouble. Absolutely. Oh, you're pregnant. We can't do anything about it. Like you don't have to do deployment. You don't have to go to war. You don't have to do the hard shit. You don't have to go someplace that's unfavorable . . . Clearly, you didn't want to deploy, or obviously, you can't hack it. (Marine Corps, enlisted, White)

In juxtaposing pregnancy with markers of military masculinity, such as war and "hard shit," Allison shows how pregnancy is linked to perceptions of femininity. In the military context, pregnancy is viewed in opposition to the hard-working, self-sacrificing servicemembers who are prepared to give up everything, including their own life, for the institution. Pregnant women are perceived as prioritizing something or someone else over the military and their military peers. Since they cannot deploy, they are seen as antithesis of a military warrior. Pregnant women are portrayed as using their femininity and sexuality to escape institutional obligations in ways men cannot.

Pregnant women are exempt not only from deployments, but also from annual fitness testing, which contributes to the assumption they are antithetical to the "ideal worker" (Acker 1990; Byron and Roscigno 2014; Glass and Fodor 2011; McFarlane 2021; Ridgeway and Correll 2004). Even pregnant women in units not set to deploy are viewed as problematic, because they have frequent medical appointments and are given modified schedules and requirements. In a context where servicemembers report not seeking medical attention because they do not want to let their units down, individuals who use institutional services are viewed with distrust and portrayed as selfish (Cogan et al. 2021). Nadine noted, "If the female Marine has more than one child? I'll just say, you won't be well liked, and the common assumption is female Marines only get pregnant to get out of things."

Military policy allows pregnant and postpartum women to opt out of physical testing and fitness requirements, but servicewomen shared stories of men manipulating the bureaucracy to restrict their access to these benefits or to punish them for taking them. For example, Morgan described how the men in her unit accommodated her pregnancy in the ways the military required them to (i.e., a lighter workload, less physical activity) but retaliated against her in other ways:

> So, I got pregnant and of course they're liable for lots of things, so God forbid I pick up a single chair. But then they went and made me go clean the bathrooms for the company. . . So, I did clean for a little bit up until I just couldn't stand the smell anymore, but they would make me do weird things like that.

Morgan believed she was switched to bathroom duty as punishment for her required pregnancy accommodations, precisely because pregnant people often have increased sensitivity to odors. Even after she made it clear that cleaning the bathroom induced nausea and made her feel faint, she was still required to do it.

The perception that women *use* pregnancy maliciously and in ways that men cannot, coupled with the fact that pregnancy is visible, and men read pregnant bodies as feminine, makes pregnancy a critical femininity anchor for servicewomen, resulting in enhanced harassment. Taber (2011) argues that women in the military try to be as masculine as possible and conceal any embodied differences between themselves and servicemen. This is difficult, if not impossible, during pregnancy. Women's pregnant bodies are a physical and visible reminder of their difference from servicemen, as are their maternity uniforms.[13] The way servicewomen must modify their work during and after pregnancy marks them as failing to comply with institutional obligations and the prevailing hegemonic masculinity. As a result, pregnant servicewomen are seen as disloyal, untrustworthy, and unable to support their peers, thereby cementing their outsider status. Their perceived embodiment of femininity is the ultimate proof that they are not only incapable of being masculine insiders but are also adversative to the military and its mission. When pregnancy is viewed this way, women are seen as not only outsiders but also enemies. Servicemen respond with harassment to regulate and control women's bodies, like pressuring Kay to have an abortion, and to negatively affect women's work lives, like threatening Rebecca with a loaded gun or placing Morgan on bathroom duty while pregnant. Servicemen may also view the presence of pregnant women in the military as eroding its status as a masculine workplace (Hale 2012; Martin and Jurik 2007; Prokos and Padavic 2002; Woodward and Winter 2004) and respond with gender harassment to reaffirm the military workplace as masculine, with no place for femininity. All these actions reproduce gender hegemony, where men enact power and invulnerability through gender and nonsexual harassment.

CONCLUSION

The military is a femmephobic organization where military training actively denigrates women and femininity (Bayard de Volo and Hall 2015; Hoskin 2019, 2020). These values shape how servicemembers gain power within the institution (Barrett 1996; Hale 2008; Hinojosa 2010; Sasson-Levy 2003). In this context, women, like men, try to gain power in the military through masculine identity work, embodying masculinity, and distancing themselves from femininity (Crowley and Sandhoff 2017; King 2016; Sasson-Levy 2003). However, the effectiveness of these strategies is limited for women: Women who embody masculinity threaten the gender order and are often cast into pariah femininities (Schippers 2007). Even in interactions where women are not branded "sluts" or "bitches," the fear of these labels still constrains women's identity work, interactions, and decisions. And despite their gender identity work, women can be tied to femininity based on how others perceive their life-course events like heterosexual relationships and pregnancies, which increases their vulnerability to harassment.

Organizational and interactional authority structures enable individuals in positions of power to confirm or deny the identity work of others (Cast 2003), to treat women as "honorary men" (King 2016), or to recode women's masculinity displays as stigmatized and feminine (Schippers 2007). Regardless of whether women are performing masculinity or expressing a noncompliant femininity, they may be anchored to emphasized femininity based on how individuals interpret their heterosexual relationships and pregnancies. Though women usually receive benefits and privileges from heterosexuality in most contexts due to heterosexual domination (Collins 2004; Hamilton et al. 2019), in the military context where femininity is especially denigrated, women's risk of harassment increases when they are associated with emphasized femininity. In this context, femininity anchors act as a tool of exclusion and tether women to stigmatized identities, thereby elevating their vulnerability to harassment and weighing down their careers.

The two types of femininity anchors discussed here resulted in different forms of harassment. The women who experienced elevated harassment as related to their heterosexual relationships described experiences of sexual harassment and assault. In contrast, women who were pregnant during their military service experienced elevated nonsexual harassment, including gender and bureaucratic harassment. When women are anchored to emphasized femininity through heterosexual relationships, servicemen view them as sexual objects rather than servicemembers. Servicemen increase sexual harassment in these moments to enact their own masculinity, to regain masculinity they perceive as threatened when women are intimate with other men, to deny women's status as honorary men, and to affirm the workplace as masculine. When women are anchored to emphasized femininity through pregnancy, servicemen use gender harassment to create a work environment hostile to pregnant women, thereby cementing their status as outsiders and suggesting they are incompatible with the military.

Each act of harassment is an expression of the military's hegemonic masculinity in that men are enacting invulnerability and aggression, and women are victimized by it, thus reinforcing men's power over women. The military's emphasis on warrior masculinity and denigration of femininity is first communicated to servicemembers during training and is sustained by the interactions of both servicemembers who are attempting to stand out in the hierarchy and those in positions of power working to maintain that hierarchy. These extremely gendered dynamics are not just experienced in interaction between servicemembers but are also embedded into the physical structures, layout, and geography of military spaces themselves. The next chapter explores how military bases, ships, aircrafts, offices, and training areas are not only dominated by men but also designed to prioritize warrior masculinity in ways that facilitate sexual violence vulnerability for women.

Not Safe at Work, Not Safe at Home

Sexual Vulnerability in Military Spaces

It was a muggy, rainy, spring day in the South. I ran to the car with my blazer over my head, hoping to stay dry. The court-martial I was observing was on a break for lunch, so my base sponsor, Stuart, took me to the officer's club. As we drove the short distance and pulled into the parking lot, he explained that the club has several reserved parking spaces for commanding officers on the base plus a single space for "any 2nd lieutenant," the lowest officer rank in the Marine Corps. I was struck by how something as mundane as a parking lot could showcase Marine Corps respect for hierarchy and expectation that leaders take care of those who work under them. It reminded me of the lunch event I had attended the day before, where I observed the Marine Corps practice of "officers eat last." Officers remained seated around tables until lower-ranking Marines filtered out of the buffet line and sat down with their meals. In researching this tradition[1] I found an article written by a first lieutenant, who explains that "Officers eat last in the Marine Corps because the young men and women in their care eat first. The welfare of the Marines comes before the personal welfare of the officer." My civilian observations of the parking space and the practice of "officers eat last" offer an alternate take on this guiding principle: Respect the chain of command and you'll be taken care of. These

Hardship Duty. Stephanie Bonnes, Oxford University Press. © Oxford University Press 2024.
DOI: 10.1093/oso/9780197636244.003.0003

examples also highlight the importance of physical space. Military core values and expectations are purposefully built into the geography of military bases; they are on display in the chow hall, recreational facilities, offices, barracks. They are an essential part of how servicemembers interact in those spaces.

Stuart pointed out that despite the name, the "officer's club" was open to everyone. I was immediately drawn to the walls, which were covered with decorations, photos, and signs. Stuart explained that squadrons returning from deployment typically make plaques commemorating the experience and place them on base, including on the walls or on tables at the club. These decorations contain the name of everyone in the squadron, the squadron's emblem, its nickname, and sometimes inside jokes from deployment. From an institutional standpoint, this practice made sense to me; the plaques highlight deployment as a goal while also stressing the unity of those who deployed together. Military values become embedded in the physical space itself.

We sat at a table covered with commemorative materials. I put my plate down and stared at the phrase written underneath my fork: "make sure to give the 'ball sack' a good tap." The words "ball sack" in bold letters next to my plate of chicken was jarring. Even more so because it was not just graffiti scribbled there in haste; it was purposefully written alongside other phrases and memories important to the unit that created it. It was protected under a piece of glass to ensure its longevity. I did a quick glance around the room and realized that I was the only woman there. I immediately wondered what it must be like to be a servicewoman eating at this table, seeing that phrase and perhaps others like it scattered around the room. I asked Stuart about it, to which he replied "It's super common. A lot of these are full of inside jokes and stuff and a lot of it is sexual. Usually it's hidden better than that, though. But yeah, it's a lot of sexual stuff."

Call signs, or nicknames for those in aviation, are also memorialized on bases. Call signs are assigned by one's peers usually in their first deployable squadron.[2] Stuart said these call signs were often "racist and sexist, or at *least* sexual" and, I would add, homophobic as well. Olivia told me that the only other woman in her Marine Corps air unit had a call sign that referenced her breasts. In 2018, Black aviators reported that their military peers gave them racist call signs that that denoted Blackness or Black people or characters such "Radio," "8-Ball," and "Snoop" (Seck 2019). In 2009, an aviator reported that his call sign options were all homophobic, including "gay boy," "fagmeister," and "cowgirl" (Thompson 2010). The active-duty military force is 82.8% men, 68.9% racially White, and 82.8% ethnically not Latinx (DoD 2020), meaning that White men dominate the military, especially in leadership roles and the highest officer ranks. This is one example of how White men have more power over others in everyday interactions, such as the ability to deny a woman's masculinity attempts, to harass or ostracize, or to determine a call sign. An article in a military news outlet explained that that many call signs are based on mistakes a person made or based on a funny experience or story (Schogol 2022); however, this is likely more accurate for White servicemembers. Aviators who are Black, women, and gay have stated that their call signs invoke their race, gender, or sexuality, often in racist, sexually objectifying, or homophobic ways. Sexist call signs are usually not isolated incidents and often occur within a pattern of sexist behavior in those units (Losey 2020). These call signs, which at times exemplify sexism, racism, and homophobia, can end up in commemorative décor, allowing these oppressions to be embedded into the physical space.

Overall, the statement enshrined on my table was tame compared to others. A few months later, I saw a post on a publicly available Facebook page in which a servicewoman shared a photo of a farewell gift that one of the men in her unit received; it read: "Here's to Honor, Getting Honor, Hitting Honor, and if you can't cum in her, cum on her." Jokes like this that are hyper-sexual and hyper-masculine point to gendered interactions that, at best, exclude women and, worse, objectify or encourage violence against them. The fact that this "present" was to be given at an official event, a farewell party for those rotating out of the unit, shows how sexism and objectification of women is entangled not just in the everyday experiences of servicemembers but also at moments that celebrate their service. Perhaps the recipient takes this gift home as a memento of military service that also highlights institutional misogyny; or worse, the gift might be displayed in a military office, where it would become another emblem of sexual objectification embedded in physical space for other servicemembers, perhaps junior-ranking ones, to see.

In the previous chapter, I demonstrated how the military is a hyper-masculine space that is hostile to women, an environment where servicemembers are encouraged to denigrate femininity and embody warrior masculinity. Masculinity and misogyny are also embedded in the spatial arrangements of military bases and workplaces and built into the physical structures of the military. The military uses masculine imagery and symbols to define what it means to be a servicemember. Many of the motivational posters displaying combat, bravery, and valor feature *only* men alongside weapons, tanks, aircrafts, and other military vehicles. For example, one poster I saw on base during my fieldwork read "Marines Move Toward the Sounds of Tyranny, Injustice, and Despair. Which way would you run?" and featured a helicopter, military vehicles, and men running forward, linking the images of combat and Marines with men, men's bodies, and masculinity.

When the Marine Corps was criticized for including only six seconds of footage featuring women in its eight-minute video celebrating 244 years of the Marine Corps, the commandant replied, "We did not break it down frame-by-frame, how many males versus how many females. And I don't plan to do that" (Harkins 2019). Women's exclusion from the video may not have been an intentional oversight, but combined with the commandant's response that he would not pay attention to representation in the future shows the assumption that the Marine Corps is masculine and *will stay* masculine. This cavalier attitude about inclusion demonstrates how women's absence and outsider status is normalized. It is not surprising that these dynamics are also embedded in military spaces. Even small and mundane messages may convey exclusion. For example, during my observations I noticed a Post-it note next to the thermostat outside of the courtroom that read "Please do not adjust. Thank you!—The Court Brethren." A literal interpretation of the language on this sign effectively excludes all women who work in these law offices, demonstrating how men can "mobilize masculinity" to unintentionally, and intentionally, promote dominance at work (Martin 2001). A larger example is how masculinity is built into much of the language used in military spaces and reflected on base signage: Airman, corpsman, and rifleman are words that invoke men yet are used to refer to servicemembers regardless of gender. Some branches are moving to de-gender their terminology. For example, the Marine Corps is changing infantryman to infantry Marine and making a move to de-masculinize all their publications (i.e., not using "he" to refer to commanders). However, masculine terminology is often still the informal default and is still embedded in core Marine Corps phrases such as "every Marine is a rifleman." Catchy phrases and unintentional Post-it notes alone do not create sexual harassment vulnerability for servicewomen, but each message that supports women's exclusion is part of a larger environment that builds tolerance for harassment and normalizes the denigration of women. In totality, this language and imagery seeps into the daily life of all servicemembers and makes men's domination of the space seem normal, natural, and unchallenged.

When I visited military bases and air stations, I saw masculine and hyper-sexual imagery in military workspaces, courtrooms, cafeterias, restaurants, grocery stores, and bathrooms. It is important to remember that military bases are a mixture of workspace, personal space, and recreational space. Therefore, women's *work*, *social*, and *residential* areas are not only dominated by men but are also often hyper-masculine and at times misogynistic spaces. A striking example is the presence of pornography in military spaces. Despite official rules against pornography at work, women described military spaces that were covered in pornographic images, mostly imagery of naked women. These spaces included physical locations like bathrooms, cockpits, lockers, tents, bedrooms, and offices as well as online spaces like email and social media.

Rebecca explained that when she was enlisted in the Marine Corps there was only one bathroom in her office and that it was "plastered with porn. I mean, it was just like, 'Whoa, okay,' they're testing me. I'm not going to say anything. Just going to go back to my little shack and not say anything. I want out of this place." When Rebecca worked in this unit, she attended a training that highlighted the fact that pornography was banned in public spaces. She chalked this up to another example of how official military policy was often circumvented or ignored by men she worked with and did not bother reporting the images or trying to take them down. Rebecca was one of the only women in her unit and she wondered "what do they think of me out here using that bathroom?" The only thing that made sense to her is that it was a challenge from the men she worked with. She felt that they were watching to see how she would react. At the same time, she feared they would harass her if she responded in any way. She thought it would be especially bad for her if she tried to report the pornography. Her fears were warranted; the link between workplace sexism and risk for sexual violence has been found in research studies on military sexual assault. For example, Sadler et al. (2003) found that in units in which an officer allowed or engaged in sexist comments or behavior, servicewomen were more likely to be raped. Therefore, the tolerance and encouragement of pornography in the workplace not only intimidates women and makes them feel like outsiders, but it also encourages objectifying women and creates an environment that might lead to sexual vulnerability for them. When men use their dominance to allow hyper-masculinity and misogyny on military bases, they effectively concentrate men's power and control of the space.

SEXUAL GEOGRAPHY IN THE FEMMEPHOBIC SPACE

The military is dominated by men, particularly at the higher ranks. Women make up only 8.9% of the Marine Corps and only 3.3% of people in top officer positions (O7 to O10). Even in the Air Force, which has the highest percentage of women in the armed forces, women still represent only 21.1% of active-duty personnel and 10% of those in top officer positions (O7 to O10) (Department of Defense 2020). The fact that military bases are spaces that are dominated by men and where work, home, and social life are blended creates extra vulnerability for servicewomen. In their book *Sexual Citizens* Hirsch and Khan (2020) use the term "sexual geographies" to explain how physical spaces, structures, and landscapes contribute to assault vulnerability. How military bases are organized, the way barracks rooms are designed and assigned, the furniture in those rooms, decorations hanging on the walls of offices, posters in bathrooms, the location of the designated smoking area, the location of bathrooms, distance between work and the barracks/dorms, and the lighting in out-door spaces all matter for sexual assault vulnerability. It is one of the reasons why women on deployments told me they were discouraged from going to the bathroom alone at night, because this is a time and location where they are at increased risk of sexual assault from the men they serve with. When femmephobia is layered within these spatial arrangements and sexual geographies, women are vulnerable to sexual violence.

Another dimension of the sexual geography of military bases is who controls the space. Who has access to rooms? Who has work-related reasons to visit servicemember's homes? Who has keys to offices, bathrooms, rec-reational spaces, supply closets, and armories? Who has the final decision on where someone lives, where people sit on an airplane, and when to fix a broken lock on a bedroom door? Access to and control of space are shaped by social power dynamics embedded in gender, race, class, and sexuality as well as in hierarchical military power dynamics such as branch, rank, position, and occupational specialty. Are people more likely to challenge someone who is being sexist or harassing a servicewoman if that person is a private? A staff sergeant? A captain? A general?

Imagine a twenty-one-year-old enlisted Marine reporting to a new duty station. She arrives with her belongings and meets her base sponsor, a married man a decade older and several ranks higher than her. His job as her sponsor is to orient her to the base, to show her around and be the first point of contact for any questions or concerns she has. The practice of assigning a base sponsor with several power differentials sets up multiple avenues for exploitation. The fact that he is older and outranks her puts him in an authoritative position over her, in a context that stresses hier-archy and adherence to orders. Perhaps certain words of advice or know-ledge shared from her base sponsor are not meant to be orders, but they could be interpreted that way by a young, junior-ranking Marine who is trained and required to follow. Now let's say he is more coercive and actively tells her that his recommendations *are* orders or requirements. She might fear punishment if she does not listen. She might assume his authority is non-negotiable. As her sponsor, he is also a gatekeeper to base information and resources. She might fear that disobeying her sponsor would be stepping out of the hierarchy in a way that could cause issues. Now imagine that this base sponsor shows her to her new barracks room and comments that he used to live there—in that same room. This invites intimacy based on shared space. He used to sleep in the same bed she would sleep in. His clothes had been in the drawers where her clothes would be. He shares that he lived there recently, right before she arrived at the duty station. If he left something in the room, it might still be there: a roll of toilet paper in a cabinet, a shirt in a drawer, DNA on the bed.

He knows where she lives, and because he had lived there too, he will probably never forget. Even if he sponsors other Marines, he will know as long as she lives in this room where she is during her down time, or when she is sleeping. If he wanted to cultivate intimacy with her, he could use his trusted position as her sponsor to justify it, and he can easily find her. Further, his job gives him an excuse to do so. If he wanted to cause her harm, he has knowledge of her location and could use his superior rank and his position as her sponsor to request to meet. Imagine that he is the on duty Marine and has another work-related reason to be walking around the barracks, to "enforce good order and discipline." Being on duty means access to and authority over the homes of junior-ranking Marines. No one who sees him in the barracks would question his presence, either, since it is a part of the job. Finally, he has intimate knowledge of the room itself, its furniture arrangements, where the exits are, where the light switches are, how the lock works, the location of the windows and blinds. All these factors would allow him to manipulate the space more easily. He could quickly make it dark, pull the blinds to increase privacy, position himself between her and the locked door to make it difficult for her to leave. Space matters, and knowledge of space is something that can be exploited to cause harm. Unfortunately, something similar to this happened to Cecelia.

Cecelia arrived at her second duty station and was greeted by her base sponsor, Quinn. He was married, he outranked her, and he was ten years older than her. In the week she had been at the unit, Quinn had interacted with Cecelia often and encouraged her to tell him about herself. She thought she had found a mentor in him. As a twenty-one-year-old, she was new to legally drinking. When Quinn arrived at her door with a bottle of alcohol, she let him in. If her mentor was encouraging her to drink, she thought it was okay. Other women may have interpreted it as an order due to his rank and role as her sponsor.[3] They drank together, and he left. Then he came back. He left again. Then he came back. She said, "He kept coming back to 'check up on me.'" This somewhat made sense to her, as checking on her seemed to align with his role as her sponsor. However, providing a much younger co-worker with alcohol seems incompatible with this responsibility; so does showing up at her room well into the night. She said that it was during one of these "check-ins" that Quinn raped her in her room.

In recalling the incident, Cecelia reflected on the fact that Quinn targeted her in her own home, saying, "I had every right to drink in the safety of my room, trusting the thought that no one would harm me, especially being in my room." She emphasized that she had considered the room a safe space. It was her military-assigned home. However, in this case, living on base in a room other servicemembers had access to and work-related reasons to go to created vulnerability for her. Further, the fact that he outranked her and was her base sponsor meant he had power and authority over her. She said, "I trusted him as my sponsor, as my NCO. I told him I trusted him." When the military puts people in positions of power and in roles where they are expected to lead and command junior servicemembers, it also creates the perception that the military trusts those people and that servicemembers should trust them as well. The expectation of trust can override feelings of uncertainty or suspicion. Finally, the fact that Cecelia's room had previously been his room and that he told her this fact means that he might have had an extra sense of ownership and entitlement over that space. The fact that it had been his room also mattered for the legal case against him, which will be discussed below.

BLENDING WORK, PERSONAL, AND SOCIAL SPACES

All but three of the women I spoke with described pervasive sexual harassment throughout their military service. Enlisted women who live on base are at an increased risk for sexual violence since both their daily work spaces and their social spaces at home are controlled by the military. Living on base means women, who are outnumbered by men, are easily noticed, and easily surveilled. Organizational rules, based on rank and marital status, dictate who *must* live on base, who *can* live on base, and *where* those individuals are permitted to live. Married servicemembers living with their spouse, regardless of rank, can live on base in a family home or receive a housing allowance to live off base. While unmarried enlisted servicemembers in upper enlisted ranks can live off base, most unmarried enlisted personnel must live on base in group-style housing referred to as barracks or dorms. For example, "The Marine Corps believes that lower-ranking enlisted Marines living together is essential to discipline, unit cohesion, and esprit de corps. Under the Marine Corps program, junior Marines (E-1 to E-3) share a room and a bathroom. Marines in the pay grades of E-4 and E-5 are entitled to a private room" (Powers 2018). Military bases also have a variety of social spaces, including restaurants, bars, grocery stores, and gym facilities. This ensures that servicemembers, particularly those living on base, have frequent interactions with their co-workers outside of the official workspace. In fact, the military claims that bases are "a lot like living in a town. There are post offices, shopping centers, medical and dental clinics, and other businesses" (Department of Defense 2022).

Living and working with the same people and interacting with them in informal settings can produce family-like relationships and have team-building benefits. This is the rationale behind the Marine Corps ensuring that lower-ranking Marines share rooms and bathrooms. However, when men control the space, and the spatial features elevate masculinity and spotlight or denigrate femininity, women are vulnerable to harassment and abuse. In other words, within such a masculine organizational context, the spatial arrangements of the military can be exploited by men to create sexual danger for women. For example, in my conversation with Margaret, an enlisted Marine, she shared her frustration that work problems, including harassment from colleagues, frequently followed her home: "And it's not like in the civilian world, where if you have a problem, you just leave it at work. There is no 'leave it at work,' it's all work."

For Margaret, harassment continues at home because "home" is a military space where those problematic co-workers also reside. Servicewomen living on base cannot escape workplace harassment by going home. In many cases, they cannot even escape it by going to exercise, going out to eat, or running errands because those are all located on base. The unique blend of work, personal, and social spaces on military bases means that perpetrators potentially have more frequent interactions with victims *and* can also be alerted to victims' daily routines to create these interactions. This is felt more heavily by unmarried, enlisted women who are poor, as they likely live on base and might not have reliable access to transportation to leave base. Imagine a woman does not have a car. She takes the same shuttle to her office every day. She eats lunch around same time every day and usually goes to one of the on-base restaurants. Some days after work, she walks to the commissary for groceries. Other days, she goes back to her barracks and changes into workout clothing and heads to the gym on base. Or she heads to the smoke pit for a cigarette. In a space with between 8% and 20% women, servicewomen are easily noticed and stand out in all these spaces. If someone is romantically interested in a servicewoman and wants to coordinate a moment to run into her, it would be much easier to track her movements and daily routines in a confined space like a military base. An individual could learn her hobbies and where she socializes, her shopping habits (i.e., does she buy alcohol? does she eat out?), if she smokes, and what time she works out and what time she usually arrives home. This knowledge can be easily used for a variety of reasons, including positive ones—perhaps women seeking more women friends might try to arrange to take the same shuttle. Perhaps a serviceman who has an interest in basketball sees a servicewoman playing and joins her. It can also be used to track or stalk someone, which is what happened to Rosa-Maria. She explained:

I had a little bit of a stalker. It was a little weird. I just met this guy.
I think it was at, like, the bar on base. We did almost get kind of
close . . . We almost kissed . . . I decided after that, I was, like, "Maybe
we shouldn't really see each other anymore" . . . I was, like, "You
have a wife and you have a kid." For a couple of weeks, he would just
still . . . his barracks was up the hill from mine, but he would still
hang around in the smoke pit (near her barracks). There was one
time, he was like, oh, "I saw you taking a nap in your room." (Marine
Corps, enlisted, Latina)

He stalked her for two weeks. During this time Rosa-Maria tried to minimize her outings and "ignored him and hoped he would go away." Being
confined to the military base allowed him to stalk her more easily. If they
had met at a bar off base, he likely would not have come to know where
she lived and worked so easily. Rosa-Maria was not surprised he knew the
smoke pit that she would use because he knew where her barracks were
located. She was shocked, however, that he knew where her room was. She
guessed that he either looked for her in the window or asked someone
which room she lived in, which was easier to pinpoint as one of the few
women on base.

Worse still, maybe a serviceman harasses a servicewoman and is afraid
she is on the cusp of reporting him; he decides he wants to silence her
and has an opportunity to do so because he knows her daily schedule and
routine. It is suggested that this is what happened in the case of Vanessa
Guillén. In 2020, Guillén was murdered on Fort Cavazos (which at the
time was called Fort Hood Army Base), in an armory room controlled
by her murderer, Aaron Robinson. The armory room was located in a
building adjacent to where she worked (Diaz, Cramer, and Morales 2022).
She was last seen by witnesses in a parking lot near both buildings. Space
and geography matter for how Robinson was able to murder Guillén on
a military base undetected. Working in adjacent buildings and having a
view of and access to the same parking lot means he could be alerted to
her coming and going as well as her work schedule. Having a similar position but outranking her meant there were work-related reasons for him to

contact her, make requests of her, or even ask her to come to the armory room he controlled. Since he was in control of the space, he could manipulate a time to isolate her in the arms room.

Sharing work, living, and social spaces with mostly men puts a spotlight on women at multiple points in their day. Men can monitor women more easily on military bases than in other spaces because women are hypervisible and because servicemembers often live, work, and socialize in the same geographic area. This is made more dangerous for servicewomen when perpetrators are in positions of power through their military rank or job, which they can exploit to justify interactions with servicewomen they want to harass or assault.

The Danger of Standing Out

When Samantha was in an all-woman platoon, she said, "The best part about it? Not getting harassed," which shows the relationship between men's domination of space and harassment of women. Women shared that because men dominated their bases, units, and offices, they experienced pervasive harassment. For example, June was enlisted in both the Marine Corps and in the Air Force. When I spoke with her, she was in the Air Force and made it clear that she preferred this branch of service because there were more women (21.1% vs. 8.9%). She recalled that when she was in the Marines, she was one of only a few women living in the barracks on her base:

June: If you know who you are, which most girls don't at eighteen, which is when they join the military—if you know who you are, you can keep your own values and not compromise to the ten guys who come to your door every day and ask you out.

Me: And is that common? People knock on your door and ask you out?

June: Oh, definitely. All the time. People you've never seen before and they know that "the girl" lives there or whatever. Yeah, definitely. (Marine Corps, enlisted, Asian-American)

June described living in an area where many servicemen had access to her living space. As one of the only women in the barracks, she and her room location were known to servicemen she had never met, and men used this knowledge to congregate outside of her door, ask her for dates, and objectify her. The low representation of women in the military makes them stand out in military spaces, giving servicemen knowledge of, access to, and ultimately control over their living spaces and movements. Melanie explains how this surveillance and harassment was not limited to the barracks:

> I'm just, like, overwhelmed. You can't go into a dining facility without getting stared down. You can't walk around the gym without getting stared down. It's like I don't want to go out because I don't want to feel like a piece of meat. (Army, enlisted, White)

Melanie described an over-sexualized workplace where men stared at women, pressured women for sex and dates, and created a climate where she did not feel safe in any military spaces. She explained that at times she chose not to run errands so that she did not have to put up with harassment. To go to the gym or the grocery store, she had to mentally prepare herself for the inevitability of harassment. The pervasiveness of the harassment affects women's feelings of comfort and safety at work, at home, as well as in any military space. Women must constantly remain vigilant about assessing sexual violence vulnerability, which is tiresome. It leads some women to decide to stay home and forgo their errands, workouts, and social outings. This is compounded by social media, where women are also harassed by servicemen and where rumors circulate about servicewomen, sometimes even before they arrive at new units or duty stations.

Carol explained that as a woman enlisted in the Marine Corps, she made a plan to not become friends with men. She specifically stated, "When I first came, I'm not here to make friends, I'm still not here to make friends. I'm here to do a job." She adopted this strategy because she knew that rumors circulated about her before she arrived at her unit:

There are very few females; like, before I came to my unit, they all knew they were getting a female check-in, and that's, like, since I've been here, everybody knows when we're getting a female check-in. Once you're getting a female, then come all the rumors, all the stories, anything she ever has or hasn't done . . . anything that you could say about her comes with it. Now, if you want to stick with that reputation that precedes you, you can, it's not really too hard to do, you know, 'cause it's already there. (Marine Corps, enlisted, White)

Carol explained that being friends with servicemen or socially interacting with them meant that more rumors would circulate. Carol lived and worked on base and had limited contact with non-servicemembers, so her approach to not make friends with men isolated her in many respects. Further, it can be hard to avoid interacting with servicemen when they target servicewomen with requests for dates, harassing them, and congregating outside of their homes. Allison described the way men harass women new to the unit as a "swarm" and a race to see who could hook up with her first:

Guys are Facebook-stalking these girls before they even get to your unit, trying to make buddy-buddy with them before they ever get here. Then you all are swarming her when she shows up to your unit, trying to hook up with her first. Then as soon as she hooks up with somebody who's not you, she's a "slut." (Marine Corps, enlisted, White)

Speaking from the perspective of servicemen, Allison explains that once men know that a woman will arrive in the unit, they stalk her on social media, and send a barrage of messages. The women coming into the unit are not viewed as new peers, co-workers, or even servicemembers but rather sexual prey and objects who are then shunned, shamed, ostracized, sexually harassed, and victimized if they do engage in romantic or sexual relationships with anyone in the unit.

Overall, some servicewomen described pervasive sexual harassment as an inevitable consequence of living in close quarters. Kayla, an officer in the Navy, stated: "I think any time a lot of people are stuck together without a lot of space . . . unfortunately . . . [they are] more likely to get sexual harassment." Kayla's reluctant acceptance of sexual harassment vulnerability demonstrates how men's domination of space and the masculinization of space become normalized and accepted aspects of the military. This can be intensified in other settings such as on deployment or in military workspaces like ships, planes, and submarines. Kayla elaborated:

> When I was on the ship, not the harassment but more I guess un-wanted . . . unwanted attention was a little bit more common. If you think about it, you're living with 1,000 people, 75% are guys, you know, on a very small ship for seven or eight months. Not making it excusable, but just the circumstances in which you would encounter it are probably more likely . . . on more, like, a ship than . . . on shore, where you're going . . . you're going back to your house every night. (Navy, officer, White)

Kayla's explanation shows the lack of separation between work and personal space in the military. Her belief that unwanted sexual attention is more likely to occur on a ship demonstrates how the blending of work, social life, and private space can create more risk and opportunity for sexual violence because it gives servicemen more access to servicewomen in a space that prioritizes men. Interestingly, another reason Kayla likely experienced more harassment on the ship than on base is because, as an officer, she is not required to live on base. When Kayla talks about going back to her house at night while on shore, she means a private, personal space off base that is not owned and controlled by the military, again highlighting the heightened vulnerability for enlisted servicewomen.

Even in the workplace, women may be sexually harassed and assaulted while trying to perform their military jobs, especially in fields dominated by men like aviation. For example, Angela stated:

And I've had situations where I was at 40,000 ft. altitude and I'm flying with two pilots for an international flight, and one of them puts his hand on my knee, you know? There's nothing you can really do about that except remove his hand and pretend like it didn't happen, because unfortunately the culture is if you're one of the few women and you say anything, then you get labeled as a person who's going to call sexual harassment. (Navy, enlisted, White)

Angela's experience shows how men's domination of space in a small, enclosed area can create sexual danger for servicewomen. Her emphasis on trying to avoid being labeled reveals her belief that reporting experiences of sexual harassment will result in her being further ostracized rather than the perpetrator being reprimanded. Thus, women's knowledge that a space is controlled by men can encourage their silence in the moment of unwanted touching, and their understanding that the military is a masculine environment in general can *keep* them silent about such instances.

Women may be especially at risk on deployment, a time when they are isolated and away from their support networks. Erin, an enlisted Marine, explained how the base where she was deployed was a hostile place for her and the few other servicewomen who were with her because it was dominated by men:

There was probably about, on that whole base, about seven to eight female Marines. We all lived in this one little tent . . . It was horrible there. We couldn't walk anywhere without people saying things. They weren't afraid to say it out loud. They would look at you and say, like, "I just want to bend you over right here. Rip your fucking pants off." They're like, "She looks like a fighter" and it was like, "Oh well, I'll just hold her face down." Or, "That one's not so great-looking but you don't need to look at her face to find her pussy." They would say things like that all the time just out loud, so you could hear it. (Marine Corps, enlisted, Indigenous)

Erin described denying herself food to avoid being sexually harassed: "It got to where we didn't even want to go to the chow hall anymore. We hated going to the little commissary. We hated going there and just anywhere in public during the day was a pain because it was just constant." Rather than addressing the behavior of servicemen, Erin's gunnery sergeant challenged her protest and forced her and the other women to eat in the chow hall, thereby ignoring their continued harassment and sustaining the men's power and control of this space. In this way, institutional sexism and interactional sexism work together to maintain women's continued vulnerability.

MEN'S CONTROL OF SPACE

Janet was a nineteen-year-old soldier who was drinking with a friend, her friend's boyfriend, and an acquaintance. She mentioned that underage drinking was common because soldiers who were over twenty-one would buy alcohol for everyone to share. They passed around a bottle of brandy for a while until there was hardly any left. At some point, after Janet felt very drunk, her friend and her boyfriend left to have a private chat, leaving Janet alone with Liam, a man she barely knew. Janet emphasized to me that "we were not a thing; that was actually the first time I ever hung out with him. But they [her friend and her boyfriend] left to go talk and I didn't want to intrude on that. So, I was just like, okay, whatever. Yeah. I'm kicking it with this random dude." At some point, Janet realized she needed to go to the bathroom:

> I remember telling him, we were sitting out in front of the deck of
> the detachment, like the Army one, in his truck. And I said some-
> thing along the lines of like, "I've really got to pee." So, I was just
> going to go walk into the detachment and go pee and probably go to
> bed. I don't know what I was planning on doing. All I know is that
> I really wanted to pee. And he was like, "Oh, okay, well then, I'll take
> you to a bathroom." And I was like, "There's a bathroom right there."

He was like, "Girl, you are drunk, you can't go in there." But I'm like, "Okay. Yeah, that's true. I'm nineteen years old. I probably don't want to be walking in front of all the cadre right now, smelling like brandy." So, we drove—or he drove, not me. I was not in any state to be driving. So yeah, he drove me to these, it's like a camp zone. They had these restrooms, so I don't know how he knew the code for this restroom. And I didn't even think about it, but he entered a code, and I went in to go pee. And then I peed. I think I also puked, pretty sure that happened. And actually, I vaguely remember . . . when the CID [Army Criminal Investigation Division] and everybody got involved, there was still vomit in the toilet. So, I definitely know I puked. I washed up and was walking back out, and as I opened the door, he pushed me back into the restroom. And I remember I was sitting on the counter, and I was really, really drunk, like near the sink. And I remember him saying something along the lines of like, "We can't take you back. You are way too drunk." And I was like, "Yeah, that's probably right. I don't even know what I'm going to do." Eventually I'm going to have to go back. But I was gone . . . And then I remember, I put my head on the wall near the sink and I think maybe that's where I fell asleep. I'm not entirely sure, but I passed out. Because then the next thing that I remember is feeling a whole bunch of pain and trying to say "no" and "move," and push him away. But I couldn't, I physically couldn't move. And then the next thing that I remember after that, was being on the couch in the day room. Have you heard of ice sheets before? It's exactly what it sounds like. It's like literal bedsheets that they put in ice. But they weren't able to wake me up. So, what you do is you take the sheets out, you wrap the person in it and then you dump all the ice on them. So that's how they woke me up. My roommate and the sergeant on duty were there. I was like, "What is even going on?" I was still pretty drunk, still *very* drunk actually. And I was really confused. This is not where I remember being. "What the fuck happened?" I said: "I'm cold. Can I change?" So, my roommate went back up to our room and grabbed me fresh dry clothes and then came back downstairs and I was really

drunk still at the time. So, I didn't even care that I was in the middle
of the day room. I just started taking off my clothes and put on the
new clothes. And then when I pulled off my shorts, I realized that
I wasn't wearing underwear, but I knew that I was wearing underwear [earlier in the evening]. So, I was just so confused. I was like,
"Where is my underwear?" And then I, like, got a flash of, like, being
on the ground in the restroom and trying to push him away and
everything hurting. And I was like, "Oh, shit." So, I kind of started
to panic and the sergeant on duty that helped me was like, "What
happened?" She said, "Oh my God. Did he take advantage of you?"
And I just started bawling and said something like, "Yeah, I think so."
(Army, enlisted, biracial)

Liam used his power and control over space and his knowledge of military rules to orchestrate an opportunity to rape Janet. First, Liam told
Janet that going to the more public bathroom could result in her getting
in trouble for underage drinking, a citation that could affect her military career. Servicemembers can be punished in a variety of ways for underage drinking. Living in a space where co-workers and superiors can
easily monitor their social activities can increase the fear of getting caught
for this offense. Liam played on this fear to convince her to go to a more
isolated location. He had a car and knew the code to a private, secluded
bathroom. After raping her, he put Janet back in his truck, drove to the
living quarters, and called her friend. He told her, "Janet's not waking up.
You have to come get her, and don't let anyone see you." He knew that if
he carried Janet her to her room, he would be more likely to be caught.
He was hyper-aware of how it would look for him to transport an uncon-
scious woman through the parking lot and into a more crowded space.
    Liam was court-martialed for the rape. There was physical evidence
from the rape kit and witness testimony that he was with Janet uncon-
scious in his truck. Janet said, "He kept my underwear. He used to say it
was a trophy. They [investigators] found them in his truck." Despite this
evidence, he was not convicted. She shared that one of the jury members
who did not want to convict said: "Well, if she didn't want that to happen,

she shouldn't have drank so much." In this case, Liam's ability to manipulate the military space and military rules was exacerbated by the military's culture of aggressive masculinity and denigration of women. Liam exploited these conditions, while the institutional values of men's domination allowed him to avoid punishment.

Control of space is also related to who makes decisions about the use and maintenance of physical spaces, including who makes room assignments on work-related trips, and who makes decisions about when to repair things like doors, locks, and windows. For example, Samantha recalled that when she was enlisted and required to live on base, she submitted a request to have the lock to her door fixed after a serviceman continually tried to break in.[4]

> In my barracks room, I was having people—someone was trying to break in at night. He very clearly knew that I was in there. You couldn't lock the door permanently. I tried to get someone to fix it. I asked someone, "What can we do?" And he said, "Why don't you just get a bat?" I was just trying to get someone to care—I can't lock my door, and someone is trying to get in all the time. I ended up doing . . . setting up my own alarm with spoons. Actually, before I did that, instead of fixing the problem they said, "Well, if you can't be by yourself, we'll just put someone else in there with you then." They had no interest in fixing it. I think they even said, "We don't have money to fix the locks." So, I set up the spoons. (Marine Corps, officer/enlisted, White)

Samantha's experience demonstrates how servicewomen's concerns about safety in military spaces, including their own homes, can be dismissed by men who control those spaces. Unlike an individual living off base, Samantha *must* rely on the military and other servicemembers to fix her locks. By forcing Samantha to live on base and requiring her to seek institutional assistance for home repairs, the military increases her dependence on men who may not perceive sexual threats as problematic. If the military requires people to live on base, it should ensure the safety and security of the homes it provides. Men's domination of the military means that men are more likely to be in positions of power but also in charge of small decisions that can make a big difference in women's vulnerability to sexual assault. Thus, it matters not only what those in high positions of power think about sexual assault vulnerability, but also what those who have spatial authority, like those who field and prioritize maintenance requests, think about sexual assault vulnerability. Melanie shared that people in her brigade were assigned CQ (charge of quarters) duty in pairs where "you and another person are sitting in the barracks to make sure that people aren't drinking underage or messing around and the MPs [Military Police] don't get called. And one of our concerns was if you're going to have two people on duty, they both need to be the same gender." Women were afraid of being alone with a serviceman late at night in the barracks because they felt like it created sexual violence vulnerability. Melanie and other women tried to ensure that women would only be paired with women, but "we went to our NCOs, they blew us off. We went to the SHARP [Sexual Harassment/Assault Response and Prevention Program] representative who is supposed to be the one that handles sexual assault; he blew us off and just didn't care. Several females expressed their concerns about being with a male on duty at night in the barracks and everybody just kind of ignored us." Women's attempts to make spaces safer for them can be thwarted by men's positions of power in the military hierarchy and their dominance in decision-making positions when those men do not recognize sexual violence vulnerability as an institutional issue.

Challenging the Masculine Space

Cecelia reported Quinn for sexual assault, and she had a rape kit conducted a few days later. Quinn's DNA was found. The prosecutors in her case seemed to think it would be easy to convict since they had her statement, Quinn had lied about his whereabouts that evening, and they had his DNA. However, the defense claimed that because Quinn had lived in the room prior to Cecelia, his DNA would be all over the room. This became a point of contention in the case, and eventually the prosecutors decided to try Quinn for fraternization[5] and adultery[6] (he was married) rather than for sexual assault. Sometimes prosecutors choose to try adultery over sexual assault because it is easier to legally prove that sexual intercourse occurred than it is to prove that consent was not given. Even still, the defense argued that Quinn's DNA being found during the examination of her body did not mean that intercourse occurred. They claimed that his DNA was in the room before she moved in and that it transferred to Cecelia without genital contact between the two parties.

In judicial cases where servicemembers intentionally exploit the power, control, and trust that is given to them based on rank and military position, the military has a choice to remove the person from their trusted position, take them to court-martial or an administrative separation board, or offer a non-judicial punishment. In this case, Quinn was taken to court-martial and convicted of fraternization and adultery. However, Cecilia did not feel as though the charges reflected the severity of what happened to her. She felt that the military failed to take her case seriously. In the sentencing hearing, the prosecution asked for Quinn to be demoted several ranks. One of the prosecutors tried to convince the members of this by highlighting how inappropriate it was to bring alcohol to a junior Marine's room. He stated: "If he wants to fraternize with lance corporals, let him be a lance corporal." If the jury members had agreed, he would have been significantly demoted, which would have taken away some of his institutional power. However, the members decided on a lesser punishment, and he remained at a rank that could still allow him to oversee junior Marines, despite evidence that he had used this position to cause harm.

In this case, the sexual geography of the duty station and the military's reliance on hierarchy created a situation of sexual vulnerability for servicewomen, which was then intentionally exploited by Quinn. Those asking how this could have been prevented could start by examining the message it sends to other servicemen that a man accused of rape and convicted of fraternization and adultery is allowed to remain in a position of power over junior Marines. This builds tolerance for harassment, reinforces expectations of men's dominance over the military space, and sustains sexual vulnerability for servicewomen.

Furthermore, when the military keeps a harasser or a rapist in a position of power, that person may become a serial abuser. Marie was raped when she was a cadet at the Air Force Academy by a senior at the academy who used his leadership position to isolate and assault cadets. Her rapist was the point person for the academy's Aero Club, meaning cadets relied on him for club access and scheduling flying hours. Marie describes how his position of power made her, and many other women cadets, vulnerable to rape:

The guy who raped me was a senior, and he was the point of contact for the Aero Club. So, I wanted to fly on the weekends, and he was the person I was supposed to email to be able to access the Aero Club. So, he said he would help me study for the tests I would need to take to check out their planes on the weekend. So, I met him in the library, and he raped me in the library. Right. So, I didn't tell anybody, but what I wouldn't find out for months is that he raped a bunch of us. There were five women who eventually reported. So, I mean multiply that by . . . the many who didn't report, an unknown number. Two weeks after he raped me, he sodomized a teenager. And he got caught in California. A woman who was . . . she was in a wheelchair because she had cerebral palsy. And she had to go to the emergency room because she was bleeding. Sorry, I'm . . . it's sickening. She reported because she had to go to the emergency room. And so, there was a prosecution in his case. The military took over the case, even though she was a civilian, even though it happened at home—off base, they still took it over. It surprises people when I tell them that. I think it's a little-known fact that the military can do that. So, he was sentenced to—you know I need to look this up again— but I think it was fourteen months, and then he served eight. Yeah, he served eight months. And then two weeks after he served, they caught him soliciting sex from a fourteen-year-old. So, they sent him to prison for the rest of his sentence. So, I think he ended up serving the full fourteen months, if you want to call that "full." He was never prosecuted for any of the crimes against cadets. By that time, I had reported; at least three of the other women had reported. Two had reported before me. That's what I didn't know is that two women had already reported before me, and he was still in that position of trust . . . that point of contact position [for the Aero Club]. He wasn't removed from that point of contact. (Air Force Academy, White)

The Air Force Academy left a senior in a position of power over younger cadets despite knowing that several women had reported him for rape. His position as the Aero Club point person subsequently ensured that young women would be required to interact with him. They would meet with him where he suggested because he was in a position of authority over them, and he suggested secluded areas, where he raped them. While the military did eventually court-martial and put him in military prison, the Air Force Academy's failure to investigate the earlier cases of rape against cadets shows how institutional inaction can empower and embolden rapists, even if unintentionally.

It is important to note that the military can easily dismiss individuals from positions of power such as a club point person. The institution can also move to dismiss cadets from the Academy or to remove servicemembers from the military without a court-martial through an involuntary separation or an administrative separation process.[7] At commanders' disposal are several policies, administrative rules, and bureaucratic measures that can be mobilized against people who engage in sexual violence. However, the women I spoke with rarely described these tools (administrative flags, non-judicial punishments, administrative separation boards, etc.) as being used against the men who harassed or assaulted them. In some cases, these bureaucratic tools and policies were used against women who reported sexual violence, which is explained further in the chapter on administrative harm and bureaucratic harassment. Sadly, Marie's Air Force career ended before it really started:

My rapist—gave me herpes. The herpes went to my brain. I ended up in the intensive care unit . . . And it wouldn't be for months that I would get my medical records and see that my very first spinal tap the day I was admitted into the ICU tested positive for herpes . . . All of that time my neurologist knew what the virus was . . . he didn't treat it. You know, he was an ass. I think he just thought I was—fill in the blanks—you know, a slut . . . whatever. So, he literally didn't treat me. But in that time [the four months before her doctor treated her] it went from meningitis to encephalitis, meaning the virus went to the tissue of my brain. And I had damage. It went to my temporal lobe. I couldn't finish my math major because I couldn't focus on the equations anymore. I had damage to my vagus nerve, which controls digestion, so I was, um, throwing up all the time, even after the infection was gone.

Marie had her medical records and herpes diagnosis withheld from her for months, which drastically impacted her health and daily life. Additionally, she believed this information was purposely withheld from her because the doctor assumed she was promiscuous, revealing more layers of harm that stem from stigmatized femininities. She tried to take time off, but the medical conditions continued to affect her. She said: "It was technically a medical discharge, but I just couldn't handle the pain, and the cognitive deficits, and yeah, so I left after two-and-a-half years of being there."

Some of the servicewomen I spoke with shared experiences of elevated harassment while on deployments dominated by men or while on ships or planes with mostly men. However, conditions of vulnerability to harassment and assault are persistent across women's military careers. It's not just that women suffer from the behavior of one "bad" serviceman, or even a couple of bad servicemen; rather, women experience different levels of harassment from multiple people across their entire time in the military, in a context in which harassment is normalized. The sum of these experiences with harassment, as well as the collective non-response from others to this treatment, puts women in difficult positions when trying to report harassment and sexual assault. When women try to disclose or report, other servicemembers view them as problematic. For example, Angela tried to tell higher-ranking officers about an attempted rape she experienced from someone in the unit:

> He showed up at my door, and was pounding on my door, wanting to borrow something for his flight suit. I opened my door and he forced himself into my room. And . . . he basically tried to get on me, and luckily enough I was able to get him out of my room. And later, the next day, when I was doing a pre-flight, I was in a flight station with the two lieutenant commanders and said, "Listen, I had a situation last night with so-and-so, it was really awkward," and they both were like, "We don't want to hear about it." Because they liked him. They liked the guy. (Navy, enlisted, White)

This experience, alongside the experience of being touched on a plane by a higher-ranking officer, solidified for Angela that military spaces were sites of men's power, domination, and control. The lieutenant commanders' failure to acknowledge and reprimand the lower-ranking man in their unit for attempted rape is just one example of how men use their positions of power to protect masculine privilege in military spaces, at the expense of servicewomen, and even in the context of violence against servicewomen. This demonstrates the power of interpersonal interactions in sustaining sexual harassment vulnerability as Angela's experience was downplayed by her military leaders.

CONCLUSION

While the military claims its spatial arrangements are designed to promote camaraderie, they have extremely gendered consequences when the devaluation of femininity and the promotion of a violent masculinity is embedded in the space. I have outlined how spatial arrangements lend themselves to exploitation when they are dominated by men and are designed to erode privacy. When servicemembers are required to live on base, and are on base for their work, recreational, and social activities, women's lives can be easily monitored and surveilled by potential perpetrators. While all servicemembers experience a reduction in privacy due to these arrangements, servicewomen, being a numerical minority, are more easily tracked and surveilled because they stand out. Further, the work-related access to servicemembers' personal spaces, such as assigning individuals to patrol the barracks, provides those who wish to cause harm an institutional excuse for predatory behavior. This predatory behavior is not reprimanded but encouraged by the institution and other servicemembers. Masculine dominance is normalized through hyper-masculine décor and imagery that is embedded in military spaces, including work offices, social spaces on base, and in the barracks. Further, men use their positions of power to preserve masculine privilege and to downplay sexual harassment and assault in military spaces. Most women who try to challenge men's dominance of space or try to create sexually safer spaces are usually thwarted from doing so. Those who try to report sexual harassment and assault are often ignored, isolated, or harassed more, which again preserves men's dominance in the space and does nothing to change vulnerability. Some women, like Cecelia, successfully report their victimization and can access military resources. Cecelia's rapist was also tried in the military justice system, showing institutional support for her victimization. However, in the aftermath of his guilty verdict, he remained in the Marine Corps at a rank where he could still oversee junior Marines and potentially cause more harm. Therefore, the interplay between spatial arrangements, organizational domination by men, and organizational support for preserving men's positions of power not only serve to exclude women from institutional belonging but place them in positions of sexual vulnerability. When masculinity and femmephobia is embedded in institutional values, military policy, and bureaucracy, it creates similar gendered consequences, which will be discussed in the next chapter.

Administrative Tools of Harm

The Bureaucratic Harassment of U.S. Servicewomen

Angela was a successful sailor working in aviation.[1] She had positive evaluations, sufficient training and qualifications, good physical fitness scores, and a degree in her field, and was on track for her next promotion. She had been in her unit for eighteen months when a new commander transferred in.[2] That is when her work experiences, and eventually her military career, changed for the worse. Her new commander often made negative comments about women. Shortly after his arrival to the unit he tried to ground her from flying and tried to move her to a desk job. She said:

> Well, you know I had heard that he obviously didn't [want women
> in the service] . . . He'd make jokes about how he thought women
> shouldn't be in the Navy and this and that, and I never took any-
> thing to it, and then slowly some of these things started happening.
> All of a sudden I'm not getting put on flights, those things are
> occurring . . . and he's trying to pull my [flight] qualifications—you
> know, it just didn't add up. (Navy, enlisted, White)

Angela had the qualifications and flight experience and had flown for her position in the unit many times, yet the new commander tried persuading

Hardship Duty. Stephanie Bonnes, Oxford University Press. © Oxford University Press 2024.
DOI: 10.1093/oso/9780197636244.003.0004

her to move to a non-flight job. She could not help but connect this to his own personal sexism, which he flaunted in the unit. When she did not comply, he tried to force her to take the desk job by grounding her from flights. He simply did not put her on the flight schedule. She believes that his hope was that she would seek to transfer or would accept a transfer out of his unit because she was no longer flying. Angela did not voluntarily transfer. Angela then failed an exam where only two of her answers were marked as incorrect. Her commander used the fact that she "failed" the exam to continue grounding her from flights, this time being able to cite a reason for doing so. She then was prohibited from retaking the exam by her commander despite a protocol where anyone failing an exam can and should retake it within ninety days. She continued:

> He said, "You are not flying anymore, that's it, I'm the skipper." And I said, "Well, with all due respect, sir, I'm required to take the exam again." Then he just refused to let me take it.
>
> And then they [the command] tried to take my qualifications away from me, and I told them they couldn't do that because they didn't follow the procedure for allowing me to retake the test in ninety days. So, my master chief took me into his office, and he told me repeatedly that I needed to convert and change my rate.[3] Even though I had a bachelor's degree in aeronautics and I had over three thousand flight hours, he wanted to convert me to PS, which is the equivalent of someone who works in an office and does accounting. I'd worked nine years specifically to fly, and they wanted to put me at a desk doing paperwork . . . But he was expecting me to convert, and I refused to convert, so I put in my resignation, and he told me I wasn't allowed to resign, and then I pulled up the instruction that stated that I was. And he tried to pull my qual[ifications], and then I got the instruction that said he couldn't do that, and I put in my resignation, and walked out of there, before he could do that. So, I submitted my paperwork to be in inactive reserve status. . . . I ended up resigning and turning in and going inactive because I couldn't take it anymore. (Navy, enlisted, White)

Subsequently, Angela was reprimanded for *not* retaking the exam in the ninety-day time period despite being prohibited from doing so. His goal was to use her exam failure, the formal reprimand for not retaking the exam (despite being ordered not to), as justification to take away her earned qualifications, which would make her *ineligible* for a flying position. This would not just force her out of the unit but would completely change her military career, trajectory, and post-service options. The commander in this situation relied on the bureaucratic and discretionary power granted to him by the military to damage Angela's military career. He was unsuccessful in prohibiting her from resigning only because she knew of a military policy that outlined a process for her to resign. This reveals how knowledge of bureaucratic rules and policies can be a source of power and resistance.

Importantly, the new commander tried several tactics to move Angela into a different position and out of the unit. First, he created a work environment that was hostile to women by making sexist comments. Then, he specifically targeted Angela through setting a flight schedule that excluded her, hoping that these unofficial penalties would force her to accept the desk job he wanted her to take. Ultimately, though, it was his power and discretion in the military's administrative system and his careful manipulation of bureaucratic policies that allowed for him to build an official case against her, and to achieve his desired result of removing Angela from his command.

Angela's experience reveals how the misuse of bureaucratic policies can be facilitated by a hierarchal structure where power in decision-making is based on rank. In the military, individuals with higher rank are afforded greater respect, responsibility, and power, as well as greater discretion in evaluations and policy implementation. Additionally, those with higher rank have more experience with bureaucratic rules and regulations. This can enable commanders to manipulate existing policies and exploit the fact that many servicemembers might not be familiar with the rules and/ or might be hesitant to question their superiors. Additionally, unlike in contexts where an employer's discretionary firing of pregnant women (Byron and Roscigno 2014) or a landlord's discretion in evictions (Tester

2008) may be used to demonstrate harassment and build a case against perpetrators, a commanding officer's discretion is a *protected* aspect of military operations and considered essential to military effectiveness. Thus, there is often no way to *prove* discrimination.

Angela's commander's expressed reluctance to work with women is not an isolated incident; rather, it is indicative of attitudes shared by many servicemen and supported by the military's femmephobic environment (Vogt et al. 2007). Altogether, the military provides the culture, structure, and tools that servicemen can use to control and damage servicewomen's careers. In Angela's case, because her commander oversaw setting the flight schedule for her unit, administering and monitoring tests required for certification, and recommending transfers, his unchecked manipulation of the rules, regulations, and evaluative procedures allowed him to achieve the goal of getting Angela out of his unit. This harassment, which I call "bureaucratic harassment," caused Angela to terminate her Navy career and left her feeling like the military "is not a place for women." In Angela's experience, once the institutional rules, policies, and procedures were used against her, she could no longer tolerate the hostility toward women and wanted out.

BUREAUCRATIC HARASSMENT

This project started with the question of how sexual abuse remains highly prevalent in an organization that has longstanding and evolving policies, prevention strategies, and education programs that address sexual violence as well as victim services and legal assistance. I wanted to understand what processes and mechanisms sustain sexual violence vulnerability, and what institutional and interpersonal factors contribute to harassment. I found that the military's bureaucracy was central to answering these questions. It certainly is not the case that the military does not have enough policies to address sexual violence. Rather, the military's bureaucracy is mapped onto the gendered and masculine values and meanings of the military context in ways that make it a tool of harassment rather than an avenue for victim assistance.

Like Angela, over half of the women I spoke with focused on the myriad of rules, regulations, policies, and citations that were used against them to achieve sexism, harassment, and discrimination. They spent a lot of time telling me about specific administrative rules that negatively affected their lives. They discussed in great detail not only how their commanders used discretion in rule implementation, but also how they seemed to have an infinite number of avenues for punishment through the administrative system. This is an interesting contrast to how bureaucracy is usually discussed as it is related to workplaces. Some argue that bureaucracy promotes equality by increasing transparency in job descriptions, performance evaluations, and organizational policy (Bielby 2000; Reskin 2000). Bureaucratic practices have been linked to reducing discrimination in the workplace through limiting subjectivity and therefore leaving less room for personal biases in recruitment, hiring, decision-making, promoting, and firing. This is because bureaucracy has been understood as a system of rules and processes that standardize policies regarding employment, making criteria related to hiring, promoting, and firing seemingly objective and depersonalized. With the same criteria applying to all potential and actual employees, opportunities for marginalized groups can increase in bureaucratic organizations (Bielby 2000; Guthrie and Roth 1999). Some argue that discrimination and inequality are more prevalent in non-bureaucratic organizations because individuals will resort to stereotypes and biases in decision-making without clear rules and regulations (Reskin 2000). However, the women I spoke with described a flexible bureaucratic system that functions as large arsenal of administrative weapons often mobilized against them. They said that policies and rules were applied at the discretion of officers and NCOs and did not enhance equality. Rather, servicewomen saw other servicemembers, usually servicemen, using institutional policies, regulations, and reprimands as *tools* of discrimination and harassment. The existence of bureaucratic harassment shows how institutional sexism adapts to the updated military administration that has

more inclusive policies, sexual harassment and assault prevention and response processes, and avenues to report discrimination.

Bureaucratic harassment is a force by which some servicemen harass,
intimidate, and control individual, as well as groups of, servicewomen
through bureaucratic channels. Bureaucratic harassment is the purposeful
manipulation of legitimate administrative policies and procedures,
perpetrated by individuals who hold institutional power over others. It
is used to undermine colleagues' professional experiences and careers.
Bureaucratic harassment refers to both the specific actions of individuals
who actively manipulate bureaucratic policies and the organizational structure that enables harassment and protects perpetrators. In fact, knowledge
of bureaucratic procedures and access to bureaucratic channels are sources
of power in themselves that can be used to cause harm. Bureaucracy is
central to this type of harassment as it is both the source of power and
protection of perpetrators and the tool that they use to harass co-workers
or subordinates. The manipulation of administrative rules and regulations
is made possible by the interplay between a gendered and raced organizational climate and bureaucratic features such as discretion, hierarchy, and
the blending of work and personal life.

Over half of the servicewomen in this book experienced bureaucratic
harassment. As with many forms of workplace harassment, bureaucratic
harassment is often motivated by sexism, with the intention of limiting
the victim's professional career. Organizational features such as hierarchy,
discretion, and organizational expectations that commanders control
the personal lives of servicemembers facilitate bureaucratic harassment.
Individuals in positions of power can use their authority to manipulate policies through discretionary implementation of rules, regulations,
and evaluative procedures. Additionally, servicemen can mobilize social power based on race and gender to gain institutional influence over
women of color regardless of rank, meaning that Black, Latina, and
Indigenous women are vulnerable to bureaucratic harassment not only
from commanders but also from their peers. Bureaucratic harassment is
also used to intimidate servicewomen out of reporting incidents involving
sexual harassment and abuse.

Race, Power, and Hierarchy

Tactics of bureaucratic harassment include revoking servicewomen's qualifications to remove them from positions or units, issuing minor infractions with the intention of delaying or stopping promotions, threatening to withhold military benefits, selectively implementing rules and punishments, giving negative evaluations, and retaliating through the administrative system for reporting experiences with other forms of harassment and abuse. In Angela's case, her commander used a series of administrative sanctions combined with his authority to both prohibit her from retaking the exam and punish her for not retaking it with the goal of officially pulling her flight qualifications. This would make her ineligible to fly and would force her out of his unit. In Joanna's case, a military peer attempted to issue a series of administrative sanctions for small or nonexistent "infractions." In her role as an Army officer, Joanna oversaw many soldiers and was responsible for approving or denying their leave requests. If she approved a soldier's leave, she forwarded the leave information to another soldier who tracked personnel movements for everyone in the unit. It was through this routine process that a soldier of her same rank tried to mobilize the military's administrative system against her:

> So, my senior enlisted guy requested leave, I approve it, then my battalion commander has to approve it. So, I forward it to the captain [who tracks personnel happenings in the unit] and this motherfucker denied it. He has no authority to do that. So, I fight him on it, fight for my enlisted guy's leave. So, he turns around and *gives me* a "counseling statement." It said I was disrespecting a superior officer. He is *the same rank* as me . . . And he says my attitude is detrimental to unit morale and he has no other option but to recommend a dishonorable discharge. (Army, officer, Latina)

While the counseling statement filed by her peer had little bearing on Joanna's career because he was not her commanding officer and did not outrank her (in fact, a superior officer discarded it), her peer tried to establish a paper trail documenting that she was not a competent leader. Despite their equal rank, a White man at the rank of captain attempted to mobilize the social power derived from his race and gender to exert bureaucratic power over a Latina soldier. By citing Joanna's "attitude" in the infraction, he used tropes surrounding women of color as quick to anger and unprofessional (García-López 2008). Notably, *only* Black and Latina women reported that their "attitudes" were cited in infractions or performance reviews, demonstrating the gendered racism that motivates bureaucratic harassment in these cases (Texeira 2002). Stereotypes that support oppressive systems are highly adaptive and can be invoked to oppress, discriminate against, or disempower women of color (Collins 2000). Based on these tropes, specific actions or statements by Black women and Latinas are more likely to be interpreted negatively.

Similarly, another serviceman of her same rank attempted to establish a paper trail against Joanna, claiming she was overweight even though she recently gave birth. She said:

> I need to have a pregnancy profile in place. So, a pregnancy pro-file involves having an Army doctor signing an Army piece of paper saying that I had a baby. What the hell is wrong with our regular doctor saying this? Well, I guess the Army doctor is special (laughing), so they want me to take time out of my civilian day . . . not paying me . . . and have me go to an Army doctor . . . so that they don't have to have me take a PT [Army Physical Fitness Test[4]] for six months after I give birth. But since there's no pregnancy profile in place, I am now subject to these regulations. And I am like, "Well, are you going to send me to the doctor?" And he said, "No." Well then, fucking fine! So, then he put an administrative flag on me to say that I am a fat soldier.

Even though this officer was the same rank and did not have any authority over her, Joanna was forced to spend a significant amount of time responding to the administrative flag and trying to get it removed from her record. Joanna's experience also highlights the micro-processes of harassment that emerge when military standards and policies are based on men's bodies (McFarlane 2021) that exclude pregnancy, further casting women as inappropriate members of the military. By targeting her post-partum body as problematic and using this to administratively punish her, her colleague invoked the stereotype that mothers are not ideal workers (Byron and Roscigno 2014; Ridgeway and Correll 2004).

While Asian-American and White women reported experiences with harassment, including bureaucratic harassment, only Latina, Black, and Indigenous women were victims of harassment from those who did not outrank them (understood as "contra-power harassment"), and like Joanna, this often occurred throughout their military careers from multiple people. This demonstrates how in a White masculine institution, social power based on race and gender can be translated into bureaucratic power (Mckinney 1992; Rospenda et al. 1998). This makes Black, Latina, and Indigenous women, regardless of rank, particularly vulnerable to bureaucratic harassment from servicemen, especially given their underrepresentation in the officer corps (Burk and Espinoza 2012). This is compounded by the fact that Black and Latina women are more likely than White women to stay in the military for a longer period of time (Moore 2002), which is attributed to their more compromised social location in society and fewer high-paying employment opportunities outside of the military. Exacerbating this issue is the fact that, among servicewomen, women of color are at times placed in less-skilled jobs than White women, which disproportionately reduces their employability when they leave the service, and which may contribute to their disproportionate longevity in the military (Moore 1991). In this context, bureaucratic harassment in the form of a threat of a disciplinary action including reduction in rank and therefore pay, or a discharge from the military, which if dishonorable would sever veteran benefits, may affect women of color more severely than White women.

Bureaucratically Punishing Reporting

Servicemen also use bureaucratic harassment to prevent women from reporting abuse. For example, Samantha met significant resistance when she tried to report sexual harassment from her supervisor. Her gunnery sergeant frequently sexually harassed her and the other women in her unit: "He would drop pencils near his desk and ask the females to bend over and pick them up." This same man also aggressively grabbed her in the barracks where he was drinking with women ranked lower than him, violating the military policy against fraternization between members of different ranks. Recalling this experience, she stated, "I used to wrestle in high school, and he came up when I was in a room by myself and he, like, grabbed me [saying], 'I heard you're a wrestler, let's wrestle.'" Samantha tried to report the issue, despite being discouraged from doing so by several leaders in her unit. Ultimately, her major coerced her into not reporting the harassment through administrative means:

> They told me they would cancel all of my leave for Christmas if they had to investigate. It was clear that this was a threat. I was asked, "Do [you] really want to ruin this man's career? If we have to go forward, we will have to cancel your leave." I ended up just dropping it. (Marine Corps, enlisted/officer, White)

The major's position of power in the military hierarchy gave him the ability to grant and take away leave without citing a reason. Since the reason for canceling leave would not be revealed on documentation, Samantha could not prove it was related to her attempt to report harassment. This enabled her superior to misuse the bureaucratic system to keep her from reporting sexual abuse. She did try to "request mast," a military policy that allows individuals to go outside the typical command structure. However, access to this policy can be denied by those in power or through men protecting other men. When Samantha tried to request mast on her major and talk to his boss:

> The sergeant sent us back. We got counseled and yelled at for not following the chain of command. And we were almost formally reprimanded. His assistant wouldn't let us go talk to him. It . . . we just were brought back to the same starting point . . . They have

so much power over you—it will come bite you anyway. The sergeant just called down to the major and said, "Hey, sir, did you know that you have some 'devil dogs' in here trying to go around you?"

Samantha was not allowed access to an official military policy because a young, enlisted Marine who set the schedule for the higher-ranking officer she wanted to meet with used his position to protect the major in the unit. Importantly, this could lead to rewards for him as an enlisted lower-ranking Marine. However, the fact that he felt comfortable calling the major on Samantha, who outranked him, is evidence that men *know* the system is designed to protect masculinity, particularly when allegations of sexual abuse come up.

Further, the term "devil dog" takes on particular meaning when used in this way. According to Marine Corps legend, Germans nicknamed U.S. Marines "Devil Dogs" during World War I at the Battle of Belleau Wood. The legend explains that the Marines were exhausted, exposed to machine gun fire, and hit with mustard gas while trying to take a hill. They were wearing gas masks, but they were crude in design. The story claims that the Marines were sweating, had bloodshot eyes, and were foaming at the mouth through their masks, making them appear like "dogs from hell" or "devil dogs" to the Germans (U.S. Marine Corps 2022a). The nickname merged with the Marines' success at that battle, solidifying their reputation as an elite fighting and killing force. Even though the phrase existed before the Battle of Belleau Wood, this story is so widespread it appears on the Marine Corps website explaining battalion history and is easily recollected by Marines. Yet when used in a derogatory manner to describe victims trying to report sexual assault, the term "devil dogs" conjures up imagery of a "rabid feminist" foaming at the mouth in an attempt to take down servicemen. When Marine Corps images are filtered through misogyny, women who report harassment are seen as internal enemies and "social justice warriors" who are anti-men and anti-military. Women who try to report sexual assault are treated like enemies within rather than deserving of institutional resources and compassion. The enlisted man who used this phrase to describe Samantha and her friend was reaffirmed in his sexism when Samantha almost received a formal punishment for trying to request mast.

Samantha realized that her commander, and even those at her same rank, had complete power over her. After suffering from the harassment and assault she experienced, she grew anxious about the further harm that she would endure from losing her leave:

> At that point I was so upset I just wanted to get out of there and go home for Christmas. The thought of losing that Christmas leave—I mean, all I wanted to do was go home and get out of there. So yeah, we dropped it.

Samantha was subjected to further harassment under the bureaucratic system and, ultimately, she was denied access to official reporting channels for sexual abuse. In effect, Samantha's major prioritized the career of her attacker over hers. In this way, bureaucratic harassment can protect perpetrators and silence victims of sexual abuse, further alienating servicewomen from the institution.

Recall Janet, who was taken to a remote bathroom on base and raped by another soldier. She woke up in the dayroom and realized she was missing her underwear and stated that she had been sexually assaulted. Soon after, she officially reported the rape. She had been drunk when she was raped, and her commander contemplated punishing her in the form of a judicial or nonjudicial punishment for underage drinking. While he took time deliberating on this, he made the decision that she could not attend graduation for her Advanced Individual Training. While her classmates were graduating, celebrating, and socializing for the last time before heading out to their first duty stations, Janet was isolated in the barracks: "I wasn't allowed to do anything or go anywhere. I just had to basically sit in my barracks room all by myself." Graduation came and went and while Janet's commander "did decide that I had been through enough and that he wasn't going to pursue any sort of punishment for me, other than I wasn't going to be able to participate in the graduation," she later learned from classmates that her name was not even mentioned at the event. She felt like being isolated and forgotten was a form of punishment. Further, making a rape victim suffer alone in her room and stress about being punished for underage drinking sends a clear message that reporting assault is not welcome.

When Janet received her paper diploma, she discovered that the honors she had earned in training were not listed, erasing this achievement. Reflecting on this, she stated, "And they took that away, too. And I should probably just let it go. But I think forever, I'm going to feel a little slighted about it." Janet felt like this was her punishment for reporting. She was not punished through the military justice system, but she was isolated during graduation while her classmates celebrated, she was stripped of her honors, and finally she was barred from taking leave to visit her family before going to her first duty station, citing the investigation against her rapist as the justification. Janet said:

> I was supposed to have gone home to see my parents. I was going to take a couple of weeks of leave to visit my family before I moved to my duty station. But I wasn't able to do that because of the ongoing investigation. They wouldn't let me leave. That was really tough for me, too, because, like I said, I just wanted to go home.

Therefore, military leaders and commanders punish rape victims who report assault by using the investigation as justification for taking away things like earned and approved leave. Further, if Janet were able to see her friends and family, to talk to her parents, to be physically away from the space where she was raped, to not remain isolated in a barracks room, she would have more avenues for healing. By taking away Janet's leave, her commander severed potential pathways for support but also sent the message that reporting sexual violence leads to unofficial military punishments. In this context, it makes sense that Samantha dropped her case so that she could go home for holiday leave, receive love and support from family and friends, and get away from the base where she was harassed and assaulted.

The military has an array of victim-friendly policies such as victim-requested expedited transfers, access to victims' legal counsel/special victims' counsel,[5] and coordinated victim services from legal, medical, and mental health professionals. These policies connect victims to key resources and are designed to ensure sexual assault cases are not simply dismissed. At times, though, these policies can be used against victims. For example, Penelope was raped by a man in her unit. She found out through workplace gossip:

> I was black-out drunk, and I didn't even know that it had happened until I went in to work on Monday, and he was bragging to people about how he had slept with me. And yeah, so I reported it, and I was immediately pulled from my unit. They made me move all my stuff to another room and did a full investigation. Hours and hours of talking to the CID, which is the Criminal Investigative Division . . . They decided that I had a founded case, so they weren't saying that not necessarily exactly what I was saying was true or false, but they were saying, "Yes. Something did happen." And that warranted me to be able to get transferred somewhere else if I felt more comfortable, which I did. They told me that I was going to be able to go to the duty station of my picking. And I was in a relationship at the time, so I chose to go to [southeastern state]. And then when my orders came down, I had orders to [northwestern state], so they couldn't have really moved me farther away from where I was trying to go. (Army, enlisted, White)

Penelope felt betrayed by those working on her case. She agreed to a transfer after being told she would be able to pick her next duty station, only to be transferred thousands of miles away from that location. At the duty station where she was attacked, she could still drive to see her boyfriend, but once she got to her new duty station, she was thousands of miles away and had to fly. She stated, "My life is flipped upside down by the incident and then I had to move three thousand miles away at the same time, so it's kind of a lot to deal with, all in like a month."

Not only did Penelope experience sexual violence, but she was disappointed that the military failed to address and respond to her assault in a satisfactory way. The move also affected her case, as she told me that she did not want to travel across the country for trial proceedings when:

> All they're trying to do is slander and try and make you out to be the bad person . . . So, we sent a letter over to the legal counsel over at [military base] saying that I was not willing to participate in that, and requesting a non-judicial punishment for him, and I'm pretty sure that he ended up getting a letter of reprimand for providing alcohol to a minor and that was it . . . I, like, slept in late for work one day and had to do fourteen days of extra duty, and he got less than that. Yeah, I slept through my alarm, and I had more of a punishment than he did. It's definitely an interesting system, I guess.

Offering a transfer to victims of sexual assault is a military policy often touted as victim-friendly. Yet the way it was used was not to support Penelope's wishes, but rather to move her far from the base where she was assaulted and far from the base where she desired to go. The way this "victim-friendly" policy was implemented resulted in Penelope declining participation in the legal process against her attacker as she would be required to fly back and forth to her former base. Therefore, the military's bureaucracy can be mobilized against victims even in cases that are eligible to proceed to court-martial. Further, even policies designed to help victims can be used against them in harmful ways.

Organizational Expectations

The potential misuse of discretionary power in military bureaucracy is exacerbated by the way professional and personal life is blended in the organization and the resulting expectations for commanders. Not only does the military regulate how servicemembers dress, behave, and speak at work, but some services also restrict how they dress, behave, and speak in civilian spaces. Commanders are expected to control and regulate many aspects of servicemembers' personal lives. For example, the Marine Corps has a "civilian attire policy" that dictates when and where Marines are "authorized" to wear civilian clothing, including the stipulation that "Eccentric or faddish styles are not acceptable within the grooming standards of the Marine Corps"; Marines cannot wear "eccentricities of dress" or "clothing articles not specifically designed to be normally worn as headgear (e.g., bandannas, doo rags)" (U.S. Marine Corps, 2018). Ambiguous rules surrounding non–work-related choices of servicemembers, combined with the high level of discretion afforded commanders, can result in harassment and racial discrimination. This is especially true when "Commanding Officers have the ultimate responsibility for determining when hairstyles are eccentric, faddish, or out of standards," as outlined in Navy Guidelines (Navy Personnel Command 2020). Hair guidelines and expectations affected Iyana:

> I am an African American female, and I don't have a perm. So, my hair is naturally curly and "fro-ish," I guess, if you will. I remember my first base, my second supervisor—like, one day I'd straightened my hair—and one day he came to me and said, "Your hair looks really nice." And I was like, "Thank you." And he was like, "No, it looks really, really nice, because there was this one time a couple of months ago where you had your hair like a certain way and it was extremely faddish but I didn't know what to say so I didn't say anything. But you never did it again." And I was like, "What?" . . . And from that day, like, I never straightened my hair again. Like, that was . . . And aside from that, you know, there were a few other incidents where people would say, "Is your hair in standard, or you might wanna check, or is that faddish?" (Air Force, officer, Black)

Military hair standards have historically been based on White women's hair, and commanders often interpret the military rules around hair and clothing in ways that exclude the hairstyles of Black women. This means that Black women experience negative attention and even official sanctions for wearing their hair the way it naturally grows. Definitions of a fad or "eccentricities of dress" are highly subjective and can make Black women easy targets for citations and bureaucratic harassment. Further, the fact that these hair and dress standards based on White bodies are codified in military rules and can produce military punishments demonstrates how the military is a raced institution with "direct control" procedures in place that preserve white dominance (Acker 2006, 454; Ray 2019).

Commanders are also expected to care for everyone in their unit, both professionally and personally, and to give advice to servicemembers about non–job-related issues, behaviors, and actions. Commanders also can make rules about behavior in non-work settings that, like laws, have severe consequences if broken. For example, a Military Protective Order (MPO) operates like a temporary restraining order in the civilian world (Tozer 2011). In domestic violence situations, an MPO is a short-term order that prohibits abusers from having contact their victims, requires them to stay away from the victim's home, or even forces them move into the barracks (Tozer 2011). Unlike a temporary restraining order in the civilian world, there is no court hearing required to issue an MPO, meaning that commanders may issue MPOs whenever they find it appropriate. Commanders' level of discretion and ability to issue directives with near-legal standing is a significant aspect of military bureaucracy.

Commanders might be motivated to control the personal lives of those who work for them to maintain their own reputations. For example, a military lawyer I spoke with told me:

> You don't want to be the commander with all of the "problem Marines," so you stop the problems before they end up in our office or before they become real issues. Like, if you have someone who is always fighting with his wife, and you think it would become domestic disturbance down the line, you are going to want to get involved before that happens. Or if you have someone with a drinking problem, they are going to get into trouble with that eventually. You

try to intervene before then, so you don't look like a bad commander.
(Marine Corps, officer, White)

Thus, servicemembers' personal lives can be a reflection on commanders
and their leadership. If commanders have several reports of servicemembers
with poor behavior, or they have servicemembers who end up in disciplinary hearings, they will have to explain this to their bosses. Commanders,
then, might have even more of an incentive to advise, control, and restrict
those working for them. This can become problematic when commanders
have a high level of discretion and there is little oversight over these
interactions.

This blending of work and non-work space, and the blurring of professional and personal oversight by commanders, creates more opportunity for harassment, including the manipulation of evaluation procedures.
Supervisors are routinely required to complete performance reviews
for individuals in their units. In the Marine Corps supervisors must assess qualities regarding character (e.g., courage, effectiveness under
stress, initiative), leadership (e.g., leading and ensuring the well-being
of subordinates), and intellect (e.g., decision-making ability and judgment) (U.S. Marine Corps 2012), all of which are highly vulnerable to the
supervisor's opinion and discretion. In the Air Force, individuals are rated
on their adherence to core values such as "how well the Airman adopts,
internalizes, and demonstrates our Air Force Core Values of Integrity
First, Service Before Self, and Excellence in All We Do. . . . Consider
the amount of effort the Airman devoted to improving themselves and
their work center/unit through education and involvement" as well as
on "Esprit de corps and community relations," where supervisors must
"Consider how well the Airman promotes camaraderie,[6] embraces esprit
de corps and acts as an Air Force Ambassador" (Department of the Air
Force 2022), which are also open to interpretation. Additionally, military supervisors can consider non–work-related factors when completing
evaluations. Maura's experiences reveal how formal military policies and
informal expectations can blur the line between work and personal life

when a commander's discretion results in administrative consequences for intimate choices. Maura said:

> His voice would change when speaking to me; it would go up a bit and was mocking-like. There were also . . . like, many little comments he made. And then I got engaged and the EPRs [Enlisted Performance Reports] he gave me were damning. I hadn't done anything but excellent work. I worked over forty hours a week. It was the sort of things I got assigned to . . . Like he would say, "I need you to go to the base liquor store for our picnic next week." Things you don't ask a military person to do. There were other enlisted people who didn't outrank me and never got handed any of those jobs. But they were all male. The attitude he had and the damning EPR . . . he gave me scores that were one off from what I needed to be promoted. It would take me forever to make rank at that point with those scores. He was mad at me because I was leaving and marrying an officer and he saw me as a traitor for marrying an officer as an enlisted . . . you know, and he was an enlisted. (Air Force, enlisted, White)

Maura's supervisor treated her differently from men and made derogatory comments to her, which themselves are examples of workplace harassment. However, it is the evidence of her *heterosexuality*, her engagement, that served as a particular point of anger for her commander. Recall the power that the slut discourse wields in the military, and how men use this discourse often against women who date and marry servicemen. Their motives for joining the military are questioned; their marriage symbolizes a breakdown of the brotherhood and cements the fact that women do not belong. When military peers are able to police women through slut discourse and then are backed up by commanders who can punish women through the military bureaucracy, servicewomen experience organizational, professional, and interactional harm. Upon finding out that Maura was engaged to the officer she was dating, her commander turned to the administrative system and exploited his power within the military bureaucracy to cause her professional harm. Dating between enlisted and officer ranks is known as "fraternization" and is prohibited in the military. In this case, the commander should have reported Maura's fiancé for fraternization, as this offense is only levied against the higher-ranking individual. However, instead of reporting an officer who outranks him, the commander chose to address the violation by giving Maura low marks on her performance review. Here, again, discretion abets the commander's punishment, allowing him to give her a low score without documenting the reason. Maura, in turn, cannot prove it was due to her dating choices and cannot fight the score. When commanders' discretionary power over bureaucratic policies and procedures intersects with expectations about behavior in non-work settings and is mapped onto gendered tropes, it empowers them to control and penalize non–work-related actions, such as Maura's personal choice of whom to marry.

Some servicewomen accept this type of discretionary punishment as appropriate. For example, when I shared this instance with an officer in the Marine Corps, she said, "He probably ranked her low on judgment as dating an officer is considered bad judgment and absolutely deserves some sort of punishment from the commander." She did not see anything wrong with formally reprimanding Maura for marrying an officer. Although fraternization rules exist to protect *lower*-ranking individuals from being exploited by *higher*-ranking individuals, she still supported the punishment of the lower-ranking servicemember. This demonstrates that some instances of bureaucratic harassment are accepted and normalized. Within an environment that privileges masculinity and denigrates femininity, some servicewomen may accept as normal, and even participate in, sexist practices that discriminate against women. This has implications for other similar military protections. For example, the military has protections in place for biased evaluations in the form of an additional rater. The role of the second rater is to check the ratings and evaluations performed by the immediate supervisor and to ensure that evaluations are not extremely inflated or harsh. While this can be a mechanism for monitoring evaluations, it did not function as a check against biased evaluations for the women in my sample. None of the victims of bureaucratic harassment discussed the second rater intervening on their behalf.[7] However, if the evaluation categories remain subjective and open to interpretation, the immediate supervisor might be able to cite a reason for the negative evaluation that would satisfy the second rater, though the reason/explanation might still be rooted in sexism.

Thus, the military's bureaucratic structure allows and facilitates this form of harassment. Unchecked access to discretionary policies and complete authority in how to run their units, including writing performance reviews and approving benefits, gives commanders extraordinary power in the military workplace. This power can be mobilized to do harm to servicewomen, especially given the expectation that commanders may regulate servicemembers' personal, as well as professional, decisions. In this way, bureaucratic harassment disrupts servicewomen's professional lives and carries distinct consequences, which I discuss below.

CONSEQUENCES OF BUREAUCRATIC HARASSMENT

Bureaucratic harassment is experienced at a personal and an organizational level and, even if ultimately unsuccessful, negatively affects victims and leaves them open for further abuse. For example, when Maura received a negative review after getting engaged to an officer, she stated, "It would take me forever to make rank at that point with those scores." Being kept at a lower rank made her ineligible for trainings, positions, or opportunities reserved for servicemembers at the next rank as well as kept her at a lower pay grade. A negative counseling statement, such as the one Joanna's co-worker filed, can have a similar effect. Furthermore, when an individual is slow to make the next rank, they are seen as being a weak servicemember, and this can be used to separate them from the military.[8] Losing one's earned qualifications, as Angela was threatened with, can dislodge one's path within one's military career track, result in a transfer or being removed from a unit entirely, and render one's training useless in the civilian world. Therefore, the original administrative strike can have multiple negative consequences.

Perpetrators of bureaucratic harassment use legitimate military procedures and processes to harass their subordinates or peers. The use of these legitimate channels often includes documentation that is detrimental to victims' careers, meaning that women spend a significant amount of time trying to respond to, recover from, or remove an administrative strike. Some women must attend classes or workshops in response to the cited infraction. The perceived legitimacy of the harassment when it stems from institutional rules shows women that the military as an organization facilitates and supports servicemen who want to cause them harm. In this context, it becomes victims versus the institution.

Bureaucratic harassment also has consequences outside of the military career. For example, June had a fairly positive experience in the Marine Corps. Upon deciding to enroll in college, and therefore not to re-enlist, she requested to leave the military early so she could start the fall semester on time. This is a somewhat common request with established procedures that June followed. She recalled:

> I turned in all my papers and I turn in my package to the Marine Corps and then my officer says, "If you ask again I'm going to kick you out with an admin discharge, other than honorable." And so, I had like three-and-a-half years of good service, no bad conduct marks, you know, I had good conduct marks, and I just said, "Okay," and waited and then I got out with an honorable discharge. (Marine Corps, enlisted, Asian-American)

As a result, June stayed in the military through her contract, starting school a semester late and losing her opportunity to play soccer at an institution that recruited her to do so. These consequences, she weighed, were better than what she would have faced receiving an other-than-honorable discharge. Forcing a servicewoman to leave the military through an administrative separation, especially if listed as "other than honorable," would not only end her military career but also revoke post-service benefits and negatively affect civilian employment opportunities. In June's case, this is particularly salient because an honorable discharge is necessary to receive veterans' funding for her education.

Kay experienced an attempted rape that introduced this book. Her experience is a poignant example of the post-service consequences of bureaucratic harassment:

> He tried to rape me. I ended up running out the car and just getting away from him and catching the little shuttle and going back to my barracks and crying. I remember I was like, "Forget this." I had this number from my therapist, and I said, "I'm very depressed. I want to hurt myself." They took me to a mental hospital, and I was there for, like, a week with crazy people—like, crazy people who were detoxing from drugs . . . When I got out, they put me back into my regular command. Nobody knew what happened, supposedly. I reported what happened when I got back to my command . . . And he [her attacker] actually came to the window [where she worked] one day and he just, like, stood there. And he said: "How are you doing?" And I . . . just wanted to burn his face off . . . Come to find out, I reported it, they investigated it, and it was his word against mine and of course because I was technically "crazy," they didn't believe me . . . Then when I went to get out of the Navy, I got this code that said I have a personality disorder. (Navy, enlisted, Black)

It is clear Kay was suffering from the experience of an attempted rape. Yet her institutionalization was used to question her credibility and to dismiss her sexual assault case rather than as evidence that she had experienced trauma. Kay further explained that because she was marked as having a personality disorder, she was unable to receive medical benefits from the military. Personality disorders are considered pre-existing conditions, meaning that veterans' benefits can be withheld. Kay's case is not unique; the Committee on Veterans' Affairs has accused the military of improper use of a personality disorder diagnosis to medically separate servicemembers to avoid paying for post-service medical benefits (Draper 2011).[9] In these instances of bureaucratic harassment, experiences with other kinds of abuse can be used against victims to separate them from the military, as well as sever responsibility for post-service medical needs. Kay's experience points to an institution that prioritizes preserving its masculine culture over creating a workplace that is inclusive of women.

Scholars argue that the military shapes meaning both within the armed forces and the civilian world (Hale 2012; Sasson-Levy 2003). Civilians' respect, glorification, and adoration of the military (Belkin 2012) means that military categorizations and the outcomes of military legal or medical systems have significance in civilian spaces. For example, when hiring a veteran, civilian employers can request a form (DD-214) that documents an individual's record of service, including how that service ended. Victims of bureaucratic harassment who received any military punishment, cited misconduct, or other-than-honorable discharge will forever carry this with them on their record. Therefore, the stigma of being labeled by the military as having a personality disorder, like Kay, or being dishonorably discharged, as June could have been, carries additional weight when this information is readily available to civilian employers.

Collective Effects

Within a gendered institution, the active manipulation of bureaucratic rules, regulations, and policies can be used to protect the organization as a masculine space. Importantly, the gendered and raced context of the military not only shapes who is likely to be given power through rank and discretion but also determines the actions, behaviors, and individuals that are targeted through bureaucratic harassment. In addition to limiting individual women, bureaucratic harassment can be used to undermine groups of women or women in general. For example, under the combat exclusion policy (repealed in 2013 but effectively in place until 2015), the U.S. military did not deploy women as members of combat units. However, women were routinely "attached" to combat infantry units. The subtle difference meant that women were not *technically* deployed into combat but were unofficially deployed into combat situations. The Female Engagement

Team (FET) was one model of all-women teams attached to infantry units in combat zones. Olivia, a lieutenant who had been selected to go on two FET deployments, stated:

> There was a major, he was like the operations officer, he used to be, like, all the time he would say, "I don't think women belong in the infantry." You know, he would say things like, "It would be a disaster to have women in the infantry." (Marine Corps, officer, White)

This officer's sexist views had a direct collective impact on Olivia's team. She explained that originally, the FET had one lieutenant, an officer rank, in charge of four or five teams of enlisted Marines attached to infantry units. The lieutenant was not attached with them to the infantry units but managed them from the base in Afghanistan. While in combat zones, each team was headed by a sergeant, an enlisted rank. Prior FETs recommended that a lieutenant lead the teams on the ground because sergeants cannot make decisions during operations meetings where other team leaders are officers (e.g., lieutenants, captains, and majors), nor can they make financial decisions for their teams. This meant that when leaders made decisions in the field about where to go and what actions to pursue, the FET teams' goals were often de-prioritized. Attaching a lieutenant to the FETs would give the women-only units more power to discuss and negotiate with other officers as well as control over their own budget.

Though this recommendation was set to take place in future deployments, the same major who made it clear that he did not think women belonged in the infantry ended up blocking this policy change, thereby limiting the FETs' power in combat zones. The major's decision limited deployment opportunities for women officers because now fewer lieutenants would deploy with the FET team. Further, he ensured that the FETs remained dependent on officers from the exclusively male units in combat situations. This demonstrates how bureaucratic harassment can occur at the collective level through policies created to block the success of groups of servicewomen and preserve men's dominance in combat decision-making.

Olivia spoke out after discovering that the recommendation was blocked. She was subsequently the target of individual-level bureaucratic harassment:

> I went into the CO's [commanding officer's] office and talked to her about it. I was the XO [executive officer] . . . so her second-in-command. She told me that this was the decision from the operations officer and that this was how it was going to be. I one hundred percent disagreed with this and let her and the major know it. I told them that this was undercutting our effectiveness and capabilities and that this course of action ensured that the FET teams would be limited and restricted in theater . . . So anyway, then they called me into the office and basically . . . they just told me I would no longer be going on the deployment. That's when they said, "You are mutinying," [and] they kicked me off.

Despite her experience leading a prior FET deployment, Olivia was fired from her position as the executive officer and dismissed from the unit, just a week before they were set to leave. She explained:

> I fought this policy because I felt like it was made for sexist reasons. This man had said so many times that he didn't think women should be in the infantry and that they weren't capable. The decision [not to attach lieutenants to each team] wasn't made to better the FET team or to help the mission or even to ensure the safety of my Marines.

Despite the clear gender implications of the major's decision to block this policy recommendation, Olivia's objection was interpreted as an act of rebellion rather than a legitimate attempt to enhance her team's effectiveness and expose a sexist action. The servicewoman commanding the FET team supported the major's decision to block the policy recommendation and agreed to fire Olivia from the deployment. In effect, by punishing Olivia for voicing her concerns, Olivia's superiors reinforced the military's masculine command structure and sustained the prevailing sexism that limits women's opportunities and experiences in the U.S. military.

Olivia's experience demonstrates how one leader can employ bureaucratic and administrative policies at his discretion to limit the military experiences and success of both an individual woman and groups of women. In this way, individuals may continue to limit women's ability to serve in combat despite the military lifting its ban on women in combat. This is notable given that when the ban was lifted, the Marine Corps commandant recommended that women in the Marine Corps should remain excluded from certain combat specialties, despite the ruling that all military occupational specialties must integrate (Baldor 2015). Further, James Mattis, then Secretary of Defense, stated to the Corps of Cadets that "we cannot do something that militarily doesn't make sense, and I've got this being looked at right now by the chief of staff of the Army, commandant of the Marine Corps . . . this is a policy that I inherited, and so far the cadre is so small we have no data on it" (Copp 2018). Mattis went on to say that "clearly the jury is out" on integration of women into the infantry (Copp 2018). Therefore, even though policy requires integration, it is unlikely to be implemented by servicemembers when leading officials speak out against it. Therefore, even though policies exist to create more equal opportunities, commanders know how to circumvent them, to use them to cause harm, and to stop them from being effective.

CONCLUSION

This chapter examines the relationship between bureaucratic systems and workplace harassment by documenting how the purposeful misuse of organizational rules, regulations, and policies can negatively affect women, constituting a distinct form of harm. In the U.S. military, bureaucratic harassment is a way for servicemen to degrade women's military experiences and damage servicewomen's professional lives. As more women move into combat units, they may experience increased resistance and harassment. Yet, despite rules and policies embedded within the military's bureaucratic structure to help mitigate or reprimand abuses, this structure has adapted, and sexism is enacted through bureaucratic harassment, in much more enigmatic ways. As women peel back these subtle layers of institutional misogyny, they come to expect harassment. Many women left the military after realizing the institution was complicit in their harassment and sexual abuse experiences, including Angela, the woman in the Navy who was grounded from flying.

Therefore, the military as an institution facilitates and protects men's domination and creates sexual assault vulnerability for women by emphasizing warrior masculinity and denigrating femininity in military values, training, and interactions. When misogyny built into the physical space combines with the fact that men control most military spaces, the geography of military spaces can contribute to sexual violence vulnerability. This chapter shows that when sexism permeates the institution, the organization's rules, policies, and bureaucracy become tools of inequality, discrimination, and harassment. Though the military has policies designed to assist victims of harassment and assault, access to these policies is restricted by those who use their power to silence victims or punish them for trying to use reporting streams. Further, even victim-friendly policies can be manipulated to cause harm. The military's rules and policies then adapt to and reflect the organization's emphasis on valuing warrior masculinity and denigrating femininity. Similarly, the military's values also conform to these gendered dynamics. In the next chapter I show how the military's emphasis on family, trust, and caregiving is filtered through a femmephobic and hyper-masculine value system in ways that also create sexual vulnerability for servicewomen.

A Failed Promise

The Military Family Is Actually a Brotherhood

Sandra's forthright response to my question of why she decided to enlist in the Air Force caught me a bit off guard. Within the first few minutes of our conversation, she stated: "I came from a home with a father that was a drug addict, and it was just a rough childhood, growing up . . . a lot of cops involved, too. I just wanted to get away from all of that, start fresh." She described a childhood of neglect, instability, and abuse entangled with her father's addiction to drugs. When her father eventually abandoned them, her mother was left struggling to raise four children in poverty. Sandra told me: "I've been on my own since I was fourteen years old." She meant financially, but in her childhood and adolescence she was also on her own emotionally, trying to navigate the transition to adulthood without guidance against a backdrop of neglect and abuse.

As I spoke to more women, responses like Sandra's no longer surprised me. A lot of them saw the military as a chance to flee not only abuse or neglect but also poverty or drug temptation. Joining the military can be an escape from the grip of, as Janet put it, "small-minded small towns." When I asked Janet why she joined the military, she responded: "There were a lot of factors, but the biggest one is, my oldest sister got addicted to meth." Janet's physical and mental well-being was deeply affected by her sister's addiction. In her teens she had to "protect" or "guard" the family's house

Hardship Duty. Stephanie Bonnes, Oxford University Press. © Oxford University Press 2024.
DOI: 10.1093/oso/9780197636244.003.0005

from her sister, who would break in and take anything she thought she could sell to help finance her addiction. One night Janet was watching the house while her parents were out of town. She invited three friends over to "hang out and drink." In the middle of the night after she was asleep, Janet's sister came to the house and physically assaulted her.

As Janet's sister attacked her, she scolded her for underage drinking: "She yelled at me that I had a problem. And that's how it all started; she was yelling at me for drinking with my friends. And because I was eighteen and, I mean, I wasn't supposed to be drinking. But I was angry at her, so I yelled at her back and said something along the lines of, 'I've got a problem?! You've got two kids and you're on meth.'" Janet was irked by the hypocrisy of her meth-addicted sister reprimanding her about drinking. She was angry that she was woken up abruptly and violently. These emotions sat with her all the next day, and she started to ask herself "What am I even doing?" That night stood out to Janet as a catalyst for why she joined the military. She reflected on her sister's life and her own. She wanted to be nothing like her sister but admitted that she had been partying a lot. She was also struggling to pay for college without support from her parents. She started to wonder what her life would become if she stayed in that town, in that house, and if she continued the relationship patterns she had with friends and family. She explained:

> So, I was trying to work two part-time jobs because I was eighteen years old, I had no experience. And I was trying to go to school full time. So, I was really struggling to make ends meet there. And then I was meeting all these people, and everybody was like, "Hey, come party, come party." So, I went to a couple of parties. And then after that whole experience with my sister, the very next day, while I was working at a frozen yogurt shop, a recruiter came in, an Army recruiter. And he was in full uniform and asked if he could hang his business cards on . . . we had a bulletin board. And a flier, and so I was like, "Yeah, that's not a problem, go ahead. Also, why should I join the Army?" And he said, "Why should I give you $40,000?" And I said, "All right, I'm in." (Army, enlisted, biracial)

Janet's path to joining the military is like that of many of the women I spoke with. Against the backdrop of childhood trauma and drug addiction in the family, fraught relationships, a lack of financial security, and a real fear of what their life would become if they stayed in their house or hometown, many turn to the military. It is not just a job and stable access to money, but the military also provides housing, medical benefits, education benefits, and an opportunity to move, usually far from home. These benefits make it possible for people in abusive situations to escape. Allison joined the military to escape her abusive mother and an abusive boyfriend:

> I was really trying to get the fuck out of Dodge, because I was in a really bad place. Like, I needed to get out. My ex was horribly abusive and strangled me and sodomized me. And like, you're twenty years old, how the hell do you get out of a small town? How do you leave? Where do you live? So, joining the military was like, seemed like the only way that I could literally go . . . where I will have a roof over my head. I will have medical insurance and dental insurance and I will be able to leave this place. And the military will train me and give me a job. I can work. (Marine Corps, enlisted, White)

Feminist criminologists have extensively documented that girls often run away to escape abuse in the home (Arnold 1990; Belknap and Holsinger 2006; Chesney-Lind and Jones 2010; Flores 2016; Lopez 2017). Often this is studied in the context of the criminal processing system, where girls escaping abuse run away to the streets and as a result are arrested for truancy, drug violations, sex work, or other nonviolent and/or status offenses. A significant number of young women who also experience trauma and abuse, like Sandra, Janet, and Allison, turn to the military for stability and the opportunity to escape. Research suggests that many women who join the military have experienced abuse, including sexual violence, prior to their service. For example, Sadler et al. (2003) found that 39% of servicewomen had experienced sexual violence prior to their military service, with 25% experiencing child sexual abuse.

While some people turn to the military purposefully seeking an escape, others join when they feel they have run out of options. The military provides material resources such as a place to live, money, healthcare, and a pathway to higher education—resources that, in a capitalist country without many safety nets, are often expected to be provided by families. In this way, the military acts as a near-total institution (Woodward and Jenkings 2011) as it takes on the role of a family-like provider for its members. This highlights another reason many women in my sample joined the military: to fill the family void in their lives. As I spoke to Sandra, whose story opened this chapter, she circled back to her abusive father: "Like I said before, that stability I didn't have growing up, it really entices people in that community [the military], because everyone wants that belonging, that's part of it." The military does not just fulfill this role materially; it also works hard to cultivate the idea of deep social bonds between servicemembers. It promises a family. This promise is also desirable for those who come from supportive homes but are seeking camaraderie and strong relationships in their work life. In this chapter, I show how despite the promise of a family, the military actually delivers a brotherhood that excludes women and makes them vulnerable to harassment and assault.

THE MILITARY FAMILY IN RECRUITMENT AND TRAINING

During recruitment, the military uses broad familial language and vocabulary around caring, obligation, and bonding, as well as a narrower brotherhood discourse, to invoke the idea that the military is a family. Websites, fliers, and recruitment pamphlets promote access to the military family alongside more tangible benefits such as healthcare, education benefits, and tax-free housing or a housing allowance. Online articles advertising the military list among the benefits "being a part of a larger family with a proud history—the military tradition" (military.com 2018). Branch-specific recruitment and promotional materials similarly highlight the benefit of family: "Being a Marine gives you the equipment and knowledge that allows you to be a leader within your family, your community, and our Country. You become part of a brotherhood that exists in and out of uniform" (militaryspot.com 2018). The use of the words "family" and "brotherhood" almost interchangeably helps cement in the minds of recruits that these concepts are the same. Recruiters also discuss unity, brotherhood, and family as benefits of joining. Women told me that recruiters and Officer Selection Officers told them things like "Welcome to the family" or "You're getting a career and a family" when they decided to join. Though the term "brotherhood" invokes a masculine version of family, whereas "family" is a broader, more inclusive term, the military uses them interchangeably in its recruitment materials.

Touting membership into a family as a benefit is a powerful recruiting tool. For many people, the draw of joining an admirable and tight-knit community is particularly important. Once women join, the military continues to promote, promise, and encourage the idea that the military is a family. This is especially true during training, when recruits learn to see the military not just as *a family* but as *their new family*. The institution starts to create a division between civilians and servicemembers, and between the pre-military self and the new military self. Military training is intentionally psychologically and emotionally stressful and conducted in a setting where trainees are isolated from their other support networks (Callahan 2009). This physical and mental stress is where servicemembers are taught to rely on one another and to begin to think of the military as *home*. For example, Kay explained her experience in training for the Navy:

> They [the drill instructors] tried to trick us around, like, the middle of boot camp. Because we were all . . . everybody was miserable. And they were, like, who wants to go home? And I was, like, this is a trick. I'm not raising my hand. A couple people raised their hands, and they got sent all the way back to the beginning of boot camp. (Navy, enlisted, Black)

By taking the individuals who expressed a desire to go home and placing them back at the beginning of boot camp, to restart training, drill instructors make clear that the military *is* home. Recruits learn that adopting the military as their new home and buying into the institutional values, practices, and goals is essential to their success. Individuals who express a desire to stay are not punished and, thus, are rewarded for expressing trust in the institution. This shows that the idea of a military family is entangled with expectations of institutional loyalty.

One experience that exemplifies the entanglement of institutional loyalty, military identities, and the military family is an exercise that enlisted Marines participate in called "the crucible." Taking place at the end of Marine Corps boot camp, the crucible is a physically and psychologically draining exercise where servicemembers are deprived of sleep, are given little food, and must complete fifty-four hours of physical tests and activities that simulate combat. Vivian stated:

> A lot of what you do depends on trusting your fellow marines. In Marine Corps boot camp, you do this crucible, and the whole point is to complete this whole two-day experience as a unit. You have to trust that the other person is covering. Like if you are running, you trust the other person is going to shoot the enemy while you are running. (Marine Corps, officer, White)

At the end of the crucible, a small ceremony celebrates trainees' transition to becoming Marines. The hike ends at an Iwo Jima monument, which memorializes six Marines who worked together to raise a United States flag during the battle of Iwo Jima in World War II. This statue is a symbol of teamwork, self-sacrifice, and loyalty to both the military and the nation. This is where trainees are presented with their eagle, globe, and anchor, a small badge they will wear on their uniforms, and are called Marines for the first time. A commander interviewed about the crucible for a military news outlet stated:

> From that point forward, the new Marines call the drill instructors by their rank. They've spent the three months referring to themselves in the third person, and each of their drill instructors as

"sir." "They're seeing now that they're actually our brothers," says Phillips. "They're not recruits, they're not pieces of crap, they're not idiots, they're United States Marines. They did what I've done." (Clark 2016)

The crucible is an example of how physically and mentally stressful training is used to emphasize the importance of teamwork in achieving success, to develop trust among servicemembers, and to build loyalty to the military institution. By completing the physical and mental transformations necessary to survive boot camp or training, servicemembers also develop a military identity that is distinctly different from their former civilian selves (Hall 2017; Koeszegi et al. 2014). After shedding their civilian identities, their military identities take precedence. Nadine told me, "You don't say, 'I'm in the Marine Corps.' You say, 'I'm a Marine.'" Not only are servicemembers taking on and embodying new military identities, but they are also bonded to others who have been through the same transformation. This idea that servicemembers are unique and different from civilians affected the women I spoke to. Many women wanted to start fresh, and they invest in their new military identities. Others were far from their own families and hoping to develop new bonds. This is especially true for women who left neglectful homes or abusive partners. They have a new group of people to identify with, a group that the military claims are their new family. The military further pushes the idea of family through institutional expectations of protection, trust, and caregiving among servicemembers.

"I Got Your Back:" Military Expectations of Caregiving

The military infuses the notion of family and brotherhood into its organizational goals and expectations to serve the institution and its mission. Take the common Army statement "No soldier left behind." This phrase may conjure up an image of soldiers on a battlefield turning back to bring those who are injured to safety. That vision, or some version of it, blends conceptions of war with the ideals of protection, sacrifice, and also care-giving. The message is clear: Servicemembers take care of each other even if they must risk their own lives to do so. This phrase, and others like it, are introduced in training, built into things like the Soldier's Creed and the Airman's Creed, and are referenced throughout servicemember's careers. Diane told me: "They taught us, you were always there for your brothers and sisters. You always hold their back. You never, never leave a Marine behind. You always helped them carry their weight when they're going through something." Diane explains how the caregiving expectation is coupled with the idea that the military is a family and that other Marines are her siblings. This lesson also communicates that the military is most effective when servicemembers work as a team and when individuals help one another, even if self-sacrifice is required.

While the "no soldier left behind" slogan invokes combat imagery, it is used in many other contexts as well. Servicemembers use the phrase to explain why they adopted their deployment dogs, to justify drinking the last beer at a party, and to encourage non-combat caretaking. For ex-ample, a military newsletter article about alcohol and drugs states "battle buddies at every level—junior Soldiers, noncommissioned officers and officers should not 'leave a Soldier behind.' We can't afford to lose even one Soldier to an alcohol- or drug-related incident" (Knight 2013). Here, the phrase plays on the notion that servicemembers have a family-like ob-ligation to take care of one another physically, emotionally, and mentally. One of the most salient examples of this expectation is in how the mili-tary teaches servicemembers to recognize distress and to prevent suicide. Mallory states:

> Well, the military is big on PT [physical training] and suicide pre-vention. Those are the two things that have really . . . I guess you could say honed their skills in on. And I'm very, very thankful that they have because there's a lot of soldiers that don't really like to do PT, that really can't do PT, and it's there to help them, and then you have a lot of soldiers who are not getting the help that they need and ignoring them or they're overlooking their symptoms and their

signs and their calls for help. And that's why the suicide prevention was put into place by us, why it has been enhanced, why there's more people now looking out for more soldiers due to the fact that the su- icide rate went up. (Army, enlisted, Black)

Clearly, the expectation that servicemembers recognize suicide warning signs and assist servicemembers who might be depressed is an institutional priority. The military encourages and even insists on servicemembers un- dertaking acts of family-like caregiving,[1] like providing emotional support and looking for signs of distress, from the top down.

The military's focus on caregiving and protection of other servicemembers is so entrenched that it can result in feelings of guilt if a suicide occurs. For example, Mallory explains how she feels responsible for the suicide of a friend:

> I was like, "If I could have done something, if I could have . . ." I didn't even hear or see the signs while talking to him. I just, I didn't, and I blame myself because I'm like, "I wasn't paying attention." I was so wrapped up in what I was doing and my life that I wasn't paying at- tention to him. I wasn't giving him the attention he needed for what he was going through.

Feelings of guilt and self-blame are commonly experienced by family and friends of individuals who commit suicide (Bartik et al. 2013; Shields, Kavanagh, Russo 2017; Tzeng et al. 2010). In the military, servicemembers who are trained to recognize signs of distress and prioritize suicide pre- vention might feel like they failed the institution as well as the individual.

Servicemembers are not only trained to recognize suicide and de- pression, but the military also expects them to cover for those who are stressed, depressed, or unable to perform their work. Self-sacrifice under the banner of doing whatever is necessary to support the team, unit, or institution is lauded in the military. It can be easier to encourage self- sacrifice when servicemembers are trained to think of one another as family. For example, Mallory continued:

It gets a little sticky because then the NCO is like, "Well, if you see that person not doing it, why don't you do it? If you're not doing anything, you could do it . . . you can help them out." . . . I was one of the ones that got stretched thin trying to pull what I was doing and what somebody else was supposed to do. But it's not about them or me. It's about us as a team because . . . it's about the team as a unit, not just an individual person. If I can do my job and do yours and make us look good, then I'm going to do it.

Mallory's willingness to cover for an underperforming colleague if it will benefit her unit is similar to how individuals are socialized to prioritize familial relationships over relationships with non-family members and over the self (Muraco 2006). She went on to say:

It all comes back to us being a family and all of us looking out for each other regardless of how you feel about a certain person. If you see them and you notice that they're not how they are, you notice something different in them, you're going to take the necessary action to see what's going on with them.

Mallory describes an entanglement of family, self-sacrifice, caregiving, and prioritizing the group over the individual in military life and work. She emphasized that it is her job not only to cover for other soldiers who might be depressed or stressed but also to approach that individual and help them work through their issues. Black women, like Mallory, might be more likely to take on caregiving responsibilities for other servicemembers due to broader societal assumptions that Black women are strong and can endure the strain of taking on the problems of others. This often leads to burnout for Black women who feel as though they have to live up to the image of strength and suppress their own needs to take care of others, as when Mallory said she was "stretched too thin" (Beauboeuf-Lafontant 2007; Martin 2002).

The expectation that servicemembers care for one another is so important that they are sometimes reprimanded if they fail to do so. For example, Katherine explained that a man with her same rank was drunk at a party while they were deployed. She stated:

> And the lieutenant colonel had come in that morning and told my colonel, "Oh, by the way, I found one of your captains incredibly intoxicated walking down the middle of the road." . . . So my colonel starts lecturing me on . . . "We need to be good wingmen, we need to watch out for each other." And he can't believe I would allow one of my peers to "just wander off like that." (Air Force, officer, White)

Part of the lieutenant colonel's discontent is that a drunk captain in his unit reflects poorly on the Air Force and could damage his reputation as a leader. Reprimanding Katherine to better recognize and address such behavior demonstrates a top-down expectation that servicemembers are to engage in caregiving. However, like the rest of the military, this expectation is gendered. Katherine was one of many captains at the party. However, she was both the only woman at her rank at the party and the only one reprimanded by the lieutenant colonel for not helping her peer. She believed that the expectation of caregiving was greater for her than the captains who were men. Although women may be expected to take on a greater share of carework than men, many women noted that they were not themselves recipients of caretaking from other servicemembers.

Excluding Women

The military invokes family discourse in recruitment materials and training exercises and encourages acts of family-like caregiving and trust among servicemembers. While institutions and local context can supply the vocabulary for individuals to use and model one vision of this implementation, it does not predetermine or dictate how individuals will construct those families (Holstein and Gubrium 1995, 1999). Meanings around family are also shaped by interpersonal interactions. Although the military uses the words "brotherhood" and "family" interchangeably, women realize through interacting with other servicemembers that the military family is actually a brotherhood from which they are excluded.

Many servicewomen's experiences do not align with the military's construction of family, nor with how they see the military family at work in the lives of servicemen, particularly in relation to caregiving. Most servicewomen can describe incidents of servicemen receiving caregiving. One woman described an instance where two Marines stood up for another Marine who was the target of homophobic remarks from a soldier. Others discussed how servicemen often rely on their leaders or peers to pick them up when they are too drunk to drive, and told stories about men helping each other study for academic tests, train for physical fitness challenges, and other instances of providing emotional, tangible, or financial support in times of need. Some servicewomen, mostly officers and non-commissioned officers over thirty, specifically emphasized their role as caregivers. They described offering financial assistance to servicemembers, mentoring them in their military careers, and talking them through depression, trauma, relationship problems, and suicide ideation. However, most women did not describe being recipients of such care themselves.

The concept of the military family is taught during training but is experienced through the countless interactions between servicemembers. Witnessing family caregiving in the lives of servicemen but not personally receiving this care is a passive disruption to servicewomen's sense of belonging, which can lead to feelings of exclusion from the military family. Reflecting on these interactions amidst the expectations of military caregiving, Cristina noted:

What was interesting was that throughout basic training, you're always taught . . . "pick up a soldier" and "we never leave anyone behind" and "look out for your brothers and sisters." But as soon as someone deviates from the conventional, you know, you have to have this type of personality or you have to act this type of way, as soon as you deviate from that, you're kind of seen as an outsider. (Army, enlisted, Latina)

Cristina explained that women who were seen as deviating from the conventional were often labeled "sluts" or "bitches." As discussed in Chapter 2, in a femmephobic context like the military it is difficult for women to avoid being cast into these stigmatized femininities. This implies that those who embody or approximate the hyper-masculine military warrior can access family-like benefits more easily. When I asked Cristina to elaborate, she shared a story of a women in basic training whom she regarded as "very friendly" and "willing to take care of people" but who was ostracized by other servicemembers who perceived her as "slutty." Cristina lamented her own participation in this behavior, and the lack of caregiving that was extended to this person, saying:

> I felt like I was in high school. Like, they would just talk behind her back, and it was just a lot of gossip. And it was really nothing I could do. It was just kind of that situation where I myself still wanted to be part of the group, but in order to be part of the group I had to do what, you know, what others were doing, meaning ignoring her, which is kind of neglecting our friendship . . . and I think it was very ironic, because you're always taught . . . you never leave anyone behind. And you hear that from our drill sergeants. But my drill sergeant ignored her, just shunned her.

While all servicemembers are taught the military-as-family narrative in training, access to the family is constrained in interaction with other servicemembers and withheld from those perceived as "outsiders," and in the military context insider status is deeply gendered.

Some servicewomen spoke more directly about their exclusion from the military family. Vivian described feelings of isolation when she was prohibited from joining the Wounded Warrior program:

> The enlisted Marines at the hospital sought me out and were like, "You qualify" . . . But the officers on base refused to let me in. So, I didn't get to take advantage of the services that the program provided, like relaxed working hours, and assistance driving to and

from doctor's appointments, and it was something like a thirty-minute drive. At the time, they were giving me basically unlimited narcotics, which I did need for pain. But it put me in a position of having to suffer through my pain to drive safely, or to be pain-free but possibly be driving under the influence. I didn't benefit from the family-like support that the military created in the Wounded Warrior program. And I didn't feel like I had any recourse because it was a colonel who denied me. I was alone on an island, and I felt like I had to beg other officers to pick me up from a surgery that I was not legally allowed to drive myself home from. (Marine Corps, officer, White)

The Wounded Warrior program is a tangible benefit available to servicemembers and veterans that provides support for those who "incurred a physical or mental injury, illness or wound during or after service" (Wounded Warrior Project 2022). The inclusion criteria from the program itself are broad, but servicemembers need approval to join. Vivian's request was denied by a colonel, a high-ranking officer, who told her that the program "wasn't for me, it was for people with battle-field injuries or cancer" even though she met the qualifications set by the hospital running the program. Vivian's commander used his discretion and drew his own formula for eligibility based partially on warrior masculinity. She felt ostracized by being excluded from the program and worried that she could not rely on her colleagues for support. If she had been able to join the program, Vivian would not have had to worry about driving to her own appointments and could have had support in focusing on her health. Vivian's experience demonstrates how servicewomen can be denied the relational benefits of the military family as well as tangible benefits designed to provide support and family-like caregiving to servicemembers. This can be especially challenging when servicemembers are isolated from other support networks due to frequent moves and the transient nature of military postings. In Vivian's case, she was stationed in Hawaii, thousands of miles from her family and friends, and this made her feel even more alone.

While the military defines family broadly and creates expectations of caregiving for all servicemembers, it is experienced narrowly and constrained by gender. Instances of women experiencing the benefits of the military family rely on men allowing them access, either in interaction or through official channels like approval for the Wounded Warrior program. As Vivian's example shows, inclusion often hinges on men's perceptions of women. At the same time, men may label women with one or more problematic feminine identities (i.e., "bitches" or "sluts") or elevate harassment against women they perceive as feminine, as discussed in Chapter 2. Even women who joined the military expecting a hypermasculine space and women who take care to embody masculinity were victims of harassment and treated as outsiders. Therefore, it is more accurate to describe the military family as a brotherhood where men are gatekeepers to inclusion. In the next section, I show how this brotherhood not only excludes women but also makes them vulnerable to sexual violence.

WATCH YOUR BACK: CORRUPTIONS OF MILITARY CAREGIVING

Military values of trust, caregiving, and loyalty are central to the construction of the family narrative (Brownson 2014). Women are encouraged to trust and look out for other servicemembers, and to prioritize their peers and the military hierarchy over themselves in ways that are not reciprocated. There are also some men who actively exploit expectations of caregiving and trust.

Trust can be exploited to cause harm and protect men's power in the institution. In such a context, the lines between training, orders, and harassment become blurred. Servicewomen may be unsure of how to respond when the person causing harm is someone who outranks them and is someone they are supposed to trust to look out for them. Cristina's drill sergeant during training used his position of power to flirt with soldiers under his care:

In the commercials—you know, advertising for the Army commercials—you always hear your drill sergeant is your role model, and your leader, and somebody that you look up to. And they're the top soldiers in the Army. But I felt like that was not the case at all . . . You see, when you're in basic training, you're deprived of a lot of things. You're deprived of a clean shower . . . we were always dirty. We . . . and I . . . we stank. And my drill sergeant, he was always very . . . he was the only drill sergeant that had, like, cologne on . . . And the females would say comments: "Oh, drill sergeant," "Oh, he's always good-looking" . . . And then it got to a point where, you know, they would call him "daddy." He knew this, and he would say, well, "How 'bout goodnight daddy" before he left for the day. And that was okay to him. (Army, enlisted, Latina)

Cristina was disappointed by someone she trusted exploiting the power he had over her and other Army recruits by lingering in the barracks and inviting sexual attention. In doing so, he corrupted the military expectation that Army leaders are parental, trustworthy figures. He even sexualized the military family by having the recruits call him "daddy." Cristina's drill sergeant was in a position of power as someone who could start or end these women's careers through his evaluations and recommendations. Positions of power and expectations of trust are further compounded by the fact that drill instructors' interactions with servicewomen extend into all aspects of their lives, where they are isolated from non-military support networks for several weeks. In fact, one of the goals of boot camp is to force recruits to realize that they have no privacy and that they are always being watched and observed. In a situation where young women are told that they have no power, no say, and no privacy, and when instructors prey on recruits, harassment becomes entangled with and inseparable from training rituals. Women learn that this behavior is normal and should be expected. These lessons also get infused into how servicemembers interact with one another.

One evening, Julia, a young enlisted Marine, was socializing with some of the men who lived in her barracks. They were playing video games in her friend Greg's room. After a few hours, they moved outside to the smoke pit—a designated area where smoking is allowed and where Marines often congregate. Some of the Marines around the smoke pit were also drinking, which is not uncommon. Julia noticed that one of the guys, Allen, was extremely intoxicated. Greg also noticed. Allen was drunk enough to warrant concern and together they told him it was time to go. They each put one of his arms around their shoulders and helped him walk the short distance back to the barracks. Supporting his weight, they helped him walk up three flights of stairs, pausing for him to take breaks and steadying him along the way. When they got to the third floor, Greg peeled off. Julia remembers this moment. At the time, she did not think it was problematic because he lived on that floor. He also asked if she was okay to walk Allen to the fourth floor alone. She said "okay" but she was smaller, shorter, and lighter than Allen and helping him up the next set of stairs alone was "a bit difficult."

When Julia got Allen to his room: "He said he wanted to come to my room . . . He said, 'Let's keep hanging.' He sounded depressed and he said he didn't want to be alone." Julia was adamant that Allen not come to her room, and she encouraged him to go to his bed and lie down. She made excuses to leave while standing outside his door, but Allen then asked her to come into his room:

> He just kept inviting me in there. Then he started talking about how he was going to kill himself. And then he was . . . I think he was using his mental health. Because I've been depressed. He was . . . sort of very aggressive with his words and kind of using it against me. Saying over and over he is sad, depressed. (Marine Corps, enlisted, White)

Julia stayed outside of his room while he stood in the doorway. She said goodbye and encouraged him to watch a show or lie down. She stressed to me that she did not want to go into his room. However, she also worried about his mental health. She did not want to leave him alone when he was talking about suicide. While she contemplated what to do next, he physically pulled her into his room by her arm. This alarmed her. After he pulled her into the room, he moved away from her and sat down, which made her feel less afraid. As soon as he sat down, he started talking about killing himself again. She debated leaving, but the messages from training about taking care of Marines hit her. She decided to try to help him because:

> I saw a Marine in distress, I didn't want to leave a Marine like that. I've had depression . . . And if they [the Marine Corps] harp on suicide so much, I think it's really hard to leave somebody who is even hinting at suicide ideation. The main thing that got me to even take away alcohol or kick him up to his room was, "Okay, if he kills himself tonight, I'm one of the last people who had seen him." You can't leave another Marine behind.

These messages swirled around in Julia's mind as she tried to decide what to do. She wanted to leave but kept returning to her obligation not to leave a Marine behind. The expectation that she always take care of other Marines meant to her that she had to protect Allen from self-harm.

However, Allen did not see Julia as a fellow Marine whom he should protect and care for. He viewed her as a sexual object. Soon after she was in his room, his comments turned sexual. She tried to shut him down by reminding him that she was gay.[2] "I think I said, 'We play for the same team'" and "I mentioned I had a girlfriend" and he responded: "But you're so attractive." This is when Julia knew that there was no talking to Allen or convincing him to leave her alone. She made a plan. She turned on the TV and set up a video game for him. She handed him the controller and turned to leave. That's when Allen got "very aggressive with his words" and "picked me up, put me on the sofa, and then . . . and pulled me into the bed. Yeah. And that's where I have the most obvious memories." Julia also mentioned Allen tried to reach up her shirt. After a brief struggle on the bed, she was able to push him away, climb off the bed, and run out of his room.

The incident haunted Julia. She kept returning to the idea that she had an obligation to stay with Allen to make sure he didn't hurt himself. This sense of duty, instilled in her by Marine Corps training that emphasized recognizing and assisting servicemembers in distress, led her to continue interacting with Allen despite her discomfort. She knew that the right response to a servicemember in distress was to care for them, and she did not want to be blamed by the institution or her peers if Allen killed himself. However, this put Julia in a vulnerable position. Furthermore, Julia said multiple times that she thought Allen was using mental health to coerce her to come in his room. That is, she believed he used the fact that Marine Corps training is hyper-focused on teaching servicemembers to stick together, especially when suicide ideation is mentioned, to manipulate and try to pressure her to stay with him. Allen's actions are an example of the way some people can exploit the military's caregiving expectation to enact sexual violence.

The next morning, Julia "analyzed the hand marks on me. It was like a physical handprint, like a bruise, inside my thigh. And I'm really glad I went to medical and caught those in photos . . . And that's where there was the physical evidence that supported what I said, which is likely why the members convicted him." Julia reported Allen for assault and sexual assault, and he was convicted at court-martial of the former. At court-martial, Julia was repeatedly questioned about why she went into his room. Even though the military trains its servicemembers to not leave a Marine behind and it teaches them to watch out for and be sensitive to suicide ideation, her staying in the room was still questioned at trial. He was not convicted of sexual assault for trying to touch her breast. This bothered her because she felt like this part was calculated by Allen. She felt he used his depression to lure her into his room to hook up with her and when she declined his advances, he tried to physically force her.

The military's prioritization of suicide prevention over sexual harassment and assault prevention also contributed to this dilemma. At no point was it considered problematic that no one stepped in to assess sexual violence vulnerability. Imagine if the military harped on sexual assault in the same way it does suicide. If the military encouraged servicemembers to evaluate interactions for sexual violence potential and to intervene accordingly, Greg may have decided to walk the rest of the way up the stairs with Allen and Julia. In this situation, either one could be vulnerable to sexual violence and the presence of another person has the potential to keep everyone safe. However, the women I spoke with did not describe sexual violence training in this way, explaining that sexual violence content was often delivered through PowerPoint presentations and that messages of bystander intervention of sexual assault were not infused into lessons on how servicemembers should care for one another.

Many servicewomen described feeling an obligation to care for other servicemembers and an expectation to trust other servicemembers, especially military leaders and commanders. Not only do military slogans invoke the word "loyalty,"[3] but many military training exercises are based on developing trust among servicemembers, trust in commanders, and trust in the institution (Clark 2016; Verweij 2007). Trust and loyalty are important for forming bonds among servicemembers who are expected to sacrifice for one another as well as potentially sacrifice their lives in combat situations (Harrison 2003; Verweij 2007). However, trust and loyalty are often not given freely to women, especially women who report sexual assault.

At the court-martial trying Julia's attacker, most of the Marines from her unit showed up to support Allen. She expressed being especially let down by that because "they were in my unit, *too*. They were supposed to care about me, *too*." This pain was compounded for Julia by the spatial dynamics of the law office located outside of the courtroom where the case was tried. Prosecutors and defense counselors worked in the same building, separated by a single lobby and waiting area with benches facing one another, divided by a vending machine against the wall. On some occasions, Julia and her family waited in the same area as members of her unit there to support her attacker, witnesses for the defense, and friends of her attacker. Without space away from people supporting Allen, she was constantly reminded of the broken promises of trust, family, and loyalty during her full three days showing up to court.

Despite developing new policies and education initiatives related to sexual violence over the last fifteen years, the military does not infuse caregiving for sexual violence victims into its trainings, narratives, and instructions in the same way it does for issues like combat trauma, suicide

ideation, and ensuring physical training success and academic achievement. While the military does address sexual violence at the policy and
administrative level, it does not prioritize sexual violence at the interactional level where servicemembers are taught how to interact with and
treat one another. At the same time, victimization is a feminized identity
in the military context, and is often portrayed as the antithesis of warrior
masculinity. These factors combined so that victims of sexual harassment
and assault who come forward are often demonized as military outsiders,
or even as enemies within.

Vilifying Reporting

Despite the military having anti-harassment and sexual assault education,
policies for reporting harassment and assault, and rules against retaliation
for reporting, when the women I spoke with tried to report they were
often harassed, isolated, and ridiculed by military peers and superiors.
Cristina shares:

> This male, he was very popular . . . And an allegation came up against
> him from a female . . . And apparently, she was sexually assaulted
> by him. And I remember that everyone was really, really upset, and
> they gave her a lot of . . . they gave her a hard time . . . because es-
> sentially an allegation will have consequences for him. People were
> saying things like, "Well, if it wasn't for her, he would have graduated
> with us." Actually, he came from a poor town . . . He was kind of seen
> as someone that was trying to better himself, making a better life
> for himself by joining the military. They would say . . . "He was just
> a good kid. He was trying to do the right things . . . and this bitch
> comes along and she fucks up everything for him." And "It's her, she's
> a slut. She's the one that led him on." But I feel like he did . . . he might
> have done something that he shouldn't have. But because he was so
> popular, . . . that the girl who brought up the allegations was sort of
> demonized. (Army, enlisted, Latina)

While the victim in this case was able to access the reporting system, she was punished informally by other servicemembers, who ostracized, harassed, and vilified her for reporting. These interactional dynamics really matter, and Cristina clearly explains the importance of status and popularity in shifting blame from those who commit sexual assault to their victims. By labeling this woman "a slut," other servicemembers call into question her status as a victim because it is problematically assumed that "sluts" always want sex and cannot be sexually assaulted.

Once they question her credibility as a victim, her motives for reporting are also reframed. She becomes stigmatized as "a bitch" who maliciously misused military reporting streams to ruin a serviceman's life. The portrayals of him as a "good kid" and as someone "trying to better himself" through the military cast doubt on his role in the assault. These dynamics shift how military policies available for sexual harassment and assault victims are viewed and used.

When victims come forward, they are not only maligned but can also be portrayed as in opposition with other servicemembers, and therefore undeserving of caregiving. When Marie was a cadet at the Air Force Academy, a classmate, who was a man, often emailed porn to the entire class:

> One time he sent out this email of a woman having sex with a horse. I didn't even know that was possible until I saw this video, actually. He emailed it to everybody—to the entire class within that squadron, so it was, like, thirty-five people he emailed it to. Yeah, I thought it was disgusting and I said something. I said something to another upperclassman, a woman, and she thought it was disgusting as well, so she reported it to our commander . . . So, he [the commander] decided to talk to this boy about sending the porn. Well, when he talked to him, he also said that it was me who had complained. And the squadron basically ostracized me. They told me that if I was ever shot down in Afghanistan, they would let me die . . . that they wouldn't save me. (Air Force Academy, White)

In this case, even though her commander (an active-duty officer) decided to step in and verbally reprimand the student who sent porn to
the class, he also identified Marie as the person who reported. Whether
this was intentional or not, the fact that her classmates turned on her
and began to socially isolate her sends a clear message that women must
accept sexual harassment as a part of their military service. She continued, "And, I mean, the whole military concept is . . . is around this
idea of teamwork. So, everything from class papers to, you know, physical training—everything—you need your classmates. So, because this
kid who was sending out the porn was liked by everybody, and I took an
issue with it, they . . . they were pissed. They were pissed, and they told
me they would let me die."

On top of the social isolation caused by this treatment, Marie's
classmates retaliated against her when it was time for peer evaluations.
Peer evaluations are used at the academy, and in the military more
broadly, for ranking servicemembers and can affect things like graduation, promotions, and the ability to stay in the military. After Marie
was assumed to have reported the pornography, her classmates ranked
her last in their unit, which had detrimental effects for her position in
the academy. The imagery of her classmates, and those she was supposed
to rely on in war, letting her die in a hypothetical combat situation also
made her "feel worthless." She was not part of the military family. She was
not a battle buddy. She was the enemy, vilified for speaking out against a
student who violated military rules about pornography. However, if reporting sexual harassment and assault was lauded by the institution, and
encouraged at multiple levels of training, she might have been commended
rather than denigrated for calling out this disrespectful behavior.[4] The fact
that she was portrayed as an enemy and ostracized by her peers reveals
that her classmates' values and loyalties are influenced less by specific military policies and rules, such as those banning pornography, and more
by interactions between servicemembers, such as the commander outing
Marie as the person who reported and thereby characterizing her as a
tattletale.

The victim identity, which a servicemember takes on when they report harassment or assault, is not only a stigmatized femininity that is denigrated, but one that is also vilified. Those who report are not seen as trying to address problems in the institution, but rather as the *cause* of problems in the institution. In the end, Marie concluded that reporting was useless, saying, "It's a real big deal [the negative peer evaluations]. I mean, if that would have happened again, would I have reported? Hell, no. Not if my life depended on it." Marie knew that her daily life at the academy, her military future, and her life in a combat situation depended on what her military peers thought about her. She learned through these interactions that other cadets turn on those who report sexual harassment. When women who report are seen to experience social ostracization and negative career effects, and are portrayed as enemies, other women begin to accept and normalize harassment and acquiesce to men's domination of the spaces where they live, work, study, and socialize. I discuss this in depth in the next chapter. For sexual assault victims, though, it makes them reject the military completely.

REJECTING THE BROTHERHOOD

The military brotherhood makes servicewomen vulnerable to sexual violence. This is problematic for all servicewomen who are promised and desire to be in the military family, but especially women who joined to escape abuse, negative home lives, and families that had hurt them. Violence often occurs within families, with many instances of child sexual abuse being perpetrated by an adult family member (Russell 1984; Sedlak et al. 2010), yet individuals can struggle to admit this because it runs contrary to dominant constructions of family as safe, nurturing, places (Mitra 2013). Similarly, servicewomen who have heard the family narrative repeated throughout their service, and who have been trained to think of violence as enacted by military insiders on those defined by the institution as enemies, might not anticipate violence *within* the institution. However, when sexual violence occurs it can sever the notion of the military family altogether. Servicewomen may feel an additional layer of harm since the institutional promise of family did not live up to their expectations nor the military's portrayal of this narrative.

Against a background of abuse, some servicewomen may be particularly susceptible to the military's promises of stability, support, and family-like caregiving. For women like Sandra and Janet, who opened this chapter, they realize that they traded one violent space for another when the military replicated the abuse they sought to leave behind. It was the same for Cecelia, who experienced sexual and emotional abuse prior to enlisting in the Marine Corps and was raped shortly after transferring into a new unit by her base sponsor, a married man a decade older and several ranks higher than her. In the victim impact statement she read at the court-martial trying her rapist, she explained how being victimized by someone she trusted echoed her past experiences with violence:

> I came to the Marine Corps to be empowered, learn how to be strong, and how to lead. To find myself, to find a family who was close to me. But once again I was wronged by someone who was close to me. Someone who was supposed to protect me. (Marine Corps, enlisted, Latina)

Cecelia stressed that the military being portrayed as a family was a powerful motivator for why she joined the Marine Corps. Cecelia was promised a family when she joined, and she was excited and eager to experience this stability after an abusive childhood. When she first got to base, she viewed Quinn as a mentor and, likely due to his age and rank as well as his status as a Marine, a potential source of protection. Initially she trusted him in this role and disclosed her past experiences with sexual abuse. Recall from Chapter 2 that Quinn used his role as her sponsor to continually show up to her barracks room. One night, he brought alcohol to her room and asked to drink with her. From her perspective, being new to base and a recent twenty-one-year-old, she thought she could trust him, that he was looking out for her, that this must be a normal part of the military bonding. However, she explained that Quinn raped her that night in her room.

After reporting him for rape and going through the court-martial process, Cecelia reflected on how he used his position of trust to exploit her and assault her. In her victim impact statement, she described a loss of trust not only in him as a person, but in the Marine Corps as an institution. She ceased to see the military as a place that would foster family for her and viewed it instead as a sexually dangerous place. Almost all the women I interviewed who were sexually assaulted speak this way about the military. They completely reject the notion that the military is a family, they reject the military as an institution, and they see the miliary as complicit in their victimization.

Sexual assault and the institutional response to sexual assault distances women from the idea that the military is a family and decreases the salience of a military identity for these women (Stets 2005; Stryker 1980; Stryker and Burke 2000). Jennifer describes how her disillusionment with the Marine Corps was a process:

> In my instance I wanted closure because I felt that it would be a sense of justice. I wanted to still believe in the military. You go through so much, especially to get into the Marine Corps. You don't want to believe it is not the dream you imagined it to be. You don't want to be disillusioned; you have already been sexually assaulted. You've been taught that you should be able to trust these people to give their lives for/with you in war. (Marine Corps, officer, White)

Jennifer juxtaposes the message she received in training that she should be able to entrust her life to other servicemembers with the reality that she cannot trust them with her body. Servicewomen who experience sexual violence do not feel connected to people they were told to think of as "brothers," which can lead to them connecting the military family narrative to their vulnerability to sexual assault. When the Marine Corps failed to give Jennifer the justice that she craved, she realized that it was not just that she could not trust Marines in the way she was taught, she could not trust the organization to respond or protect her.

Diane re-examines the messaging she received about the military family in recruitment and initial training through her later experiences with sexual harassment and assault in the Marine Corps. She states:

> I was told that I was going to join a brotherhood and a sisterhood that people were, people are going to look out for me and I'm going to look out for people, and that's not what it was. It's a great idea. Great idea. Great ideology. So wonderful concept . . . But seeing what other female Marines go through, no Marine gets left behind, unless you're a female because you don't count. That's . . . kind of the gist that I picked up. That's not necessarily what they teach, but that's what I picked up. No Marine gets left behind, unless you're a female . . . And I went in trying to belong somewhere. I went in thinking that I'm going to have a family . . . that's not going to abandon me. My mom was in and out of prisons . . . I have abandonment issues that I'm trying to work through. But, like, the Marine Corps just kind of like solidified that kind of just, well you don't have a family and you really are alone and there's nothing you can do about it. (Marine Corps, enlisted, White)

Diane exemplifies someone who joined the Marine Corps hoping for a family because of a lack of stability in her home life. She was drawn in by the promise of family and she was motivated by the messages in boot camp that Marines take care of one another. She believed in these institutional narratives and values and worked hard to protect and care for her peers and then later her junior Marines when she was in. However, once she left gender-segregated boot camp, she realized through interacting with other servicemembers that not everyone thought of women as members of the military family. She said:

> The schoolhouse showed me what I was really involved in. I was sexually assaulted by another Marine. And the saddest part about it was they taught us, you were always there for your brothers and sisters . . . Well, I had two other Marines watch it happen and they were laughing at me while it [the sexual assault] was happening . . . And

that was the harsh reality to me. And I found out what I was really involved in. I found out that I was in a man's world and there was nothing I could do about it because I was already a Marine. Like, I couldn't get out, I had to serve.

Diane was sexually assaulted in the library located in her barracks. She was reading and relaxing and told me she "had sweats on, really baggy clothes. And that's important because Marines like to say, 'Well, what was she wearing?'" By describing her clothing, Diane hopes to portray herself as "not asking for it," which reveals that she anticipated being blamed for her own assault by others in the Marine Corps. She went on to explain:

> These three drunk Marines, they come up and they're laughing and being all kinds of loud. And one of the Marines, they sit down on my back and they start touching me. And I'm like screaming for help. And "the duty," he's literally just right below us, and I know he can hear me because I have a very loud voice, and he just let it happen. He didn't do anything. "The duty" didn't do anything.

This is a situation where she would have expected other servicemembers to intervene, to help or protect her, and yet the other Marines stood by and laughed and one "even sat down on my legs to keep me from kicking." She learned through interacting with servicemen that the military caregiving, protection, and family she had been promised and hoped for was not for women. She also saw that men would protect each other even as one of them sexually assaulted her.

The Marine on duty refers to the person assigned to "unaccompanied housing" duty or what many Marines refer to as barracks duty.[5] Marines on duty patrol the barracks, monitor visitors and deliveries, and are charged with looking for and reporting any violations or misconduct. They are specifically instructed to "intervene when you observe Marines abuse alcohol, become disruptive, mistreat other Marines, or in any other way put themselves and others at risk" (U.S. Marine Corps 2020). When the Marine on duty ignored her screams, it solidified for her that others did not view sexual assault as problematic, not even among people tasked with keeping Marines in the barracks safe from harm.

Diane felt duped by the institution because it was only once she was already in the Marine Corps and contractually obligated to spend four years in service that it was revealed to her that the military was not a family and was actually a brotherhood where women were denigrated and vulnerable to sexual violence. She felt trapped in an organization where perpetrators of sexual violence were encouraged and protected by other servicemembers. She filed a restricted report for the sexual assault, which meant that she was able to receive mental health support, but no legal action would be taken against her perpetrator. Some victims chose to file a restricted report because unrestricted reports require that the entire command be notified of the assault. In Diane's case this was crucial because she knew the interactional culture was hostile to people who reported assault. When I asked why she chose restricted over unrestricted reporting, she told me, "I didn't want to be condemned by my own unit." In Diane's case, interacting with other servicemembers sent a clear message that women were not members of the family, were not protected within the organization, and were even vulnerable to violence. For other servicewomen, this message is also supported at the institutional and policy level when women are unable to access reporting streams or victim-friendly policies.

When the institution deprioritizes victim experiences, it further demonstrates that the military devalues victims of sexual assault. After Penelope was raped, she was offered an expedited transfer and was promised she could go to a duty station of her choosing. An expedited transfer is a policy designed to be victim-friendly. It allows victims to transfer out of a unit and even to a new base so that they do not have to live and work near their attacker. However, as detailed in the last chapter, this policy is not always enacted in ways that the victim desires or even in ways that help the victim. Rather than fulfilling Penelope's request to go to a state in the Southeast, the military sent her to the Northwest, isolating her from her support network and impacting her ability to easily travel to testify against her rapist at court-martial. After this experience she said:

> Because since the assault, I am not the soldier that I used to be. I was super gung-ho about the Army; super motivated, and I loved it—and then this happened and I kind of lost all respect for the organization and my leaders (Army, enlisted, White)

Not only did the sexual assault and her command's response change Penelope's outlook on the military, but it also altered her sense of self—she no longer felt like "the soldier that I used to be." She did not view herself as a part of the institution, and she rejected the idea that the military was an inclusive organization. She continued:

> So, I have a hard time respecting and being motivated to be a part of an organization that I feel in a way let me down . . . I don't even like putting on the uniform anymore. I had this big idea that the Army was going to be this awesome thing and experience for me, and that's not what it turned out to be. So, it's unfortunate that I had this experience right off the bat, but at the same time I kind of got to see the Army for the worst that it can be. The way the whole process ended up working and how I got moved three thousand miles away, it's just—I don't think that I'll ever be able to get over the fact that that happened, and I just don't want anything to do with the Army anymore because of it.

Here, Penelope distances herself from the Army in general, as well as specific indicators that she is associated with the Army, such as her uniform. Penelope's frustration with the military justice system combined with the assault shows how she feels exploited at multiple levels. She explains how her disappointment with the military's response to her sexual assault is directly linked to her desire to detach herself from the Army. It is interpersonal and institutional betrayal.

Recall Kay whose experience with attempted rape during her service was detailed in the last chapter and opened this book. After the attempted rape, she was sent to a mental institution because, during this traumatic period, she stated she wanted to hurt herself. Ultimately, Kay's experience at the mental institution was used against her to drop her case. Her hospitalization was used as evidence that she had a personality disorder. Assigning her a personality disorder code removed her eligibility for post-service medical benefits, a consequence that she believes was a direct punishment for reporting the assault. She went on to express other issues with how the military handled her case:

> They don't protect you. Like, that's something I will say about the military that has to change. If you accuse someone of sexual assault or any type of assault or anything, they don't protect you. They just make you continuously see this person. You know what that does to somebody? (Navy, enlisted, Black)

Kay reported her attacker through official reporting streams. She hoped that while the military investigated, there would be an attempt to ensure that she did not have to work in the same unit, building, and office as her attacker. When nothing happened and she remained in the unit with her attacker, she asked for a transfer. This request was ignored, and she was forced to continue to see him every day at work. She tried to talk to peers about this, but many of them had ostracized her. She wasn't sure if it was because she reported the assault or because of how the assault affected her:

> So I had an emotional meltdown. I mean, when I tell you that I was acting like . . . I had . . . when I got into the fight with my friend—we can talk about it now, we laugh about it—but I cussed him out. . . in front of my superior officers, like in front of my bosses. I cussed him out and slammed the door, and threw stuff, punched a hole in the wall. I could have gotten arrested just for that alone . . . for destroying government property. . . . I went upstairs and threw chairs and stuff.

You know how messed up I had to be to be like that? . . . I was to the point where I was enraged. I had never been that angry in my life . . . I saw, like, red . . . So, to get to that point where I'm around all these people who've been in the military for, like, some of them decades, and no one advocated for me, no one helped me . . . especially the women. Nobody cared.

Kay acknowledges that she was angry, confused, and emotional. These are all normal reactions to trauma and to sexual violence, especially when the victim is forced to continually interact with the attacker and be made to feel unsafe at work but also in any other space on base, including her home. What should have been seen as a normal response to her assault was instead viewed as problematic from other servicemembers who chose to ostracize her instead. She also highlights how women are at times complicit in this treatment and contribute to the climate that supports harassment.

When Kay sought out the chaplain for spiritual leadership and a listening ear, he told her: "You're just sad. Just start working out. You're just sad. You go home every day and watch TV, don't you? Like, yeah, just start working out and get some hobbies. You'll be okay." She pushed further: "I remember asking him, 'Can I please go to another duty station?'" A victim of sexual assault in the Navy is eligible to request an expedited transfer to another base if they filed an unrestricted report, but this request has to go through their commander's officer, not the chaplain.[6] When she asked, the chaplain told her to "Just suck it up, just toss it out." It is unclear if the chaplain knew about the policy or not, but it is clear that he did not offer spiritual or emotional support in the aftermath of her victimization. Not only did the military leave her vulnerable to sexual violence, but she was further ostracized for reporting her victimization by servicemen, servicewomen, commanders, spiritual leaders, and medical experts.

After the attempted rape and the military's negative response to her experience, report, and symptoms, Kay wanted out of the Navy. Recall from the introduction to this book that after Kay was able to leave, she stated, "I burned my uniform. Like, when I got my separation papers, I burned my uniform. And I was like, 'peace' . . . I like did not look back." In summary, the institution dropped her case and used symptoms of her trauma against her to create documentation that would allow the military to move to force her out. Other servicemembers ostracized her after she reported or ignored her complaints that she was forced to interact and work with her attacker. Finally, Navy leaders and peers viewed normal responses to her assault, such as anger and depression, as her own personal problems, despite the institution's emphasis on caregiving. All these factors proved to Kay that the military was not a family that she was a part of. It was not a place that ensured that she, or people like her, were taken care of in any capacity, as she was denied legal, medical, social, and even spiritual support. She sought to get out of the Navy as soon as possible.

Citing regulations relating to hair, dress, body weight, and physical fitness, scholars claim that servicemembers' bodies are not their own but are rather tools of the military (MacLeish 2013). Servicemembers are tasked with maintaining their bodies as instruments of the institution (MacLeish 2013) and are officially sanctioned if they are "overweight" or cannot perform physically. Even Kay stated that "they feel like they own your body" when discussing how she and other women she knew had been pressured to have abortions by miliary doctors and leaders. For Penelope and Kay, they reclaimed their bodies by denigrating and destroying one of the physical markers of military insiderness and ownership, the uniform.

CONCLUSION

The "military as family" narrative is encouraged by invoking family discourse in recruitment materials and training exercises, and membership to the military family is often explained as a key benefit of military service. The military encourages family-like caregiving and trust to serve its institutional goals, such as loyalty to the institution and mission effectiveness. Since servicemembers are separated from their family and friends and isolated in military spaces, they may seek to form family-like bonds with others. The family narrative is especially attractive to individuals seeking to escape negative home lives and abusive families. While the military uses the words "brotherhood" and "family" interchangeably to explain this key benefit of membership, in interaction women realize that the military family is a brotherhood that excludes them and can create sexual violence vulnerability for them.

Research has found that the extreme stress and mental duress of military training often creates loyalty to the institution and camaraderie (Callahan 2009; Hale 2012; Harrison 2003). Verweij (2007) argues that trust, loyalty, and love among servicemembers are needed for survival in combat situations. Servicemembers are taught in training that there is no greater bond than the one they will share with those with whom they train, serve, and deploy (Citroën 2018; Halvorson 2010). The military views caregiving, trust, and loyalty as essential for mission effectiveness and therefore encourages servicemembers to protect, care for, and trust one another. However, these values and expectations get filtered through the femmephobic military context, and women learn through interacting with other servicemembers that they are not the recipients of this caregiving and protection in the same way that men are. Further, some servicemen exploit the expectations of trust and loyalty to cause harm. Servicewomen I interviewed discussed how they felt compelled to help and engage in carework that left them vulnerable to sexual violence.

An additional layer of the military brotherhood is revealed when victims report sexual harassment and assault. Women who reported their victimizations were ostracized by their peers, blocked from accessing military policies designed to assist victims, and even harassed further. Women learn that using military policies and reporting streams invites more mistreatment. Some women believe that it is not just that the institution cannot protect them from sexual assault, but that the military is complicit in their victimization. This can occur even when a servicewoman is assaulted by a non-servicemember but still receives a negative response from her command. For example, Melanie was raped by an Iraqi policeman while on deployment and reported it to her command. She stated:

> They basically told me nothing was going to get done because even if they went to his command, they would just high-five him, and that was what my command told me. So, I ended up just hating that command team because I felt so let down by people who are supposed to

be fighting with me . . . We all sat around the table and they pretty much told me—they're like, "Well, we don't recommend this goes anywhere because even if you do say anything, nothing will happen because he's Iraqi. They won't care." They were like, "You can go to the chaplain if you want, but he probably can't do anything either because he travels and he's not here right now." So, they pretty much kind of just dismissed me. (Army, enlisted, White)

Even though Melanie was not raped by a U.S. serviceman, she expresses her disappointment with how her command handled her report. Further, the soldiers dismiss her rape by relying on stereotypes that the Iraqi forces would not care or engage in disciplinary action against her attacker. In doing so, they vilify Iraqis and dismiss Iraqi men as sexist as well as blame non-action in response to Melanie's rape on Iraqis rather than on the command. Simultaneously, the soldiers actively silence Melanie and exacerbate her suffering by dismissing her. The fact that this occurred on deployment, a time when team and family-like bonding is essential to individual and organizational success, heightened Melanie's outsider status.

When her military leaders and peers as well as the institution itself did not offer her support or resources or even seem to care about her rape, her perspective on the institution shifted. She continued:

Well, I didn't really have any . . . it's like so nobody really cared that I was hurting or what happened, and it seemed like the very people I was trying to protect kind of turned on me and they wouldn't take me seriously. It's like for our final photo, it was like a group shot before we redeployed, we went back to the same place to take that photo and I had to stand next to the damn same guard who attacked me. And I was just like—I couldn't grasp what the hell made them think that was okay.

Melanie viewed the military as an institution composed of people she could *not* trust, which led her to leave the Army as soon as she was able. In explaining this decision, she stated, "I feel like the camaraderie and the teamwork and people watching out for each other just isn't there." Rather than stressing the family-like bonds she had with other servicemembers, Melanie emphasized her colleagues' lack of care for her. It is clear that caregiving is not the expectation, at the interactional and organizational level, when it comes to sexual assault victimization. The military's values on carework and teamwork are ultimately filtered through a masculine and warrior lens that results in expectations of care for things like suicide ideation and combat-related trauma but not in cases of sexual violence. The military could encourage servicemembers to watch out for and protect each other from sexual violence in the same way that it encourages them to recognize depression and suicide ideation, but it does not fight sexual violence at the interactional level. Leaders do not systematically reprimand servicemembers who fail to shut down harassing statements like they do when they fail to help a drunk peer. This leaves victims to manage and handle sexual victimization on their own. When servicemembers try to report victimization, they are vilified and further harassed, isolated, and punished. Therefore, the military family is actually a brotherhood that not only excludes women but also creates and sustains sexual assault vulnerability for them. The military's emphasis on caretaking, trust, and loyalty is also entangled with prioritizing the brotherhood and actively de-prioritizes victims of sexual violence. This is made clear by the reality that assault victims are ignored, ostracized, and vilified when they disclose, report, and seek institutional support and help from their colleagues and superiors. In cases like Diane's where servicemen laughed while she was assaulted, assisted her attacker, or ignored her screams, women learn that servicemen are protected by the institution and by other servicemen even when they perpetrate sexual violence. The lesson is encapsulated by Diane's statement "No Marine gets left behind, unless you're a female." The military brotherhood is not only off limits to women, but it also plays an active role in their vulnerability to harassment, assault, and victimization.

Sexual assault often shifted how women viewed the military culture, the institution, and servicemen. Rather than view misogyny, harassment, and sexist talk as normal or just part of being in the military, victims of sexual assault connected these behaviors to the military's ongoing issue with sexual violence and often confronted it, disclosed to leaders, or used official reporting streams. Melanie explains this process when she shared that "the sexual assault" was one of her most prominent military memories "because that changed how I viewed everything." She told me that prior to the assault, she had trusted other soldiers and she was more likely to let sexist talk go or "just kind of laugh about it and ignore it." After the assault, she said, "I'm more serious about it." Melanie explained that she took jokes about women or inappropriate comments more seriously after she was sexually assaulted. After her assault, Melanie realized that she is an "outsider within" (Collins, 2000) the organization and believed standing up to sexual harassment would not further risk her sense of inclusion. Rejecting the notion of the military family, already existing as a feminized and vilified "other" for reporting sexual assault and seeing the military as complicit in sexual violence victimization shapes how women view harassment. Of the nineteen women sexually assaulted during their service, sixteen (84.2%) confronted harassment in interaction during their service.

Not everyone confronts or reports the victimization they experience in the military. Some fear being vilified for reporting in the ways described in this chapter. Other women know that victimization is viewed unfavorably in a femmephobic context that values aggression, domination, and violence. Some women want to avoid being seen as a victim in the military space as this is a stigmatized feminine identity in the military context. The next chapter explores how the military's emphasis on warrior masculinity shapes how victims of sexual harassment understand, process, and explain their experiences.

Eschewing Versus Embracing a Victim Identity

Responses to Harassment

The military's mission as an organization is to be a supreme fighting force, to dominate enemies in combat, and to emerge victorious in war through superior weaponry, tactics, and intelligence.[1] Servicemembers are trained to be tools of domination, to use their bodies and minds to be warriors. They are instructed to be tough, aggressive, violent, and skilled in fighting, even if their military job[2] is not combat-related. The Marine Corps phrase "Every Marine is a rifleman" has been used for decades to claim that every Marine is "ready, willing, able, and basically trained to conduct combat operations regardless of primary"[3] military occupational specialty (Curtis 2021). When former Secretary of Defense James Mattis was a major general speaking to around two hundred Marines deployed in Iraq, he stated: "There are hunters and there are victims. By your discipline, cunning, obedience, and alertness, you will decide if you are a hunter or a victim. It's really a hell of a lot of fun. You're gonna have a blast out here!" (Ricks 2006). In many ways to be a military warrior is to be a *victimizer*. What does this mean for individuals who are victimized, in the form of sexual harassment, by other servicemembers? How can servicewomen understand and make sense of being a victim in a space that only values dominance? How do they respond to sexual harassment

Hardship Duty. Stephanie Bonnes, Oxford University Press. © Oxford University Press 2024.
DOI: 10.1093/oso/9780197636244.003.0006

in an organization that associates victimization with femininity, which is actively denigrated in the institution? How can they respond to harassment when admitting victimization is considered feminine weakness, and reporting victimization results in further isolation and harassment? Half of the women I spoke with remained silent and adopted individual strategies to handle harassers. Some adopted this strategy because they did not think the military would adequately address their victimization, and some did so to avoid calling attention to their status as victims in a space where this identity is denigrated. Ultimately, the hyper-masculine culture of the military both produces harassment and serves as a barrier to women recognizing harassment and using official reporting streams.

Throughout this book I have explored how the military facilitates sexual violence vulnerability because femmephobic and hyper-masculine meanings are infused in the spatial arrangements and geography of military bases and entrenched in organizational values and polices. Encouraged by these same meanings, servicemembers also interact with one another in ways that produce and reproduce femmephobia through sexual harassment, sexual assault, and the vilification of reporting. This chapter focuses on how these gender dynamics also shape and constrain women's actions, responses, interactions, and identities, especially when it comes to harassment victimization.

SILENCE AND AVOIDANCE

Almost all the women I talked to (N = 47) described personal experiences with sexual harassment and shared examples of working in an environment where inappropriate sexual, sexist, and racist comments were made toward them. Rather than confronting or reporting this behavior, half of the women remained silent and tried to ignore it. Women did not come forward or report harassment, in part, because men dominate the organization and do not prioritize sexual victimization as an issue. Sarah served in the Air Force, which has the largest representation of women out of all the branches. Still, she felt that men's domination, especially in top positions, ensured that masculinity is privileged in the institution and hindered reporting. She said:

> I think for me it was uncomfortable because he was a higher-ranking person than me. This guy would allude to the lack of sex life with his wife. And it's like, I don't exactly know how to react in a way that is what you, as my superior, want to see. Like, if I say, "Ew, that's gross and it makes me uncomfortable," how are you going to perceive me—as this innocent little girl who can't handle a little, you know, some talk or whatever? (Air Force, officer, White)

In the past, confusing and convoluted rules for reporting and the perception that one is unable to go outside the chain of command to report have been cited as barriers to reporting for women who are harassed in the military (Jeffreys 2007; Pershing 2006; Sadler et al. 2003). In the current military context, there are multiple reporting streams for harassment. Officially, individuals can also report outside of the chain of command for a variety of issues, including harassment. However, the women I spoke with still described barriers to reporting at the interactional level. They did not feel comfortable accessing these policies. Women like Sarah, unsure of the consequences she might face by reporting a man who outranked her, would rather remain silent. Sarah's hesitation to confront comments that made her uncomfortable was partially because she was unsure if her superior was being sexually suggestive toward her, and also because she knew that he is protected by his position in the military hierarchy, his influence over her career advancement, and his status as a man. In a masculinized workplace where femininity is denigrated, Sarah fears being perceived as feminine, or worse an "innocent little girl," if she calls attention to inappropriate comments. It is clear that Sarah associates the act of challenging sexism with vulnerability to a stigmatized feminine identity, one that might invite further denigration. This interplay constrains how many women respond to harassment.

As described in the previous chapter, the military is a place where sexual assault victims are often vilified for reporting abuse and are even blamed for their own attacks. In this context, one is unlikely to come forward about harassment, which many might view as a lesser offense. Instead, women are incentivized to adopt individual strategies for managing harassment rather than report it at the institutional level or confront it at the interpersonal level.

Some women implemented avoidance strategies or other nonconfrontational responses, such as altering their appearance, in an attempt to limit instances of future harassment. For example, instead of reporting an officer who harassed several women in the unit, Molly, a woman who was enlisted in the Air Force at the time, chose to avoid him. She stated:

> A specific person who was very high-ranking in comparison to me, he used to . . . kind of, like, tease girls. He was married, and he used to tease girls by poking us in the sides when he walked by. I remember feeling very uncomfortable about it. And I didn't know what to do, but because he was so high-ranking . . . he was higher-ranking than my boss and this issue wasn't recognized, so I kind of just put up with it. I avoided him. I found myself just trying to avoid running into him. I would pay attention to where he was, and I wouldn't go near him. If I had to see him, I would stand far away and make sure he couldn't touch me, you know? I made sure I was always facing him when I had to see him or talk to him. He moved out of the unit a year or so after, and that was that. (Air Force, enlisted, White)

Due to military hierarchy and the lack of clarity on reporting high-ranking officers, Molly did not confront or report a man who harassed her and other women, even after she was touched by him repeatedly. Even though there were Air Force policies prohibiting unwanted touching and sexual harassment, Molly claims that the issue "wasn't recognized," likely because she knew that it would be difficult to access reporting streams or that she might be harassed and ostracized by others if she did successfully report, revealing the importance of the interactional level in accessing these options. The military culture that maligns victims who come forward renders useless the military policies and resources designed to assist victims.

Instead of reporting, Molly tried to minimize interactions with her harasser. This took significant time, energy, and organization. She had to
anticipate where he would be and at what time. At work, this was a distrac-
tion from her military duties as she found herself planning her workday
to avoid him. When she did see him, she got anxious and focused all her
attention on making sure he was not near her, not behind her, and always in eyesight. She described backing out of doorways so that she could
keep her eye on him, hoping this would keep her safe from him. Her
vigilance had to remain after she left work because she also wanted to
minimize running into him in social and recreational settings on base.
She also explained that she had to keep this process covert, trying not to
draw attention to her actions in case it resulted in increased harassment
from him. A lot of her energy, which could have been put toward her
military job, her friendships, and hobbies, was spent trying to stay safe
in a place where she was contractually obligated to work and live. She
endured this treatment and implemented these strategies for over a year,
while this man continued to harass her and others. Molly was likely not
the only one trying to avoid this man. While this shows how one person
can severely impact the work environment for many servicewomen, it also
highlights how military priorities, and a culture that brushes off or even
vilifies victims, contributes to women's continued vulnerability. If Molly
had confidence that the military would reprimand or remove her harasser,
perhaps she might have reported him. If the military created a climate that
was intolerant of harassment, a pathway for other servicemembers to address his actions might exist.

Maura explained that while she was enlisted in the Air Force, she was
often assigned to work in one-on-one situations with Kevin, a married
enlisted man who was several ranks higher than her. At first, they were
assigned on a few occasions to drive from one base to another, a car ride
that lasted about an hour each way. Recalling one of these experiences,
she said:

And he would ride with me. And I can remember on one of those
occasions, he said, "Well, it's about lunchtime; maybe we should stop
and get some lunch." And I said, "Hey, that sounds good to me." So,

he said, "What would you like to eat?" And I said, "I don't know; what do you feel like?" And he said, "Why don't you reach over here and see?" (Air Force, enlisted, White)

Maura first spent time with Kevin during these car rides where he sexually harassed her, made lewd comments, and tried to pressure her for sex. A few weeks later they were assigned to paint offices together, just the two of them. At first Maura said that it was "probably not the wisest thing" for their boss to assign Kevin and her to work alone in isolated settings. But as she recollected the story, she pieced together that Kevin likely asked for or arranged for these assignments so that he would have more opportunities to harass and assault her. She said "he probably told him [their boss] that he wanted to have me assigned to help him paint the office" because it was while they were painting that he turned from words and harassment to actions and assault. Painting lasted several days, and they were isolated. Kevin increasingly pressured Maura for sex, then groped her breast, and then raped her. In recalling the experience, she said that it is "one of my least favorite memories in life."

Two months after the rape, Maura got engaged. After a month-long engagement, she was married. Because her partner was also a servicemember, her marriage came with an opportunity to transfer to a different duty station. Two months after her wedding she was settling into a new base. She told me, "I got away from there quick" and spoke about her marriage as a pathway to escape her rapist rather than a romantic event. In reflecting on her decision to get married, she stated:

I think that one of the reasons why I was willing to accept his proposal, and to get married so quickly, and to leave [southern state] . . . was because I was absolutely desperate to get out of that office.

Maura's strategy to keep herself safe was not to report her rapist, but to try to distance herself from him completely. She internalized that her superior officers were not invested in her safety, since one raped her and the other assigned her one-on-one duties with her rapist. She also did not have trust in the military's sexual assault policies, telling me that she declined to report because "I was too afraid of rocking the boat." Maura had received messages that reporting victimization was the issue, not victimization itself, making these policies seemingly off-limits for her. Therefore, she accepted a marriage proposal from someone she later called "an abrasive jerk" and "a control freak" and someone she told me she probably should not have married, to escape a predatory man at her duty station. Interestingly, Maura relies on an institutional avenue to achieve relocation (a join spouse assignment), just not a sexual assault policy or resource offered by the Air Force, revealing her lack of trust in those policies. In this environment, women are often alone in trying to mitigate harassment and abuse in ways that affect their daily workplace experiences, their military careers, and their personal and intimate lives.

Consistent with quantitative research that finds that Black servicewomen are more likely than White servicewomen to experience unwanted sexual advances from military peers (Buchanan et al. 2008), Black, Latina, and Indigenous women discussed being harassed consistently at every duty station, in every unit, and by multiple perpetrators at various ranks. For example, Joanna stated:

> Your soldiers call dibs on you. When I'm new to a unit I already hear people say, "Ohh, look at that new captain, she's so cute, I'm-a hit that." You know, like they're going to do me. Then they fight each other over this fictitious affair we are going to have. They are for real getting angry and competitive. It's crazy, it really is. (Army, officer, Latina)

In situations with multiple harassers across all ranks, it becomes harder to adopt an avoidance strategy. Therefore, some Black and Latina servicewomen adjusted their appearance to try to escape some of this treatment. Kay described this strategy:

> When I got there, I was sexually harassed from the minute I walked through the office. Yeah, I had really taken a lot of care in my appearance when I first went in the military. You know, I wore makeup.

I would make sure my hair looked nice. I would make sure my uniform was pressed every night, and my shoes were shiny . . . I got
to my duty station I think by May or June. By the time we got to
Thanksgiving, I had completely let myself go physically to protect myself from the things people would say to me. (Navy, enlisted, Black)

Kay initially connected her harassment to her appearance, but she
quickly realized that pervasive harassment was related to her being a
woman. Even when she stopped caring about her appearance, harassment
did not end. When she tried to confront men who treated her like a sexual
object, harassment intensified. She said:

Because I was perceived as being attractive there was that whole
other thing where I was, like, a sexual object. And then once I decided not to participate in all of that, I was ostracized, teased, harassed, all those things. And also because I was a woman, I advocated
for myself as a woman. And you can't do that in the military, because
you'll get broken. They'll do whatever they can to stamp you out.

When the prevailing response to confronting harassment or reporting
sexual assault is to disbelieve and even harass the victim, women are
encouraged to remain silent and forced to adapt to this environment.
While individual-level strategies to avoid harassment are sometimes successful, such as when Maura was eventually able to leave the base where her
NCO raped her, the responsibility for stopping harassment then falls on
women, which further isolates them within the institution. Additionally,
these strategies do not actually stop people from harassing, as they may
simply move on to a new victim. The masculine culture of the military
that encourages silence in the face of harassment also ensures men's continued domination of the military workplace. In these men-dominated
and masculinist spaces, where women are expected to handle harassment
on their own, women must also develop their own ways to understand the
harassment they experience.

DOWNPLAYING HARASSMENT

At the same time that women are assessing how to respond to their experiences with sexual harassment, they are also left trying to make sense of these incidents. This can be especially difficult in a space where women are trying to avoid or downplay feminine identity markers because sexual harassment is often triggered by femmephobia (Hoskin 2019), and processing harassment can be a feminizing experience. Women risk further stigma if they acknowledge harassment, so instead many try to eschew the victim identity by reframing the motives of men who harass them.

Meredith told me throughout the interview that she was "one of the guys" while at the same time explaining constant sexual harassment from men at her duty stations. Harassment escalated when she started dating a man in one of her units and the other soldiers would ask them about their sex life, make sexual jokes about her, and make lewd gestures at her. She said:

> It made me so mad. And then I realized they don't even realize they're doing it. So . . . and if it's not malicious . . . how can I be mad? I mean, I can be mad, but it is what it is. And I . . . I'm only one person. I can't change the culture . . . this culture. (Army, enlisted, White)

Meredith re-interprets the motivations behind men's sexually objectifying talk. Seeing her colleagues as unintentionally offensive or "not malicious" allows her to avoid labeling herself a victim and distances her from a feminized identity in this hyper-masculine space that valorizes warriors. Not confronting harassment might be a deliberate choice women make to enhance their safety in the military. Reframing sexual objectification and harassment from men as harmless or unintentional allows them to cope with the pervasiveness of these behaviors while also avoiding appearing too "weak" or "feminine" by admitting to themselves and others that their colleagues are victimizing them.

Meredith maintained this strategy even when a serviceman sexually assaulted her:

They [servicemen in her unit] didn't do that to me [hit her on the butt] because I'd punch them or something. But, I mean, I remember one time I was on the jobsite and all a sudden the guys all swarmed around me. I'm like, I don't know what's going on . . . what's going on? And this one kid came up to me and he goes, "Hey, Meredith, I bet I can make your boobs" . . . He said, "I bet you a buck I can make your boobs"—what'd he say?—"I can make your boobs bounce without touching them." Alright, there's something going on because all you guys are standing around me here, so something's going on. "So, you're betting me a dollar that you can sit here, and you can make my boobs move without touching me?" He goes, "Yeah." I go, "Alright." He goes wonk [gestures that he grabs her boobs]. He goes, "It was worth a buck." And I was like, "I gotta give you props, that was pretty good, but if you ever do that" . . . you know . . . so I took it in stride . . . they knew that with me—because I was one of the guys—and I always . . . You know what I mean?

In her attempt to explain away a moment of unwanted groping, Meredith struggles to maintain the claim that she is one of the guys. She excuses this behavior both in interaction and in telling me about the experience. She claims that she is one of the guys because her reaction was nonconfrontational. Emphasizing that she "took it in stride" demonstrates that she did not get upset like other women might. She accepts this experience as just "boys being boys" (Jeffrey and Barata 2017; Weiss 2009) and uses that acceptance to try and claim membership to this masculine group. Even though this is a gendered form of aggression directed at her, the hyper-masculine culture of the military leaves Meredith very little space to respond to such a violation. Calling out the assault would force her to admit to being a victim and might also invite more violence. Because the assault was so public, she may have feared at the time that more men might assault her. In emphasizing her role as "one of the guys," she makes a patriarchal bargain (Kandiyoti 1988) and acquiesces to the violence in hopes that it will gain her access to the military brotherhood, protect her from more violence, or both.

However, both during the experience and in her retelling of the event, Meredith is conflicted by having to make a choice between being a victim or being one of the guys. Notably, Meredith's reaction to unwanted groping is contradictory to how she initially claimed she would react if a serviceman touched her. She started her account by stating that she would be physically violent if she was touched, a reaction she expects would be perceived as an appropriate, aggressive, masculine response. However, this response would also require her to apply the victim label to herself and the perpetrator label to the men in her unit, something that could complicate her attempt to gain "honorary man" (Kanter 1977; King 2016) status. Meredith does not allow herself the freedom to physically respond to men's violence (even hypothetically) because she had already experienced a gendered form of aggression that would require her to take on the feminized status of sexual assault victim. Uncomfortable at the prospect of envisioning herself as a victim, she backs away from this claim of confronting aggression with aggression and deflects to a story that reframes aggression as harmless fun, "fun" that she must acquiesce to and rationalize to survive it.

In the face of sexual harassment, many women prioritize masculinity and downplay sexual harassment by reframing their victimizer's motives and distancing themselves from the victim identity. Women may also reassert masculinity by explaining sexual harassment in one of two ways: (a) emphasizing their own masculine responses to this treatment, and (b) claiming that endurance of sexual harassment is a display of strength, a trait often associated with military masculinity. In doing so, servicewomen attempt to transform the meaning sexual harassment has for their lives. Instead of being a feminizing experience, they reframe harassment as a marker of masculinity. For example, Allison stated:

> Well, my recruiter was giving me a hard time for being a girl, and another recruiter who knew me better said to him, "Allison is not a chick; she's just a dude with tits." And it's true, you know. I don't get upset about stuff that most girls do. (Marine Corps, enlisted, White)

In this moment, Allison is denied insider status for being a "girl" by one serviceman and simultaneously given "honorary man" (Kanter 1977; King 2016) status from another. Keeping "honorary man" status in this interaction hinges on Allison maintaining her masculinity, rejecting a victim identity, and remaining stoic in the face of harassment (Connell 1995; Weiss 2009). Allison cannot admit that the recruiter's comments were sexist or that they bothered her because that would mean outing herself as a victim, risking a feminized identity and jeopardizing a masculine identity. Therefore, Allison distances herself from other women in the military and from traditional femininity by emphasizing that she does not get "upset" and implying that women who do get upset are devalued and lower on the gendered hierarchy. She also asserts her masculinity by emphasizing and agreeing with the recruiter who said she is a man in a woman's body. When servicemen read her body as feminine, they internalize this as a marker of her outsider status, which invites harassment. Stating that she does not get upset about sexism allows her to both trivialize the marginalization she faces and distance herself from feminizing emotions like "being upset" and feminine roles like "being a victim."

Her strategies for distancing herself from femininity are bolstered by a serviceman who views her as an "honorary man." The fact that he engages in defending her shows that achieving honorary man status can afford women the benefits of the military family caregiving, as he uses his status to defend her against harassment. However, to stand up for Allison, the recruiter must instruct the other serviceman to ignore her body, revealing the strictness of the gender binary in the military context.

When I asked Allison how she coped with the constant sexualized context she described to me, she focused her response on other women:

Here is my perspective on it. You're in a boys' club . . . there's going to be sexist jokes and, yeah, whatever. There's going to be a low level of misogyny probably all the time because there's 95% men[4]. Just a sheer numbers game. And so, when girls are like, "I just can't believe this" and I'm like, "Did you think you were joining the Girl Scouts?" . . . I joined the military expecting to get fucked up. I joined expecting to get screamed at, put through hell, run through the wringer, stressed out. I joined the military expecting to get tested.

Allison criticizes other servicewomen's responses to harassment and misogyny, demonstrating that the responsibility for handling harassment often falls on those who are mistreated (Hlavka 2014). Additionally, she reinforces the idea that women who do get offended are weak and those who do not are strong and tough. Just as enduring physical pain in silence is problematically considered a sign of strength (Barrett 1996; Sasson-Levy 2011), Allison similarly understands enduring sexual harassment, viewing it as another institutional test she must pass to prove her ability to succeed in the military.

Unlike Allison, who claimed to expect the misogyny she experienced in the military, Margaret had to adapt to the sexist environment she witnessed:

> I remember, we met this girl and she was really pretty, really nice. This redhead, she had a full tattooed sleeve. When we wore sleeves up, I remember my master sergeant saying this and he's married, and he loves, loves, loves his wife, but he would say things like, "Oh, I would just jizz on her arm." And it's like, "Whoa, okay. Hi." It didn't really offend me because I was in that environment, and I know that doesn't mean anything. I think you just get a hard skin to that. You're like, "Oh, it's the way it is." (Marine Corps, enlisted, White)

Rather than reframe men's intentions as non-offensive or non-malicious, Margaret claims the masculine environment has made her less sensitive to sexualizing and objectifying comments. Margaret understands not reacting to objectification as demonstrative of the "hard skin" she developed in her years of service where sexism was commonplace.

Servicewomen like Margaret and Allison interpret gendered forms of struggle (such as sexual harassment) through the warrior masculinity lens, allowing them to distance themselves from victim identities. They reframe their experience of enduring sexual harassment as another obstacle

they must face to be seen as strong, flipping the dominant view of victimization from an indicator of weakness to a sign of strength. Similar to
how the "Strong Black Woman" discourse can normalize powerlessness
and encourage silence about the sexual harassment and assault that Black
women face (Beauboeuf-Lafontant 2007; Tillman et al. 2010), warrior
masculinity and servicewomen's commitment to appearing strong can
contribute to the normalization of sexual harassment within the military.
By demonizing victimization and placing emphasis on toughness, the military culture makes it difficult for victims of sexual harassment to admit,
discuss, or report these experiences without jeopardizing the notion of
themselves as good servicemembers.

WOMEN IN COMBAT: MASCULINITY INSURANCE AND EMBRACING A VICTIM IDENTITY

Traditionally, combat roles have been reserved for men. Women were
officially excluded from combat until 2013, when the ban on women in
combat was repealed, and some units are still in the process of integrating
women. Combat exclusion prohibited women from being assigned to
units where the primary mission was to engage in direct ground combat.
The historical exclusion of women from combat roles demonstrates one
of the ways in which the military constructs warrior masculinity as something only for men. Since warrior masculinity is linked with combat experience, risky deployments, and the legal use of lethal force (Barrett 1996;
Connell 1995; Duncanson 2013; Dunivin 1994; Hale 2008, 2012) within the
military's masculinity hierarchy, servicemembers experiencing combat
and demonstrating bravery and heroism in combat situations often receive benefits in the form of respect, resources, prestige, power, and un-
questioned masculinity.

Despite the official ban on women serving in combat, women have
participated in combat and served in the U.S. military during its major
wars for over a century. In recent years, the military created several
exceptions to circumvent its own combat exclusion policy to enhance

military effectiveness in combat areas. For example, Erin was an enlisted Marine who was selected to participate in the Lioness Program. This program was designed to circumvent the combat exclusion policy that was in place until integration implementation began in December 2015. The Marine Corps deployed women under non-combat military occupational specialties, and then selected them while deployed to spend thirty days in combat zones (the maximum number of days they could spend without being considered deployed into combat). The Lioness Program was the precursor to the Female Engagement Teams (FET). The FETs trained together in the United States before deploying as a unit specifically designed to attach to infantry units. The FETs circumvented the thirty-day rule by spending thirty days with an infantry unit in a combat zone, followed by a few days at the base, and then being attached to a different infantry unit for another thirty days. These programs put thousands of women into combat situations, despite the official ban on women in combat. Many women were eager to join these programs. It was an opening to a part of military service that had been officially closed to women for so long, and they wanted the opportunity to serve, and be recognized, in this capacity. Many believed they had something valuable to bring to combat missions. Some understood that combat deployments would gain them more respect from their peers. Nadine explained, "Because if you deployed, it was like, 'Whoa, that's a combat Marine.' That's a whole other level. It's leveling up. So, I was like, that's what I'm going to do in Iraq."

As war zones shift, definitions of combat have adapted to include more than just troops in contact, or a firefight between two opposing militaries. Anne Irwin (2012) defines combat as "any time outside the wire during which the potential for and threat of combat were ever-present . . . and occasionally manifest" to better represent the lived experiences of soldiers in Afghanistan who considered themselves to have completed a combat tour. Even using this definition, many servicemembers, including men, will not experience a combat deployment. A combat deployment is highly valorized and respected in the military and sits at the top of the masculinity hierarchy. Therefore, anyone who has experienced combat can use this experience to claim warrior status. Masculinity in combat is context-specific. It emerges and is enacted differently than in non-combat or hypothetical combat situations (Hockey 2003). Hockey (2003) argues that acts of heroism one might celebrate in a hypothetical combat situation might be considered risky or dangerous in actual combat. Similarly, in actual combat situations, warrior identities are not as tied to bodies and gender as in hypothetical combat situations, where women are consistently constructed as outsiders. It invites more flexibility to the strict gender binary adhered to in other military contexts.

Combat experience may be visible by markers on an individual's uniform, cementing warrior status. If a servicewoman is eligible for and receives a combat action ribbon for engaging the enemy or being under hostile fire, this will be displayed on her uniform. Similarly, if she receives an award such as a Silver Star, the Navy Cross, a Distinguished Flying Cross, or the Air Force Cross, she will wear this on her dress uniform; these show that she experienced combat and demonstrated valor, courage, or bravery.[5] Women I spoke to recalled being shot at, shooting at others, and surviving and responding to attacks by improvised explosive devices. These experiences would make them eligible for such ribbons and awards.

Nadine explains that deployment or even combat experience can be visible from simply the uniform itself:

> I'm fresh from Iraq, still had the sand on my boots. Salty is what they call it, salty. I was salty as hell. You could tell how salty somebody is based on how faded their desert uniform is. If it's really faded, that means they've been out in the Iraqi sun for a minute. Just don't fuck with them. So, I wore my saltiest shit because I'm like, "Oh, no, I'm checking into this unit, you're going to know who the fuck I am." (Marine Corps, enlisted, Black)

Nadine explains that faded uniforms indicate deployment experience and that she opted to wear her deployment clothing to display her combat experience to other servicemembers. Women who have experienced combat can also "mobilize" combat masculinity (Martin 2001) in interaction with other servicemembers. This means that if someone is not recognizing them as having served in combat, they can bring up their experience to try to gain respect.

Women's inclusion in interactions and activities that cement warriorhood, such as sacrificing their lives for one another and the military in general, can also gain them status as "honorary men" (Kanter 1977; King 2016; Miller and Brunson 2000). The women who were in combat explained how they felt like members of the military brotherhood. Reflecting on her experience in the Lioness Program and the controversy over repealing the combat exclusion policy, Erin stated:

> They try to play up the whole sexual side of it, and that's bullshit because it's based on the type of relationships that you can form together. If I can get the guys that I work with on the front line to think of me as a brother, then I could do that in the infantry, too. We're nothing but brothers. We're a brotherhood. Had they done the move sooner [gender integration into infantry units], I would've stayed in. I would've been a career Marine with no family. (Marine Corps, enlisted, Indigenous)

Erin expresses frustration with the assumption that women in the infantry will introduce problems due to sexual attraction. She was in combat with men in the infantry and bonded with them. She described them as her brothers. The Lioness Program made such an impression on her that if the military had allowed her to continue to pursue combat roles, she would have done so. She specifically mentions she would have forgone having children of her own, demonstrating the military dichotomy between feminized and masculinized forms of family.

She went on to describe the men she worked with as "the brothers I never wanted. I don't know. I had their back. They had my back," and she was able to describe specific examples of how they helped her and how she also took care of them. Once, several Marines stood up for her when she was blocked from getting on a plane during her deployment:

> We were all in line, getting on the plane, and out of nowhere, this crew chief just stops me and pushes me to the side. It was like, "What are you doing? I'm with them!" Then all the guys turned around and

they're like, "She's with us. She's with us." They're trying to pull me on the plane, and I was trying to get by this guy who wouldn't let me get by. The guys, they used to call me "Erry." They're like, "Don't worry, Erry. We'll figure this out." They got on the plane, and they went to go get somebody higher up.

The men successfully stalled the plane from taking off until a higher-up could confirm that Erin should be on the flight. Erin's experience demonstrates how achieving acceptance among one group of servicemen does not guarantee automatic inclusion in every military space and that "honorary man" status must be re-established every time she enters a new space or interacts with a new group of servicemembers. The crew chief assumed that she was not to deploy with an all-men unit. However, Erin's experience shows that once a servicewoman has achieved some level of inclusion, she can both use this status to claim further access or others might do so on her behalf. In this case, Erin spoke up for herself and the servicemen backed up her claims. This demonstrates that she has a larger range of access to the military family than most of my other participants described. Servicewomen who experienced combat shared multiple stories of both acting as caregivers and being recipients of care, which were noticeably absent from most women I spoke with. Servicemen included her and treated her as an "honorary man" (Kanter 1977; King 2016), but again this status had to be re-established or renegotiated in new spaces and interactions with new servicemembers.

Women's status as members of the brotherhood or as honorary men also shaped how they responded to sexual harassment. Combat serves as a rite of passage into "honorary man" status because women who experience combat can claim warrior masculinity, often considered a top masculinity in the hierarchy of masculinities (Barrett 1996; Hale 2012; Hinojosa 2010). Servicemen are more likely to confirm the masculine identity work of women who experience combat, giving these women greater confidence in their interactions and allowing them to better negotiate the sexist climate of the military. "Honorary man" status does not protect these servicewomen from *experiencing* sexual harassment in the workplace. However, it shapes how these women *perceive* and *respond to* sexual harassment. Women who have experienced combat can take on a victim identity with less risk due to the "masculinity insurance" (Anderson 2002) they can wield in interaction with others. Anderson (2002) developed the concept of "masculinity insurance" to explain how some gay men can escape stigma others place on their sexuality if they perform another aspect of hegemonic masculinity exceptionally well, such as through athletic talent. For some women in the military, their combat experience serves as masculinity insurance and proves they are warriors. The warrior status and combat experience give them more freedom to adopt other identities, including those associated with femininity and victimization.

While Erin was deployed to Afghanistan, she and the seven other women on her base were sexually harassed and objectified every time they went to the chow hall. Comments included "I just want to bend you over right here" and "She looks like a fighter" and "That one's not so great-looking but you don't need to look at her face to find her pussy" were directed at them while they tried to eat. These comments infuriated Erin, who told me she "would always say something back to shut them up." She would respond with "Go ahead" or "Fucking try it. See what happens," or "Shame on you. Shame on all of you fuckers." One of the most telling responses that Erin shared with me was when she told these men:

> "How dare you talk about another Marine like that?" and "Yeah, I see all your wedding bands. I'm sure your wives would like to know what you just said about me." They just looked at me. They're like, "You can't talk to me like that because I'm a staff NCO." I'm like, "No, you can't talk to me like that because I'm a woman."

It is clear that Erin sees sexual harassment and objectification as problematic treatment of a Marine. She does not view these comments as normal, she does not downplay them, and she does not frame her experiences with this harassment as a sign of her strength. Rather, she directly confronts the harassers and shames them for disrespecting a Marine, showing that she views herself as a military insider. Erin responds to harassment in ways that would be too risky for many other women.

Erin went on to explain how this sexual harassment persisted daily, even when she confronted it. It got so bad that she and the other women refused to go to the chow hall. Then she reported the behavior to their gunnery sergeant, who did nothing to reprimand the harassers and ordered Erin and the other women to keep eating at the chow hall. Erin ignored this order. Instead, she kept reporting the harassment up the chain of command until she reached a major who seemed to listen. She told him, "We aren't going to the chow hall, because every time we go there, all we get are verbal attacks all the time. We don't want to do it anymore." Erin navigates the military space as someone who belongs because accepting a victim identity does not pose a threat to her institutional inclusion in the same way it does for women who have never been accepted.

At the insistence of the major, two captains were ordered to accompany the seven women to the chow hall and:

> As soon as we got to the chow hall, it started, and it was so frustrating that we had to go through all of that, so we could get this gunny to back off . . . We got back, and we didn't even want to talk to the major because we were mad at him for making us go. The two captains told him, they were like, "It's exactly like they say it is." He was like, "Well, why don't you guys say anything?" I was like, "Sir, I have mad respect for you, but it happens every fucking day, in front of you. It's happened in front of your fucking officers. It's happened in front of every fucking Marine here and nobody says anything. Nobody backs us up. Nobody says, 'Shut the fuck up. You're talking about another fucking Marine.'" I was like, "Nobody says that, but if I say that, if I correct someone who's telling me they're gonna bend me over right then and there, if I say something to defend myself, I'm wrong. That's what you guys are telling me. That's what I get in trouble for." Because I'm not gonna put up with that. (Marine Corps, enlisted, Indigenous)

When Erin's report is met with resistance, she doubles down and reprimands the major of her command (a breach of respect for hierarchy) for his failure to address the issue. Erin does not see sexual harassment as normal, nor does she frame it as a test she must endure to prove she fits in. Instead, she views it as undeserved and inexcusable behavior against another Marine, for which the offending servicemen should be held accountable. Her insider status, as a Marine on a combat deployment, gives her standing in interactions with other Marines and leads her to believe that it is the institution's responsibility to address her mistreatment. These are markedly different views from servicewomen who downplay sexual harassment. It is important to note that Erin's status as an "honorary man" did not decrease harassment against her, but it did give her leverage with leadership that allowed her to successfully advocate for herself in response to the harassment. Furthermore, Erin's story highlights the importance of the interactional context. She is not asking the major to report every harasser through military bureaucratic channels. Rather, she is seeking for him to model shutting down harassment as it occurs. She is asking for him, and other servicemen, to stand up to harassment, to shame harassers, and to protect victims in the moment—and he delivers. She said, "Then he started paying attention, and he started to have the staffing COs pay attention. When they heard comments, it was their job to turn around and shut it down. Because I was getting in constant trouble all the time for my comments." Once staff NCOs told harassers, "You have no right to talk to these female Marines like that" or asked harassers, "What command do you belong to?" Erin shared that "then things started to not be so bad." This is critical, since interpersonal interactions such as vilifying those who report, or ostracizing victims, are actions that influence many women to remain silent when harassed. It is interactions where other servicemembers interrupt harassment in the moment that could be folded into understandings of military caretaking in ways that would help build a climate that is intolerant of harassment.

Nadine also spoke about how her combat experience gave her leverage with other servicemembers. When she returned from deployment and was settling into her new unit, a serviceman who shared her rank tried to give her orders and denigrate her while on the shooting range. First, he tried to tell her to move to a different area, then he asked her to report her rank to him, and then he told her she was lazy. Nadine responded:

> Why you trying to talk to me like I was a little private or something like that? And I looked at him and I was like, "Don't talk to me like that." He was like, "Well, you need to get over there and you need to ... You're being lazy, da, da, da." I was like, "First of all, don't ever talk to me like that again. You and I are the same rank ... and you haven't deployed." I read him from top to bottom. But I was very, very careful to make sure that my voice didn't sound like "angry Black woman" because that's what they're expecting. I'm very cognizant that I was representative of my race. And even to this day, I'm the only Black Marine that some of them ever know or will ever know. So basically, I read him up and down as far as, "You're a Marine, but you're still a boot, da, da, da, da, da, da. You may have the rank, but ..." I read him up and down. "Don't you ever talk to me like this. If you get a couple deployments under your belt, and then come talk to me." (Marine Corps, enlisted, Black)

Servicewomen of color are vulnerable to harassment and discrimination from servicemen of their same rank. However, Nadine was able to use her deployment experience to reprimand a White Marine of her same rank who tried to act as though he outranked her. She knew the experience was gendered and raced and she had to remain aware of how she sounded to avoid coming off as the "angry Black woman" while also demanding the respect she felt she earned through her combat deployment. For Nadine, her combat deployment is an interactional bargaining tool, a masculinity resource that she can rely on when interacting with servicemen who are attempting to harass, insult, or exert power over her.

Women's experience in combat does not challenge the value of warrior masculinity, since this identity is still unattainable to most servicemembers, men included. However, this experience gives them masculinity insurance (Anderson 2002) that they can employ in interaction with others. It allows them to confront harassment because they do not carry the same fears and risks as other women about taking on a victim identity. In this context, servicewomen who access warrior masculinity and its patriarchal dividends (Connell 2005) can use their position of power to stand up to harassment, negotiate for equality, and disrupt the normative masculine context that seeks to oppress them. However, as Erin's experience shows, they need men to join them in challenging harassment and the gendered dynamics that cause harm to women in the military. If more men use their institutional and social power to reprimand harassers, the climate of tolerance for this treatment will decline and women might face fewer interactional consequences when they themselves call out harassment or try to report it.

CONCLUSION

In a context that denigrates victimization and femininity, many servicewomen eschew the victim identity, which constrains how they respond to, understand, and discuss harassment The military's emphasis on embodying a warrior portrays military identities in opposition to victim identities, forcing many servicewomen to remain silent about harassment. Additionally, servicewomen see that many women who do report harassment and assault are vilified, ostracized, and harassed further, and face resistance from the institution. Therefore, rather than confront or report harassment, women often develop their own individual strategies for managing this mistreatment. Some servicewomen alter their own behavior and attempt to avoid perpetrators or remove themselves from negative situations. Developing individual strategies allows servicewomen to try to escape harassment without calling attention to themselves as victims and without having to question men's dominance of the space. However, sexual harassment still serves as a salient reminder that women are viewed as outsiders in the military. This is the difficult reality that servicewomen face when they live, work, and socialize in military spaces. Many women recognize that sexual harassment is problematic but must reframe the meaning of this treatment to cope with and survive in a femmephobic context. Some servicewomen reframe the motives of harassers, and others claim that enduring harassment is a marker of toughness and masculinity. These strategies allow women to claim inclusion at moments of exclusion and dominance. However, they simultaneously reproduce gendered inequalities in the military workplace. The institution requires their compliance for their survival.

In contrast, women who have masculinity insurance (Anderson 2002) or who are seen as honorary men (Kanter 1977; King 2016) can confront harassers and report harassment they experience. The women I spoke with who experienced combat were able to use this experience in interaction with other servicemembers who harassed them. They confronted, reprimanded, and reported harassers and at times invoked their warrior identities to demand respect. While combat experience allows women to advocate for themselves in sexist, unequal, and harassing situations, the larger issue is the femmephobic culture of the military, which creates a situation where women must pursue warrior accomplishments in order to belong and have the power to confront troubling interactions. However, the respect some women are able to garner from some men through experience with combat does not challenge the overarching femmephobia inherent in the military. The ability of some women to be seen as honorary men rests on the assumption that most women cannot achieve warrior masculinity, which perpetuates the denigration of femininity. It also reproduces the association between warrior status and masculinity. Ultimately, the military's culture of warrior masculinity and femmephobia puts servicewomen at risk of sexual harassment and violence, it constrains servicewomen's responses to sexual harassment, and it defines those who have the power to confront this treatment.

The Need for Cultural and Contextual Change

The title of this book, *Hardship Duty*, frames the pervasive sexual violence and harassment servicewomen experience as constituting an "arduous" and "unhealthful" quality of life with "excessive physical hardship," conditions the Department of Defense (2023) defines as those that deserve hardship-duty pay and that are "substantially below the standard most members in the continental United States would generally experience."[1] The term "hardship duty" is hardly ever used without the word "pay" attached to it, but in the case of U.S. servicewomen who navigate the femmephobic and sexually dangerous terrain of the military, there is no additional compensation. I use the term "hardship duty" to highlight the immense sacrifice and spirit shown by these women, who should be recognized using the military's own terminology for servicemembers working in positions, jobs, and posts that deliver a below-standard quality of life.

Despite this hardship, women will continue to pursue military service for a variety of reasons. Some join to escape abuse or because they are seeking a family. Others see the military as a calling or a chance to serve their country. Some seek the physical or mental challenges the military can offer. Some hope to become warriors. Others join for the financial stability and benefits. The military provides a job, stable pay, and in-service benefits such as a housing allowance, free legal assistance, and health

Hardship Duty. Stephanie Bonnes, Oxford University Press. © Oxford University Press 2024.
DOI: 10.1093/oso/9780197636244.003.0007

insurance. It also provides post-service benefits such as tuition assistance through the GI Bill, discounted mortgage rates, and access to veteran medical insurance and benefits. These benefits are a pathway to upward economic and social mobility for all servicemembers but are particularly salient for those coming from lower socioeconomic statuses, especially in recent years, when military pay increases have outpaced civilian pay increases (Stickles 2018). The fact that women continue to pursue military service despite the great adversity they will face once they are in does not absolve the military of a responsibility to address these inequalities. Until the military changes its culture, values, structures, processes, and spatial arrangements, in ways that expose and challenge the prevailing culture of misogyny and hyper-masculinity rather than protect its place in the institution, women will be vulnerable to sexual harassment and violence and harmful interactions will persist. The military needs to address its femmephobic context and confront harassment on the interactional level before the many harassment-prevention and victim-friendly policies adopted over the past 20 years have a chance of effecting meaningful change.

THE FEMMEPHOBIC CONTEXT

Military training introduces men and women recruits to an organizational context that frequently denigrates femininity and constructs the notion of an ideal servicemember in opposition to women and femininity. These values shape how all servicemembers gain power within the institution (Barrett 1996; Hale 2008; Hinojosa 2010; Sasson-Levy 2003). In response, women try to gain power in the military through masculine identity work, embodying masculinity, and distancing themselves from femininity (Crowley and Sandhoff 2017; King 2016; Sasson-Levy 2003). However, the effectiveness of these strategies is limited: Women who embody masculinity threaten the gender order and are often cast into pariah femininities (Schippers 2007). Women may be labeled "bitches" or "sluts" when they try to embody behaviors usually associated with masculinity.

For example, women I spoke with were denigrated as "bitches" when they were assertive or aggressive in the workplace but also if they turned down men's sexual or romantic advances. Women were labeled "sluts" if they associated with men, if they dated men, and if they reported sexual abuse. Slut discourse was also used to call into question women's status as victims of sexual harassment and assault.

Femininity Anchors

In addition to deploying pariah femininities, servicemembers penalized femininity and curtailed the gender expressions of the women I interviewed using additional feminizing tools. In femmephobic spaces, any association with femininity invites denigration, even if that femininity bolsters the existing gender order more broadly. This creates unique constraints for servicewomen. The military reinforces an extreme gender binary where women become synonymous with femininity, despite their gender identities, gender identity work, embodiments, or displays (Bonnes 2022). This creates constant sexual danger for women in the institution. Women are at risk of harassment if they embody femininity, if they act feminine, or if others' perceptions anchor them to a feminine identity.

I developed the term "femininity anchors" (Bonnes 2022) to explain how servicewomen were feminized when men interpreted their heterosexual relationships and pregnancies as representing emphasized femininity (Connell 1987). Servicemembers attach gendered meanings to life-course events like heterosexual relationships and pregnancy in a way that tethers women to emphasized femininity. My analysis of servicewomen's experiences with harassment shows how men engage in increased objectification and sexual harassment of women when it is revealed that women are in relationships with men. Heterosexual women often benefit from heterosexual privilege (Collins 2004; Hamilton et al. 2019); however, heterosexuality for women in the military context attaches them to the stigma of femininity, and servicemen respond by sexually objectifying and harassing them. When women are anchored to emphasized femininity through pregnancy, servicemen use gender harassment to create a work environment hostile to pregnant women, thereby cementing their status as outsiders and suggesting they are incompatible with the military. The fact that pregnant women are not allowed to deploy, coupled with assumptions that mothers are nurturers, not warriors, positions them as threats to the military mission and the institution itself (McFarlane 2021).

The military is an extreme example of a hyper-masculine environment, but similar gender dynamics and the existence of femininity anchors may be present in other organizations dominated by men, such as construction, corrections, policing, and technology. The concept of femininity anchors can be extended beyond the military context, especially because such anchors are less fluid than dress, discursive practices, and other gender identity work. Previous research shows that pregnancy and motherhood discrimination are common in the workplace (Byron and Roscigno 2014; Glass and Fodor 2011; Ridgeway and Correll 2004; Taber 2011). Pregnant women and mothers report unfair termination, negative evaluations, less pay, lack of family-friendly workplace policies, and lack of paid maternity leave. The concept of femininity anchors can explain why pregnancy triggers enhanced harassment and discrimination: Pregnant bodies anchor women to emphasized femininity, an identity seen as incompatible with masculine constructions of the "ideal worker" (Byron and Roscigno 2014; Glass and Fodor 2011; Ridgeway and Correll 2004).

Gendered Space and Gendered Constructions of Family

The femmephobic and hyper-masculine context that values and rewards warrior masculinity is embedded in the military's physical space and spatial arrangements in ways that produce sexual violence vulnerability for servicewomen. Men dominate military spaces and hold more institutional power than women, ensuring a gendered power imbalance. Men control military spaces, including the locks on doors, access to bathrooms, offices, and barracks. Women in this book experienced sexual assault in their offices, in their own homes/rooms, in tents on deployment, in cockpits, in bathrooms on base, at on-base picnic areas, at on-base bars, and in military-provided hotel rooms. Clearly, the military does not prioritize assessing spaces, interactions, and assignments for sexual violence vulnerability. That is, individuals in charge of facilities, maintenance, workplace assignments, and assigning positions of power (like base sponsors) are not trained to think through how these decisions might create sexual violence vulnerability. Worse, some people might use these decision-making points to enable violence against women due to the underlining femmephobia throughout the institution.

The military family narrative hides the institution's intimate role in sexual abuse vulnerability and promotes belief in the "few bad apples" logic through a façade of inclusion. During recruitment and training, the military cultivates the idea that the military is a family that supports its members. Many seek out the military specifically for this benefit. Servicewomen must navigate an institutional context that advocates caregiving and kinship but also allows exploitation and "othering." Military expectations of caregiving and values such as trust and loyalty are designed to erode boundaries between servicemembers to promote camaraderie. However, these expectations and values are also filtered through a hypermasculine and femmephobic lens in ways that create sexual violence vulnerability for servicewomen. Victims of sexual assault shared times where they felt pressure to adhere to military expectations of loyalty or caregiving at the expense of their own safety. If sexual safety was built into the fabric of these values and expectations, and servicemembers were trained to assess situations, interactions, assignments, decisions, and policies for sexual violence vulnerability, this would change how caregiving, trust, and loyalty expectations play out in the organization. This would not only decrease the pressure on women to disregard their own safety to help others but would also encourage other servicemembers to think about providing sexual safety as an aspect of caregiving. This is even more important when the work environment blends with social and recreational spaces, creating more opportunity for harassment and more confusion around professional boundaries.

The Warrior/Victim Binary

To be a "military warrior," it is necessary to also be a "victimizer." The construction of a warrior as the antithesis of a victim creates a strict binary where victims become synonymous with enemies in many military spaces. It also replicates the gendered binary that portrays masculinity in opposition to and better than femininity, which makes the victim identity a form of stigmatized femininity. Previous research has argued that aggressive masculinity encourages violence, which may help explain why violence against women in the military is so high (Bayard de Volo and Hall 2015). It is also important to consider how the warrior/victim binary can explain why victims who come forward are ostracized, harassed, and vilified. One of the most poignant examples of this was described when Marie's classmates said they would let her die in Afghanistan after she expressed concern that a classmate had violated the Air Force Academy's pornography policy. This treatment not only normalizes harassment in the military space but also discourages people from disclosing victimization and dissuades them from using military reporting channels. The fact that "victim" is a stigmatized identity also constrains how women respond to the sexual harassment they experience. Many women adopt individual-level strategies to mitigate harassment such as avoiding harassers, traveling in pairs, and seeking transfers.

In my research, instances of women who did confront harassment in interaction or report harassment to the institution were concentrated among servicewomen who were already stigmatized and vilified for reporting sexual assault, or servicewomen who were given "honorary man" status due to their embodiment of warrior masculinity through combat experience. A victim identity did not pose an issue for these two groups of women, either because they were already seen as victims or had enough masculinity insurance (Anderson 2002) to combat the stigma associated with victimization. Sexual assault victims see themselves as outsiders to the brotherhood, as demonstrated by their rejection of the military family narrative. Sexual assault victims reject the idea that the military family is inclusive, and they recognize that it is not just an exclusive brotherhood but also a site of masculinity that creates sexual danger. They see the institution as complicit in their victimization. As a result, they are more likely to confront or report harassment than women who are not victims of military sexual assault.

Women who have combat experience wield this proof of their warrior status in interactions with harassers. Due to their masculinity insurance, they do not have the same risks that others do when confronting harassment. The actions of these servicewomen do not reconfigure hegemonic masculinity to be inclusive. Rather, servicewomen prop up warrior masculinity by aspiring to and achieving the status, and then by valuing and employing it in interaction. However, in these instances they use warrior masculinity to challenge gender inequality and question other aspects of masculinity, especially those that create exclusion, harm, and inequality through sexual harassment. While these women stand up to harassment and have some leverage with peers and military leaders, their honorary man status does not protect them from harassment. Their status is not guaranteed and must be constantly renegotiated in interaction. The fact that certain women are able to embody and enact a warrior identity does not challenge this identity's association with an aggressive masculinity. Rather, these women become viewed as the exception, and are postured against other women who are portrayed as weak military outsiders. As long as femininity is denigrated in the military and women are automatically associated with femininity, servicewomen will be disadvantaged during their service.

BUREAUCRATIC HARASSMENT

Military policies designed to assist victims are also circumvented by bureaucratic harassment. The military's bureaucratic structure can be a source of power as well as a tool that individuals can use to harass. By highlighting how servicemen can manipulate rules, policies, and evaluations to cause harm to individual and groups of servicewomen, I show how the interplay between a gendered institution and bureaucratic features work to

place servicemen in positions of power that they can manipulate undetected. By naming bureaucratic harassment and outlining its tactics and
consequences, this book makes visible an important dimension of workplace harassment and sexual abuse. This is another tool that servicemen
use to enact sexism and create boundaries around inclusion, but this time
it is documented with a paper trail.

Bureaucratic harassment can also be enacted against men of color, to
police sexuality, and to constrain masculinity among men. For example,
Black aviators in the Navy have claimed racial bias in evaluations in
training, resulting in many being kicked out of the program (Seck 2018).
These evaluations, where Black aviators failed test flights for mistakes that
White aviators did not, were compounded by commanders asking them
to perform more difficult skills than they asked White pilots. Further,
these different evaluation measures occurred against a backdrop of racist
interactions, where Black aviators were given call signs that indicated the
color of their skin (see Chapter 3). In this example, it is clear that bureaucratic harassment was used against Black aviators to remove them from
the pilot program.

Bureaucratic harassment likely occurs in workplaces, both masculine
and non-masculine organizations, that are hierarchal, where individuals
in positions of power have a high level of discretion, and where work and
personal life are intertwined. Other military and paramilitary organizations such as military academies, police departments, and correctional
facilities, as well as other top-down bureaucratic organizations such as
some academic institutions and large corporations, are likely places where
employees experience this kind of treatment. While the military has a
variety of rules and regulations that commanders can manipulate, bureaucratic harassment could also be present in organizations with little
administrative oversight and few institutional rules. For example, small
businesses and start-up companies that lack clear rules for hiring, firing,
promotion, and reporting harassment could be susceptible. In such organizations, those with bureaucratic power could easily draft a rule to
damage someone's professional experience and career. Additionally, organizations where there is an expectation to work long hours, to conduct

work in "out-of-office settings" (Morgan and Martin 2006), and to attend social events with co-workers or clients could be vulnerable to bureaucratic harassment because interactions in these settings can have professional consequences. Even within workplaces that have a formal human resources department and established policies for reporting discrimination and harassment, power based on rank, skill, or social category can be translated into bureaucratic power and protection, especially when work is organized in smaller autonomous units such as teams. When these bureaucratic features are influenced by an organizational context that supports sexism, it is likely that men will be situated in places of power and have the ability to manipulate policies, rules, and regulations to undermine their colleagues.

MISOGYNY ADAPTS

This book demonstrates how hyper-masculinity and misogyny adapt to organizational changes aimed at gender inequality. In the introduction, I discussed events that occurred at the Tailhook convention in 1991. Since 1991, there has been enhanced recruiting of women into the military. The recruitment strategies claim gender-neutral benefits such as a secure job, health benefits, education benefits, skills training, and guaranteed housing as well as less tangible benefits such as the promise of family. At the same time, the military has also enacted several policies and programs aimed at alleviating sexual assault within the institution. Since 1991, the Department of Defense has created Sexual Assault Prevention and Response (SAPR) missions and offices for each branch, which focus on education about sexual violence and provide services and resources for victims of sexual violence. SAPR also tracks data related to military sexual violence and continuously adapts its policies to enhance victim support. These policies include access to expedited transfers for victims; access to free medical, legal, and counseling services; access to a victim advocate; access to a military lawyer specifically tasked with representing victims (Special Victims' Counsel or Victims' Legal Counsel); and the ability to report retaliation for documenting an incident of assault. Once a sexual assault has been reported, the military requires a coordinated approach where all parties that interact with the victim (commanders, lawyers, medical professionals, etc.) convene monthly at a case management group meeting to discuss the case status, victim progress, and services for the victim. New policies have been adopted since I conducted interviews. For example, the Air Force now has a stipulation that if servicemembers are discharged with a personality disorder and have filed an unrestricted report of sexual assault, they are eligible for a review of their separation. Under this policy, if a victim of sexual assault has reported and is being discharged for a personality disorder, a set of guidelines should be followed before proceeding with the discharge. This process includes a mental health evaluation and a peer or higher-level mental health assessment (Department of the Air Force 2022). This policy was likely developed to curtail outcomes like Kay's, where the symptoms of sexual trauma are used against victims to end their military careers.

To gain deeper understanding of these practices, I interviewed military lawyers who worked on sexual assault cases. They praised the effectiveness of the victims' legal counsel program and the case management group. Several of them showed compassion for victims who came to their office and a few of them cried in the interview when recollecting what victims had endured. Some lawyers were specifically trained in handling sexual assault cases. Therefore, the military has well-thought-out sexual harassment and assault policies and has invested resources in addressing the issue from medical and legal angles. However, many of the women I interviewed did not make it to the legal process due to barriers at the organizational, cultural, and interactional levels. Some did not use these military resources for fear of more harassment. Others were blocked from accessing these channels altogether by higher-ups and peers. Women who were able to access legal, medical, and institutional resources found it often came at the price of social isolation and denigration from other servicemembers.

Despite these institutional-level changes aimed at addressing sexual abuse and assisting victims of sexual violence, the women I spoke with still described a work environment where they were sexually harassed. Therefore, my research raises the question of how effective these changes are if they are only on a policy or individual level. Transformations must be made on an interactional level for these policies to be fully effective. For example, while it is helpful to know that Erin would have access to the victims' legal counsel program if she were assaulted by one of the men who threatened her in the chow hall, this does nothing to address the constant sexual harassment she faced when deployed in Afghanistan. Furthermore, having a resource or policy in place does not always ensure access to that resource or policy. Women are intimidated out of reporting through the selective implementation of bureaucratic power, like when Samantha's commander threatened to take away her holiday leave if she reported her assault. Though Kay was eligible for coordinated victim services outlined by SAPR, not only did she not receive these services, but her mental health was also used against her to drop her case. The mental health effects of her sexual assault also followed her into the civilian world when her records indicated she had a personality disorder. Even when victims can access helpful policies, it might not be in a way that prioritizes them. Recall Penelope who was sexually assaulted and promised an expedited transfer that prioritized her location preferences. While Penelope was transferred, however, it was thousands of miles from where she had asked to go and away from her support networks. The expedited transfer policy for victims is important, but access to this policy in a way that prioritizes victim preferences is restricted. Therefore, institutional policies, resources, and attempts to assist victims are constrained by the sexist context in which they are enacted. This shows how misogyny can adapt to organizational changes in ways that sustain sexual abuse vulnerability.

Similarly, new military policies aimed at creating gender equality, such as integrating infantry units and opening more military jobs, positions, codes, and specialties to women, are constrained by masculine power structures and interactions that continue to privilege men. Through bureaucratic harassment, powerful individuals can unofficially continue repealed policies that contribute to inequality. Bureaucratic harassment limits women's power and participation in combat roles despite the military's gender integration programs and goals. Similarly, just like bureaucratic harassment was used to limit the power and scope of Female Engagement Teams in combat zones, it can be used to continue other military policies that have been repealed, such as Don't Ask, Don't Tell (repealed in 2011) and the ban on transgender people (lifted for active-duty servicemembers in 2016 but later targeted by the Trump administration, and then lifted again by the Biden administration). Thus, while certain forms of harassment and exclusion are no longer legal on paper, the intersection of bureaucratic discretion and workplace harassment can allow the invisible continuation of these policies and perpetuate inequality on the interactional as well as the organizational level.

Many branches of the military have made an effort in recent years to de-gender their terminology. The Marine Corps removed the word "man" from job titles and moved to make their published materials gender-neutral. An example of this is on the Marine Corps website, where the organization describes itself as "comprised not of a brotherhood or sisterhood—this is a warriorhood" (U.S. Marine Corps 2022b). These efforts mark a departure from conceptualizing men as the default Marine, which can be helpful for women's inclusion. However, de-gendering language is not enough to create inclusion for women. These changes need to be coupled with transformations in how the organization teaches, educates, and trains individuals to be Marines. If a warrior identity is still constructed in opposition to femininity and encourages the denigration of women, the pervasive harassment of women will persist.

Most policy responses to military sexual violence focus on the individual level, leaving in place an organizational context that sustains women's vulnerability to harassment. In recent years, the U.S. military has developed numerous policies and programs to address sexual harassment. These organizational policies often target individual victims and perpetrators by creating reporting streams and systems of punishment related to sexual abuse. In January 2022, President Biden signed an Executive Order requiring the Department of Defense to codify sexual harassment as part of the Uniform Code of Military Justice. The Executive Order signals severe punishments for inappropriate conduct, but punitive measures will not alter deeply embedded organizational norms because they leave in place the military structure, culture, and context that encourages and facilitates harassment and assault. Individual-level responses largely overlook the gendered values, processes, and practices that contribute to inequality at the organizational level. These responses also disregard the fact that policies developed to assist victims are filtered through the gendered institutional context, which can render them ineffective or enable the policies themselves to be used as tools of harassment and ostracization. Instead, the military should encourage interactions that build a positive and inclusive command climate, normalize pregnancy dispensations, promote a more fluid image of what constitutes an ideal servicemember, and actively work to identify and reduce sexual violence vulnerability in military spaces and interactions. Without interventions designed to challenge the organizational context, the military will continue to be an institution that denigrates femininity, encourages men to harass, and makes women vulnerable to sexual assault and harassment.

POLICY IMPLICATIONS

Despite the resilience of a military organizational context that causes harm to servicewomen, I see opportunities and make recommendations on how to mitigate some of the inequality and vulnerability servicewomen face. I recognize that changes to policy, processes, and practices are merely tools to address some instances of inequality. No policy, process, or practice can eradicate the misogyny prevalent in the military without dismantling the femmephobic and hyper-sexualized structure, goals, and culture that is built into the institution. However, what I outline here may help create better experiences for current U.S. servicewomen by making it more difficult for harassers and sexual abusers to cause harm without consequences. These recommendations are narrow and speak directly to the victimizations women described to me and the difficult experiences women had reporting, confronting, or acknowledging the harassment and abuse they experienced.

Many of the servicewomen in my sample joined the military to escape negative situations at home. Some had experienced neglect, physical abuse, and sexual abuse before joining. This is consistent with the quantitative literature that suggests that women who join the military have higher percentages of childhood sexual victimization than their civilian counterparts (Bostock and Daly 2007). This finding is not surprising given the fact that the military promotes itself as a place where members receive support, stability, and a family. Further, military leaders know that many men and women join the institution to escape. As Jennifer told me:

> A lot of female recruits come here with emotional baggage. They're trying to escape something. They were, you know, assaulted as a kid, abused as a kid, had a poor father figure they're trying to escape. So, they typically come here with a lot of issues. (Marine Corps, officer, White)

Therefore, since the military's family narrative is particularly appealing to those escaping abuse, and because having been a victim of abuse is a risk factor for future victimization (Arata and Lindman 2002; Boney-McCoy and Finkelhor 1996; Desai et al. 2002; McDaniels-Wilson and Belknap 2008), the military should be prepared to address prior victimization among its members. The institution should offer services targeted at addressing pre-military victimization such as counseling, support groups, and help lines. If a recruit or servicemember discloses victimization, they should be referred to mental health support.[2] The military should also make information about common symptoms of and reactions to victimization (depression, posttraumatic stress disorder, substance abuse, etc.) readily available so that individuals may be encouraged to seek help processing their experiences and trauma. In the civilian world, this is done through education programs in schools (Miller-Perrin et al. 2018). The military could include these discussions during training and leaders could provide frequent reminders, similar to how the military currently embeds discussions of suicide prevention into public dialogue (Department of Defense 2015). While the military does already offer an array of mental health services, people are often stigmatized for using them or they have a hard time accessing them in a timely manner (Green-Shortage et al. 2007; Sharp et al. 2015). For example, an estimated 60% of servicemembers who have mental health issues do not seek help, often citing stigma and negative attitudes toward mental health treatment as barriers to pursuing assistance (Sharp et al. 2015). Therefore, the military should work to destigmatize seeking mental health services for sexual assault and promote better mental health more broadly via swifter access to these resources. Framing mental health support as a resource every servicemember will need and use during their service could help. Explaining that mental health support is essential to unit readiness and mission effectiveness can alter negative perceptions of seeking help. Discussing mental health support as improving one's strength rather than as an indicator of weakness can also reduce the stigma.

Existing research on sexual assault in the military has identified several barriers to reporting, including procedural barriers such as the discretion commanders have in investigating a case and confusing reporting procedures (Jeffreys 2007). Servicewomen also fear the consequences that they might experience for reporting, such as being further ostracized, being separated from their units, and losing their jobs (Firestone and Harris 1999; Jeffreys 2007; Pershing 2006; Sadler et al. 2003). Additionally, servicewomen might not report because they do not anticipate a satisfactory response, or they have come to view sexual harassment as acceptable behavior (Firestone and Harris 1999; Pershing 2006). While some of the servicewomen in my sample might have refrained from reporting for these reasons, they also described additional barriers to reporting. Some women in the military do not confront or report harassment because not doing so helps them in other aspects of their military lives. Specifically, not reporting or confronting harassment can allow them to eschew a stigmatized feminine identity, that of a "victim," that they fear will bring them more trouble. Women seeking insider status in a space that denigrates femininity and where men have power to anchor women to stigmatized femininities have constrained choices. They already feel like

outsiders and must navigate a gendered terrain that includes pervasive harassment. Many see that those who do report sexual assault or harassment
are vilified. They fear the interactional and interpersonal consequences
of confronting harassment like social isolation or new or enhanced harassment experiences. Therefore, policies should be updated to acknowledge the interactional obstacles to reporting identified in this book. The
SAPR program should integrate interactional barriers to reporting into
its program and disseminate this information to all servicemembers, including military leaders and commanders. Leaders could better promote
a harassment-free work environment if they were informed of all types of
the barriers to reporting and were encouraged to actively stop the vilification of victims and those who report sexual abuse.

The military already has several policies related to sexual assault that
are helpful to victims. However, a major obstacle to victims is access
to these policies and programs. I show how bureaucratic harassment
can be used to keep individuals from reporting sexual assault and from
accessing administrative channels that could help them. Commander
discretion is a major factor in access to reporting channels. I recommend
that there be checks placed on commanders' discretion that do not have
to be initiated by lower-ranking service members. While "requesting
mast" is a military policy that allows individuals to go outside of the
typical command structure, again, access to this policy can be denied
by those in power. Therefore, I recommend that discretion be limited in
evaluations and in implementing military policies. Periodic checks on
negative evaluations to look for bias related to gender, race, or sexuality
would also be useful.

Importantly, the recommendations I am making are not oriented toward the goal of ensuring that everyone who experiences harassment or
sexual assault makes a report. Of course, the military should strive to create
an environment where barriers to reporting streams and obstructions to
victim-friendly policies are removed, making them more freely available
to those who want to use them. However, the overall goal should be to
make the military a safe place for all servicemembers and to ensure that

those who are victimized are able to access the support and resources they require to process and recover from their experiences. The military needs to infuse sexual safety into military spaces, values, and interactions to counteract the sexual vulnerabilities that are currently embedded in these organizational features. This means actively de-sexualizing military spaces and instilling the idea that servicemembers do not harm one another in existing military messages around caregiving, trust, and loyalty.

SAPR personnel should incorporate the concept of sexual geography (Hirsch and Khan 2020) and gendered spatial dynamics into their risk assessments for sexual violence. Understanding how the physical space of a military base can create sexual violence vulnerability in the ways outlined in this book can help the SAPR program identify risky spaces. Additionally, servicemembers should be discouraged from placing hyper-sexualized or sexist imagery or signage in military bases. Leaders especially should be instructed to look out for and remove over-sexualized, hyper-masculine, and femmephobic signage, decorations, and images in unit spaces to set an anti-harassment climate. All servicemembers should be trained to assess physical spaces for contributions to discrimination and sexual violence and encouraged to intervene.

While I show that the interactional level can undermine attempts at equality on the structural level, previous scholarship suggests that the interactional level can also be a site of transformation (Deutsch 2007; Ridgeway and Correll 2000) and could be used to address the military culture that is harmful to women. For example, prior research has found that command climate can shape sexual abuse reporting within a unit (Firestone and Harris 2009; Miller 1997; Rosen and Martin 1997; Sadler et al. 2003). Sadler et al. (2003) found that servicewomen were more likely to be raped in units in which an officer allowed or engaged in sexist comments or behavior. Similarly, Buchanan et al. (2014) found that when servicewomen felt that commanders did not tolerate harassment and were respectful of women in their units, they experienced less harassment and were more satisfied with their reporting outcomes. Leaders can promote healthy working environments with less sexual harm and reshape femmephobic military culture. This would include actively stepping in when victims are teased, denigrated, or harassed. It would also mean leaders modeling to servicemembers that harassment is not acceptable. This might include shutting down harassment when they see it unfold but could also include using hypothetical situations that highlight how harassment puts units at risk. Tying anti-harassment training to the language of military preparedness and highlighting anti-harassment actions as essential to military missions and effectiveness could reduce the normalization of this treatment. For example, framing harassment-free units as a force-multiplier could indicate to servicemembers that harassing other servicemembers puts a unit at risk.

Several of the women in this book were made vulnerable to sexual violence because they were required to interact in isolated and intimate spaces with servicemen who far outranked them. Servicemembers should be encouraged to assess power dynamics and men's unequal control of spaces when making decisions for those under their command. For example, leaders should be mindful of any power differentials when making assignments for base sponsors, duty schedules, and work projects. Individuals assigned to collateral duties that give them power over others should be removed if they have a report of harassment or sexual assault against them or if it is known that they have harassed in the past.

Sexual harassment and assault prevention training should begin as soon as servicemembers enter the institution. If discussions of sexual safety are embedded into basic training when servicemembers are learning other core military values, it might establish an expectation that servicemembers keep each other safe from sexual harm. It might also decrease the vilification of victims who report. Further, having drill instructors who discuss sexual safety in an informal style might create more engagement from trainees than current standard military training on sexual assault. Many of my participations shared Kelly's view that trainings on sexual assault tended to be "boring PowerPoint lectures. Basically, checking a box that says sexual assault is bad, don't do it." Sexual assault prevention training should also be more scenario-based and include a discussion of common victim feelings, reactions, and behaviors.

FINAL REMARKS

In this book, I have shown that servicewomen must navigate a highly gendered terrain that denigrates femininity and puts them at risk of sexual
violence. It is exhausting for women to undertake this work on top of their
regular military jobs, especially when women know that they will never be
accepted as full members to the military brotherhood. The threat of sexual
harassment and violence looms over them at work, but also follows them
to their personal and social spaces. Even in moments where women are not
contending with a harasser, they interact with sexist and hyper-sexualized
messages through the physical environment of military spaces. They also
fear that harassment might creep into potential and future interactions
and must remain on guard to assess the potential sexual danger in each
interaction (Hart 2021).

In many ways, women are in a battle against pervasive harassment and
sexual violence, and some view the men they serve with as their biggest
threat. Kay, whose attempted rape opened this book, reflected on this,
saying, "You know, like . . . like, you sign an oath to protect the United
States Constitution against all enemies, foreign and domestic. But some of
these enemies that I was encountering were my . . . my fellow shipmates,
you know?" Kay saw her military peers not through the institutional lens
of family but rather through the lens of war, conflict, and adversity. She
viewed other sailors as her enemy and her service as a pursuit of self-
defense and protection from dangerous individuals, as well from the Navy
as an organization that enabled them. She felt unsafe at work, in her own
home (which was on base), and walking around the base to go grocery
shopping, to the gym, or to the doctor's office.

The fear of internal enemies extends to deployed women. Nadine was
almost raped in her bed while deployed. A man snuck into her window
while she was napping, put his hand over her mouth, and tried to assault
her. She fought him off, but after that moment, Nadine told herself, "I
got to go on every single convoy. I'm not going to be left back here," and
she signed up to leave base whenever possible. She would rather risk the

dangers of a convoy, enemy fire, and combat than face the dangers that men Marines posed to her when she was on base. She said she also

> started going right back to the gym, working out, trying to get stronger, trying to get my martial arts training. Because it wasn't an issue of me figuring out the right people to trust. And I think that's what upset me the most is, it wasn't so much as me not following my better judgment . . . It's just, I can't worry about everyone all the time, and it took me a while to realize the stuff that happened wasn't my fault.(Marine Corps, enlisted, Black)

It is for Kay and Nadine, and so many women like them, that I have titled this book *Hardship Duty*. It is "outside of normal military operations" (Department of Defense 2023) for women to have to plan their days around avoiding their harassers or their rapists. It is "particularly arduous" for Nadine to have to "worry about everyone all time" or for Erin, who was told "I just want to bend you over right here" while at the chow hall in Afghanistan. It is excessive physical hardship to fear sexual violence while you sleep, eat, or use the bathroom, while working or relaxing in your home. While hardship duty pay is usually determined based on the location or duties individuals are assigned, women in this book experienced these conditions in Afghanistan, California, Colorado, Florida, Georgia, Germany, Kansas, Hawaii, Iraq, Japan, South Korea, New Jersey, North Carolina, South Carolina, Texas, Virginia, in the air, and in the middle of the ocean. Air traffic controllers, calibration specialists, computer programmers, cooks, doctors, engineers, food service specialists, human resource specialists, intelligence officers, journalists, lawyers, logistics officers, mechanics, members of Female Engagement Teams, medics, pilots, and supply administrators across ranks and from different branches were all harassed during their service. Women in this book were sexually assaulted by servicemen in their workspaces, at military social events, in their on-base living quarters, on airplanes, on ships, and while riding in cars on military bases. For women, hardship duty is not tied to a location but is intertwined in their daily lives as servicemembers, permeating their training experiences, deployments, promotions, and celebrations. It extends to their homes, workplaces, and social spaces. Can we continue to ask servicewomen to spend their entire military careers in a state of stress, strain, and conflict when hardship duty is not meant to be assigned long term, especially without compensation? It seems we can, and we will, as long as we continue to silence women's experiences and allow misogyny to be infused in military values and the concepts of hardship, arduous, and warrior. That is why this book centers servicewomen's voices, breaks the silence, and begs for a transformation of the military that includes systematically dismantling the layers of femmephobia exposed in these pages.

The data for this book come from numerous sources. Primarily, I draw on semi-structured, in-depth interviews with fifty U.S. servicewomen conducted from 2014 to 2019. Gaining access to the U.S. military and its members is difficult. Some military buildings can be considered "quasi-public settings" (Lofland et al. 2006), but access to most areas is restricted to those with permission to be on a base or training area. With limited access to military spaces, my best method for data collection was interviews with servicewomen. I recruited participants using convenience sampling; women were referred to the study by email, listservs, and social media. One benefit of convenience sampling was that I avoided formally engaging with the military hierarchy and bureaucratic structures, which could have complicated my ability to protect participants' anonymity. At first, three initial contacts served as key informants and gatekeepers and introduced me to their networks of servicemembers. I ceased snowball sampling from these networks because the twenty participants recruited this way were demographically similar (mostly White Marine Corps officers), and I wanted to include participants from theoretically important groups (Glaser and Strauss 1967).

I sought participants across military branches, across ranks (officers and enlisted servicewomen), and from different classes and races (see Table A1 for sample demographics). The sample includes thirty-one enlisted women and nineteen officers in the Air Force (n = 13), Army (n = 11), Marine Corps (n = 21), and Navy (n = 5). At the time of their interview, twenty-five women were active duty, four were in the reserves,

Table A1. SELF-REPORTED DEMOGRAPHICS

N = 50	Air Force (n = 13)	Army (n = 11)	Marine Corps (n = 21)	Navy (n = 5)	Total
Personnel Status					
Enlisted	4	9	14	4	31
Officer	9	2	7	1	19
Race					
Asian American	1	2	1	0	4
Black	1	2	1	1	5
Latina	0	2	4	0	6
Native American	0	0	1	0	1
White	11	5	14	4	34
Military Status					
Active Duty	7	5	10	3	25
Reserves	0	3	1	0	4
Out of Military	6	3	10	2	21
Marital Status					
Single	4	0	11	4	19
Coupled	2	2	3	0	7
Married	5	5	4	1	15
Divorced	2	4	3	0	9
Age Range					
18 to 25	0	4	6	0	10
25 to 30	6	4	8	2	20
31 to 35	6	2	5	3	16
36+	1	1	2	0	4
Sexuality					
LGB	2	1	6	0	9
Heterosexual	11	10	15	5	41

and twenty-one were out of the military. Among women who were out of the military, most had been active duty within five years of the interview, though three of them had been out longer.

The sample was designed to engage servicewomen's military experiences that reflect current military policies, issues, and practices. The early 2000s to 2010s brought many policy changes that shape servicewomen's lives and careers. For example, the sexual assault prevention and response program was developed in 2005, which started a decades-long process of targeted military sexual assault education and prevention, and Don't Ask, Don't Tell was repealed in 2010, which formally ended the policy that prevented gay servicemembers from openly discussing their sexuality at risk of being discharged. During this decade, women were officially deployed into combat situations through military programs designed to circumvent the combat exclusion policy (which was repealed in 2013).

The study was designed to seek variation in rank, race, military branch, and sexuality. To ensure confidentiality when recruiting online, I reached out to participants by direct message or asked participants to contact me directly to participate. Participants signed a consent form before the interview, and I assured them they could stop participating at any time. In addition to excluding specific location and base names in my research, I use pseudonyms and remove identifying information to protect participant anonymity. I continued to collect data until I reached theoretical saturation, where I heard the same experiences and stories across multiple interviews (Glaser and Strauss 1967; Lofland et al. 2006). For the themes that inform this analysis, women told similar stories across branches and ranks; nuances based on race and status as an officer or enlisted servicemember are included in the analysis.

One-on-one interviews allow for in-depth and complex analysis of responses from participants (Rubin and Rubin 2012). Interviews enable scholars to explore how people understand, respond to, and process their experiences, as well as the strategies they take in social situations (Esterberg 2002). In-depth interviews are recommended for examining sensitive issues, such as sexual harassment, as well as learning about what is important to the individuals being studied (Rubin and Rubin 2012).

Therefore, this method is ideal for unpacking servicewomen's experiences with harassment and assault.

Interviews ranged from forty-five to 205 minutes. My interview guide was open-ended and allowed servicewomen to share their experiences in their own words (Fine et al. 2000; Strauss and Corbin 1998). I asked broad questions and then follow-up questions as needed, treating interviews more like "guided conversations" (Fontana and Frey 1994; Rubin and Rubin 2012). I asked questions that encouraged vividness in participants' descriptions (Rubin and Rubin 2012), such as why they joined the military, their transition to military life, and their most memorable service experiences. Asking about a specific memory or experience is likely to bring about a more vivid, detailed account than asking about their military experiences in the abstract. Each interview consisted of the same main questions but different follow-up questions and probes, which allowed me to focus on what each participant revealed (Rubin and Rubin 2012).

Using "constructivist grounded theory" (Charmaz 2000), I analyzed data to understand participants' meanings about their experiences. The themes that guided this book emerged inductively from the data generated by interview transcripts (Charmaz 2000; Coffey and Atkinson 1996; Emerson et al. 1995). Transcripts were hand-coded and read many times to identify patterns (Emerson et al. 1995). After I identified initial codes, I went back through my transcripts and fieldnotes to identify nuances within themes. I then wrote analytic memos based on these patterns to develop themes for analysis (Charmaz 2000; Lofland et al. 2006). After reading through the memos, I returned to the data to apply focused coding for each book chapter. I reread the data to explore negative cases and narrow the analysis (Table A2).

INTERVIEW FORMAT AND PARTICIPANT COMFORT

All interviews were conducted on the phone or in person and audio-recorded. Participants were given a choice of phone or in-person interview to enhance their comfort, which is especially important when an

Table A2. TYPES OF HARASSMENT EXPERIENCES ($N = 47$)

	Women Who Discussed Harassment ($n = 47$)
Sexual Harassment and Assault	
Sexual harassment (inappropriate sexual comments, unwanted sexual attention, obscene gestures, seductive behavior, and sexual bribery and coercion)	91.4% ($n = 43$)
Sexual assault (unwanted touching, groping, attempted rape, rape)	40.4% ($n = 19$)
Nonsexual Harassment	
Bureaucratic harassment (manipulation of administrative policies and rules to punish and undermine colleagues' professional experiences)	55.3% ($n = 26$)
Gender harassment and discrimination (harassment used to disparage and demean based on gender, including sexist insults and denigrating pregnancy)	95.7% ($n = 45$)

Note: Of the 50 interviewees, 47 women shared they experienced one or more forms of harassment listed in this table. The interviews covered harassment, but I never directly asked participants about distinct harassment categories. These categories emerged during inductive qualitative data analysis. Thus, even more women may have experienced these forms of harassment during their service but did not bring it up during the interview.

interview might engage sensitive subjects such as harassment or assault (Schwerdtfeger 2009). Prior research examining victims of violence has suggested that the method of data collection can shape whether victims participate in studies (Reddy et al. 2006; Rosenbaum et al. 2006). Rosenbaum et al. (2006) found higher participation rates in studies examining sensitive information, such as questions about physical and sexual violence, when telephone interviews were used. Interview methods can also have an impact on what is disclosed in the interview. Some argue that more anonymous methods of data collection, such as a phone interview or an automatized phone survey, make it more comfortable for individuals to discuss sensitive topics due to the assurance of confidentiality (Reddy et al. 2006; Rosenbaum et al. 2006). However, others find that face-to-face interviews create a better environment for eliciting responses to sensitive questions (Campbell et al. 2009; Rubin and Rubin 2012). Participants may feel more comfortable speaking about sexual harassment and abuse in person, as face-to-face interviews allow for more trust and rapport to develop between the researcher and the participant and they have more space for discussion and support (Campbell and Adams 2009; Rubin and Rubin 2012). These different findings regarding victim comfort and interview format guided my decision to offer participants a choice between phone interviews or in-person interviews.

Overall, research suggests that participant comfort is important when researching sensitive subjects such as sexual harassment and abuse (Campbell 2002; Schwerdtfeger 2009). More specifically, recalling experiences with sexual abuse can be emotional and painful and victims of sexual abuse might have different concerns about participating and disclosing their experiences in a given study. Scholarship examining the reasons individuals participate in trauma research have found that sexual abuse survivors often mention altruism or the desire "to help other survivors" as a motivation (e.g., Campbell and Adams, 2009; Pessin et al., 2008; Schwerdtfeger 2009; Schwerdtfeger and Goff 2008). Several evaluations of participants' reactions after taking part in trauma-related research suggest that such participants found it to be a cathartic experience and noted therapeutic benefits such as that it helped them to heal and feel less isolated (e.g., Campbell and Adams, 2009; McClain et al. 2007; McCoyd and Shdaimah 2007; Pessin et al. 2008; Schwerdtfeger and Goff 2008). These studies also suggest that benefits may be enhanced when researchers and participants meet in person. Therefore, I designed my study to allow women to participate through in-person or phone interviews based on their preferences, comfort, and availability.

Victims of sexual harassment and assault are often revictimized when they disclose their victimization to friends, family members, police officers, doctors, nurses, and lawyers (Campbell 2002; Schwerdtfeger 2009; Ullman 2010). Revictimization occurs when a victim discloses sexual abuse and then is questioned in a manner that indicates disbelief, blames the victim, or expresses sympathy for the perpetrator. It was important for me as a researcher of sexual harassment and assault to be mindful of the potential for revictimization when asking questions and probing during an interview (Campbell 2002; Schwerdtfeger 2009). Therefore, I left my interview guide vague enough so that if participants were comfortable disclosing sexual harassment or abuse they could do so on their own. If they did not bring up sexual harassment or abuse during the more general questions in the interview, I introduced the topic into the interview by asking about the issue in general. I then asked, "Can you tell me about a time where you saw or heard about sexual harassment or abuse in the military?" When discussing issues of sexual harassment or assault I was mindful of when and how it is appropriate to probe, follow up, and ask for more information based on the potential for revictimization and a reading of the participant's emotions (Campbell 2002).

When interviews covered sexual harassment, assault, or rape, I engaged in interview techniques to try to decrease retraumatizing participants. If the participant disclosed a sexual abuse incident to me during the interview, I made sure to end that sequence of questions on an empowering note. Each interview was also different in the language that I used when discussing sensitive topics with participants. Schwerdtfeger (2009) notes that incorporating participants' own language surrounding sexual abuse is important to both establish rapport and avoid the participant feeling shame, judgment, and revictimization during the interview. I mimicked the language that participants used to describe their harassment and assault experiences. I was careful to never label something an assault or a rape if the participant did not use that language themselves. Scheirs and Nuytiens (2013) argue that it is important to acknowledge the role of emotion in qualitative work, stating that often emotions help researchers establish rapport and trust with participants. Therefore, whenever the interview covered emotional material, I was sure to be engaged and supportive to both comfort the participant and establish trust.

As a feminist scholar studying victimization, it is imperative to me that my participants' voices are at the center of my work and that I am representing their stories in a way that makes sense to them. I kept a list of women who expressed interest in remaining informed about the study and any publications resulting from the research. This kept communication open between me and many participants. Several servicewomen have emailed or texted over the years to share online articles about women in the military or sexual violence in the organization. Others have emailed with stories or experiences that they forgot to share or that had happened to them since the interview. I often share my work with servicewomen who participated in my study and receive responses that indicate that they agree with my analysis but also that participating in the research was cathartic to them. I received the following in a message from a participant who read my *American Sociological Review* (Bonnes 2022) piece:

> Thank you so much for sharing the article with me. I would not miss the chance to read it and unfortunately, you are very correct that the harassment and denigration of women and pregnancy are still a very prevalent problem in the military today . . . I could relate to your article and the other service member's stories . . . Again, thank you for sharing the article and I am glad that you were able to use some of my story in your research and article. You did tell my story correctly and your representation and analysis made complete sense.

After my article "The Bureaucratic Harassment of U.S. Servicewomen" came out in *Gender & Society* (Bonnes 2017), one of my participants shared it on social media with the caption "She was very easy to talk to and I felt it was worth it. It's interesting to see how she applied my experience." Another participant reached out to say: "Interestingly enough, I read your article and thought 'the exact same thing happened to me!' And then I realized it was me. I thought it was really interesting that you were able to connect stories and circumstances together into one defining theme. It felt cathartic reading it, so thanks for taking the time to share!" This shows how I was able to keep my participants' identities confidential while also representing their stories.

DATA TRIANGULATION

I triangulated my data collection by collecting and analyzing a variety of data sources, including textual sources, such as documents outlining military policies, procedures, and guidelines, and observation of courts-martial relating to military sexual assault.

Documents and textual sources often provide insight into the nature and structure of an organization (Noaks and Wincup 2004) and can serve as important points of observation of social phenomenon (Zussman 2004). It was important for me to understand the policies, rules, and regulations that are central to the operation of the military institution. Including military documents in my data analysis allowed me to understand the rules governing my participants' daily lives and careers. I analyzed documents outlining the dress codes for each military branch, housing policies, performance review forms, sexual assault program overviews, and military orders relating to sexual assault such as the Sexual Assault Prevention and Response Order, and the Family Advocacy Program Order. The documents outlining military policies, procedures, and expectations that I analyzed were found on the internet or shared with me by one of my key informants, who is a military lawyer.

I used participant observation to supplement my interview data (Lofland et al. 2006). Participant observation allows for researchers to explore important interactions between participants and to gain a better understanding of the social setting under study. In the spring of 2016, I observed two trials over the course of eight days. I observed all trial proceedings for each case, including jury selection, the court-martial itself, and sentencing hearings. For each of the eight days, I arrived with my base sponsor, a military lawyer, at 7 a.m. and stayed through the proceedings, which usually ended around 5 p.m. I also observed interactions that occurred before and after these hearings, both inside and outside of the courtroom. These observations gave me access to the backstage realm of court interactions. Observing outside of the courtroom both before and after trial proceedings gave me access to information, conversations, and interactions between servicemembers and their lawyers, friends, and family members. Often these conversations were about the case, but other times it was small talk about things like weather, children, or jobs. While in military courtrooms I took fieldnotes and noted dialogue, interactions (verbal and nonverbal), silences, eye contact, and spatial arrangements. Although my observations were limited to two courts-martial, it helped me become more familiar with military settings, traditions, and legal proceedings. The use of limited participant observation combined with in-depth interviews allowed me to better identify, understand, and describe servicemembers' perceptions (Emerson 2001). I also interviewed military lawyers who participated in these courts-martial as well as one of the victims whose case went to trial.

POSITIONALITY

Being a military outsider presented research challenges and advantages. I had to overcome the distrust that some servicemembers have of civilians (Woodward and Jenkings 2011). The military's status as a near-total institution enhanced my role as an outsider throughout this research process because as an institution it cultivates a sense of "insiderness" among servicemembers as distinctive and separate from civilians (Woodward and Jenkings 2011). The "military versus civilian" or "us versus them" dichotomy affects access to individuals in the military and it frames the interactions that an interviewer may have with a military participant (Higate and Cameron 2006). For example, being a military outsider, I was not able to rely on shared knowledge of the military to build rapport or to direct questions (Higate and Cameron 2006). Military insiders sometimes mistrust civilians, particularly those studying sensitive issues within the institution, which may have made some individauls apprehensive about particaiting in the study. For example, in the process of setting up an interview with one of my participants she wrote to me and said, "I will not bash men," demonstrating how she thought my research might be framed. She agreed to participate after I assured her that I was not seeking specific comments; rather, the interview would be a chance for her to share her experiences however she wanted to talk about them.

To build rapport that might have been lost due to my role as a military outsider, I employed a variety of techniques to reduce distance (Lofland et al. 2006). Throughout the recruitment and interview process, I tried to establish a mutual, non-hierarchal relationship where I not only answered questions about my own identity but also acknowledged similarities and differences between myself and participants (Letherby 2003). In my interviews, I tried to present in a "non-threatening demeanor," meaning that I was supportive, sympathetic, and a good listener throughout the interview. This is especially true when discussing sensitive topics such as sexual harassment and rape (Campbell 2002).

To compensate for a lack of shared knowledge based on military experience and to build rapport, I used military jargon often. This strategy established that I was familiar with the military and discouraged participants from explaining acronyms or routine military processes. I used the role of "acceptable incompetent" (Lofland et al. 2006, 29) to ask questions about assumptions that may be taken for granted among military insiders. For example, participants could not respond to questions about basic training or deployments by saying "you know how it is" or other similar replies that avoided specificity.

My outsider status ensured that military roles and ranks did not influence participation, data collection, or responses (Higate and Cameron 2006). As an outsider I avoided issues that might come with outranking or being outranked by my participants, such as awkwardness, feeling forced to answer questions, and glossing (Higate and Cameron 2006).

NOTES

CHAPTER 1

1. The definition of sexual harassment I use in this book includes inappropriate sexual comments, unwanted sexual attention, obscene gestures, seductive behavior, sexual bribery and coercion, and exposure to sexual imagery (Cortina and Areguin 2021; Miller 1997; Welsh 1999). Nonsexual harassment includes gender harassment and bureaucratic harassment. Gender harassment refers to behaviors that do not seek sexual cooperation or submission but are used to denigrate and demean based on sex or gender (Cortina and Areguin 2021), enforce stereotypical understandings of gender, and punish perceived violations of gender (Miller 1997). Gender harassment includes demeaning terms used to refer to women, masculinity and femininity slurs, and sexist insults (Cortina and Areguin 2021). Bureaucratic harassment refers to when organizational rules and policies are applied in a manner that leads to further sexual harassment or discrimination and is the subject of Chapter 4 (Bonnes 2017).
2. "Civilian Attire Policy" is the name of these regulations in the Navy and the Marine Corps. In the Army, they are referred to as "Standards of Civilian Dress and Prohibited Attire."

CHAPTER 2

1. A portion of this chapter first appeared as Bonnes, Stephanie. 2022. "Femininity Anchors: Heterosexual Relationships and Pregnancy as Sites of harassment for U.S. Servicewomen." *American Sociological Review* 87, no. 4:618–43. Copyright © 2022 American Sociological Association. doi:10.1177/00031224221110535.
2. In 2021, 9.1% of active-duty Marines were women (Department of Defense 2021b).
3. In this book, I use the word "woman" but most servicemembers use the term "female" when discussing servicewomen and I wanted to match their language here.
4. In the Army and the Marine Corps, the term "Military Occupational Specialty" (MOS) is used to describe a military job or role. In the Air Force, a military job is referred to as an "Air Force Specialty Code" (AFSC). In the Navy, a military job for those who are enlisted is called an "enlisted job rating."

5. The phrase "Be polite, be professional, but always have a plan to kill every person you meet" is attributed to former Secretary of Defense and retired Marine Corps Four-Star General James Mattis. Diane shared that she heard this phrase repeated during military trainings and throughout her service.

6. "The schoolhouse" refers to MOS training or job-related training that Marines attend after initial training and before being assigned to a permanent duty station.

7. Attending the Military Entrance Processing Station (MEPS) is a step in the military recruiting process where recruits are tested, evaluated, and medically examined.

8. Similar corruptions of military abbreviations have existed in other branches. The Women's Air Force (WAF) was referred to "We All Fuck" in the 1980s, and at the Naval Academy the acronym WUBA, which officially stood for "working uniform blue alphas" was altered to "Women Used by All" to refer to women midshipman (Burke 1996; Haynie 1998; King 2015).

9. Mallory is referring to an Army Combatives Course which focuses on hand-to-hand combat techniques. In this quote, she is either referencing that the rumor was started while she was in the combatives course or while she was practicing techniques learned in the course.

10. There are variations on this phrase mentioned by women in other services. One soldier shared that she heard, "If the Army wanted you to have a family, it would have issued you one."

11. The Air Force Academy, Naval Academy, and U.S. Military Academy at West Point all prohibit dependents for prior-enlisted and new candidates. This does not mean that one cannot have children and join, but there must be a court order proving that the candidate severed their parental rights. Therefore, Kay could have had the baby and her boyfriend could have severed his rights and still attended the Naval Academy. The 2022 National Defense Authorization Act is repealing the ban on cadets and midshipmen having dependents.

12. While Andrea was serving, the Marine Corps was only 6% women. In 2021, 9.1% of active-duty Marines were women (Department of Defense 2021b).

13. The maternity uniforms are distinctive enough to set pregnant servicewomen apart even if they are not visibly showing yet. However, not all women in my sample were able to obtain one. Joanna explained that "they make female pregnancy uniforms, but they never have them in stock, so I wore my husband's uniform." This shows that even accommodations for pregnancy, like maternity uniforms, can be difficult to access.

CHAPTER 3

1. "Officers eat last" is a tradition specific to the Marine Corps; other branches have different mealtime expectations and etiquette based on circumstances (Darcey 2012).

2. The call sign tradition is practiced by those in aviation across different military branches.

3. In the documentary *The Invisible War*, several women in the Marine Corps explained a culture of drinking that they were required to participate in as directly related to their sexual victimization. One woman was told by her boss that drinking events were mandatory. Another Marine explained that "I was ordered to drink" on

the same night her company commander followed her back from the bars, asked to talk to her in his office, and then raped her. This shows that the availability of alcohol and a culture of drinking, combined with a hierarchal power structure, means that lower-ranking servicewomen not only feel pressure to drink but fear professional and military consequences for not participating. Leaders' ability to command, order, and require socialization highlights the blend between hierarchy, social life, and work life present in the military that creates situations ripe for exploitation and sexual violence.

4. Several women in my sample described men breaking into their barracks rooms, hotel rooms, or deployment spaces and trying to sexually assault them. Some men had keys to their rooms without their knowledge, others climbed in through windows, and some tried to break the lock or the door. This was a pervasive security issue for women that they had to rely on the military to address.

5. Fraternization is a policy that prohibits servicemembers from socializing outside of their own rank and can be charged as a criminal offense if the fraternization "has compromised the chain of command, resulted in the appearance of partiality, or otherwise undermined good order, discipline, authority, or morale" (Uniform Code of Military Justice 2018).

6. Adultery is illegal in the military and can result in a court-martial. The maximum punishment for adultery according to the Uniform Code of Military Justice is "Dishonorable discharge, forfeiture of all pay and allowances, and confinement for 1 year" (Uniform Code of Military Justice 2018). Further, both parties can be tried for adultery even if only one of them is married. While no one I spoke with was tried for adultery, there have been reported cases of rape victims being tried for adultery after reporting their married attackers (Eagan 2012).

7. Involuntary separation is a mechanism that the military can mobilize to effectively fire servicemembers. In the Marine Corps and Navy, the non-judicial process that can result in a servicemember being forced out of the military is called an administrative separation (ADSEP). Administrative separation is pursued by the commanding officer (in these cases called the separation authority), usually with a recommendation from a legal advisor. There are no punitive outcomes, but servicemembers can receive an other-than-honorable discharge, which has long-term consequences for veterans' benefits and employability (e.g., by making them ineligible to retain or obtain a security clearance). During this process, the servicemember is represented by a lawyer who argues on their behalf. In some cases, the lawyer will argue that the individual should not be separated, or they will make a case for how their service should be characterized (i.e., honorable, general, or other than honorable). At times, the process will result in a hearing or a board where this evidence and information is heard. The ADSEP board will make a recommendation regarding separation and characterization of service, which will be given to the commander/separation authority before a decision is made. There are many behaviors and misconduct that can result in these proceedings, such as drug abuse, a pattern of misconduct, insubordination, or failing to perform military duties. In the Air Force, perpetrating sexual assault is specifically listed as a reason that a commander can move to separate an individual (Department of the Air Force 2022).

CHAPTER 4

1. A portion of this chapter first appeared as Bonnes, Stephanie. 2017. "The Bureaucratic Harassment of U.S. Servicewomen." *Gender & Society* 31, no. 6: 804–829.
2. Angela describes him as the "skipper of the command," meaning that he had decision-making power in the unit. "Skipper" is not a rank in the Navy but is an informal name for those in charge of aviation commands in the Navy.
3. In the Navy, "rate" can be used to refer to the job that a sailor is trained and qualified for. This demonstrates how the master chief was also encouraging her to take the non-flying position that the skipper had tried to get her to take initially. The skipper, who outranked the master chief, may have put pressure on him to do so. The outcome was that there were several people in the unit trying to push her out of her job in aviation, which only started after the new skipper came into the unit.
4. The Army has since changed some of the testing components and the test is now known as the Army Combat Fitness test.
5. A victims' legal counsel (VLC)/special victims' counsel (SVC) is a military lawyer who usually has experience trying cases in the military court system. They offer victims legal support, legal advice, and represent victims at courts-martial. The different names reflect different branches with the Navy and Marine Corps using VLC and the Air Force and Army using SVC.
6. These terms are highly subjective and can be filtered through the military's masculinized and femmephobic values. In such a context, camaraderie may be understood as what three of my participants described as "not rocking the boat" or not confronting or reporting when faced with sexist comments and remarks.
7. Joanna did discuss the role of a higher-ranking officer in preventing another soldier of her same rank from successfully filing a counseling statement against her. Therefore, the second-rater process could help eliminate the power of the discretion of one's immediate supervisor.
8. Servicemembers are only allowed to remain at a given rank for a certain amount of time before they are separated from the military. The term "high year tenure" is used to define the maximum years a servicemember can remain at a specific rank without being promoted before they are moved to separation proceedings. Additionally, if the military engages a reduction-in-force process, the decision on whom to separate is often based on records of poor service or evidence of being slow to promote.
9. From 2001 to 2018, the military discharged "over 31,000 servicemembers with personality disorder, at a savings to the military of over $17.2 billion in disability and medical benefits" (Kors 2018). In some instances, the military recognizes this as an issue. In a 2022 Air Force separation proceedings document, a "special process" is described for discharging people for a personality disorder when the person has served in an imminent-danger pay area or when the person filed an unrestricted report of sexual assault. Under this policy, if a victim of sexual assault has reported and is being discharged for a personality disorder, a set of guidelines should be followed before proceeding with the discharge. This process includes a mental health evaluation and a peer- or higher-level mental health assessment (Department of the Air Force 2022).

CHAPTER 5

1. The military does not explicitly use the term "caregiving" to describe these expectations. Rather, the institution encourages servicemembers to protect, rely on, and trust each other. Several participants mentioned that they were instructed to "watch each other's backs." When women shared what they were expected to do for other servicemembers, they described caregiving tasks. Women explained that they were instructed to protect the physical and mental well-being of other servicemembers, to offer financial advice for junior-ranking servicemembers, and to be available as officers to give rides to enlisted servicemembers who were intoxicated or stranded somewhere. Other participants discussed assisting servicemembers through mental health crises, breakups, deployment trauma, parenting difficulties, and job-related struggles. All these actions involve emotional, social, and physical labor that is often provided by caregivers or family members, and I interpret these as caregiving tasks.

2. Julia's ability to mention her sexuality in this moment was not an option for servicewomen prior to the repeal of "Don't Ask, Don't Tell" (DADT) in 2010. Prior to the repeal of DADT, mentioning a relationship with a person of the same sex could be grounds for discharge, and this disproportionately affected women. Almost half of the Army (46%) and Air Force (49%) servicemembers discharged under DADT in 2007 were women, even though men make up the majority of these branches (Shanker 2008). Even though Julia's comment did not stop Allen's aggression, her mentioning her sexuality did not pose the same risk to her military career that it would have prior to 2010.

3. The first value in the Seven Core Army Values is loyalty. The Marine Corps motto "Semper Fidelis" translates to "Always Loyal" or "Always Faithful."

4. Marie reported the incident to an older classmate, who then reported it to leadership at the Air Force Academy. After the incident was reported, the commander did speak with Marie about it. However, her peers were told she reported the incident directly to leadership. Their treatment of her was based on their belief that she officially reported the incident to the commander.

5. Barracks duty is assigned to servicemembers within a unit on a rotating basis and is not always the same person.

6. In 2022, victims of "stalking, other sexual misconduct, and wrongful broadcast or destruction of intimate visual images" can also request expedited transfers if they filed a report with the military criminal investigation organization (Department of Defense 2022). The decision to grant a transfer requires that a commanding officer verify that the victim filed an unrestricted report, and then the commanding officer must "1) consider all evidence 2) consult a judge advocate or legal advisor and 3) determine if the report is credible" (Navy JAG, 2022). The determination of whether the report is credible might allow for some discretion or bias to shape the decision to grant the transfer.

CHAPTER 6

1. A portion of this chapter first appeared as Bonnes, Stephanie. 2020. "Service-women's Responses to Sexual Harassment: The Importance of Identity Work and Masculinity in a Gendered Organization." *Violence against Women* 26, no. 12–13: 1656–80.
2. In the Army and the Marine Corps this is referred to as a military occupational specialty (MOS). In the Air Force, it is referred to as an Air Force Specialty Code (AFSC). In the Navy, a military job for enlisted sailors is referred to as enlisted job rating.
3. General Alfred Gray coined the phrase "Every Marine is, first and foremost, a ri-fleman. All other conditions are secondary." It has long been used to describe the Marine Corps, including in an article entitled "Every Marine a Rifleman" written by James Curtis in 2021 and quoted here.
4. While Allison was serving, the Marine Corps was only 6% women. In 2021, 9.1% of active-duty Marines were women (Department of Defense 2021b).
5. The combat exclusion policy was ended by Panetta in 2013. He was pushed to end the ban on women in combat due to an ACLU lawsuit (*Hegar et al. v. Panetta*) filed on behalf of the Service Women's Action Network (SWAN) and four servicewomen who served in combat and/or lead female teams on missions with infantrymen in Iraq and Afghanistan. Two of the plaintiffs were awarded Purple Hearts for being wounded in combat. The lead plaintiff, M. J. Hegar, also earned a Distinguished Flying Cross with Valor Device for actions during a medevac mis-sion in Afghanistan where her helicopter was shot down and she was injured and yet still managed to get her team to safety.

CHAPTER 7

1. The Department of Defense defines a "Hardship Duty Pay Location" as "Locations where QoL [quality of life] living conditions are substantially below the standard most members in the continental United States would generally experience. HDP-L [Hardship Duty Pay Location] is intended to recognize the extraordinary arduous living conditions, excessive physical hardship, and/or unhealthful conditions that exist in a location or assignment" (Department of Defense 2023).
2. A Marine Corps lawyer shared that when new recruits disclose sexual abuse, they usually must give a statement to the Naval Criminal Investigative Service (NCIS), which turns over the information to local police. However, they are not channeled into therapeutic or mental health services. These disclosures frequently occur during the "moment of truth" that is a part of many military trainings. Recruits are encouraged to share information that was withheld when they applied and went through the recruitment process.

Acker, Joan. 1990. "Hierarchies, Jobs, and Bodies: A Theory of Gendered Organizations." *Gender & Society* 4, no. 2: 139–58.

Acker, Joan. 1992. "From Sex Roles to Gendered Institutions." *Contemporary Sociology* 21, no. 5: 565–70.

Acker, Joan. 2006. "Inequality Regimes: Gender, Class, and Race in Organizations." *Gender & Society* 20, no. 4: 441–64.

Ainsworth, Susan, Alex Batty, and Rosaria Burch. 2014. "Women Constructing Masculinity in Volunteer Firefighting." *Gender, Work & Organization* 21, no. 1: 37–56.

Allsep, Michael. 2013. "The Myth of the Warrior: Martial Masculinity and the End of Don't Ask, Don't Tell." *Journal of Homosexuality* 60, no. 2–3: 381–400.

Anderson, Eric. 2002. "Openly Gay Athletes: Contesting Hegemonic Masculinity in a Homophobic Environment." *Gender & Society* 16, no. 6: 860–77.

Antecol, Heather, and Deborah Cobb-Clark. 2001. "Men, Women and Sexual Harassment in the U.S. Military." *Gender Issues* 19, no. 1: 3–18.

Arata, Catalina, and Linda Lindman. 2002. "Marriage, Child Abuse, and Sexual Revictimization." *Journal of Interpersonal Violence* 17, no. 9: 953–71.

Archer, Emerald M. 2012. "The Power of Gendered Stereotypes in the U.S. Marine Corps." *Armed Forces & Society* 39, no. 2: 359–91.

Armstrong, Elizabeth A., Laura T. Hamilton, Elizabeth M. Armstrong, and J. Lotus Seely. 2014. "'Good Girls': Gender, Social Class, and Slut Discourse on Campus." *Social Psychology Quarterly* 77, no. 2: 100–122.

Arnold, Regina. 1990. "Processes of Victimization and Criminalization of Black Women." *Social Justice: A Journal of Crime, Conflict, and World Order* 17, no. 3: 153–66.

Baldor, Lolita. 2015. "Officials: Marine Commandant Recommend Women Be Banned from Some Combat Jobs." *Marine Times*, September 18. http://www.marinecorpsti mes.com/story/military/2015/09/18/officials-marine-commandant-recommends-women-banned-some-combat-job/72421888/.

Barrett, Frank J. 1996. "The Organizational Construction of Hegemonic Masculinity: The Case of the U.S. Navy." *Gender, Work & Organization* 3, no. 3: 129–42.

Bartik, Warren, Myfanwy Maple, Helen Edwards, and Michael Kiernan. 2013. "The Psychological Impact of Losing a Friend to Suicide." *Australasian Psychiatry* 21, no. 6: 545–9.

Basham, Victoria M. 2009. "Effecting Discrimination: Operational Effectiveness and Harassment in the British Armed Forces." *Armed Forces & Society* 35, no. 4: 728–44.

Bayard de Volo, Lorraine, and Lynn Hall. 2015. "'I Wish All the Ladies Were Holes in the Road': The U.S. Air Force Academy and the Gendered Continuum of Violence." *Signs* 40, no. 4: 865–89.

Beauboeuf-Lafontant, Tamara. 2007. "'You Have to Show Strength': An Exploration of Gender, Race, and Depression." *Gender & Society* 21, no. 1: 28–51.

Belkin, Aaron. 2012. *Bring Me Men: Military Masculinity and the Benign Façade of the American Empire, 1898–2001.* New York: Columbia University Press.

Belknap, Joanne, and Kristi Holsinger. 2006. "The Gendered Nature of Risk Factors for Delinquency." *Feminist Criminology,* 1, no. 1: 48–71.

Bielby, William. 2000. "Minimizing Workplace Gender and Racial Bias." *Contemporary Sociology* 29, no. 1: 120–29.

Boney-McCoy, Sue, and David Finkelhor. 1996. "Is Youth Victimization Related to Trauma Symptoms and Depression after Controlling for Prior Symptoms and Family Relationships? A Longitudinal, Prospective Study." *Journal of Consulting and Clinical Psychology* 64, no. 6: 1406–16.

Bonnes, Stephanie M. 2017. "The Bureaucratic Harassment of U.S. Servicewomen." *Gender & Society* 31, no. 6: 804–29.

Bonnes, Stephanie M. 2020. "Service-Women's Responses to Sexual Harassment: The Importance of Identity Work and Masculinity in a Gendered Organization." *Violence against Women* 26, no. 12–13: 1656–80.

Bonnes, Stephanie M. 2022. "Femininity Anchors: Heterosexual Relationships and Pregnancy as Sites of Harassment for U.S. Servicewomen." *American Sociological Review* 87, no. 4: 618–43.

Bostock, Deborah J., and James G. Daley. 2007. "Lifetime and Current Sexual Assault and Harassment Victimization Rates of Active-Duty United States Air Force Women." *Violence against Women* 13, no. 9: 927–44.

Brownson, Connie. 2014. "The Battle for Equivalency: Female US Marines Discuss Sexuality, Physical Fitness, & Military Leadership." *Armed Forces & Society* 40, no. 4: 765–88.

Bryant, Clifton. 1979. *Khaki-Collar Crime.* New York: Free Press.

Buchanan, NiCole, Isis Settles, Angela Hall, and Rachell O'Connor. 2014. "A Review of Organizational Strategies for Reducing Sexual Harassment: Insights from the U.S. Military." *Journal of Social Issues* 70, no. 4: 687–702.

Buchanan, NiCole T., Isis Settles, and Krystle Woods. 2008. "Comparing Sexual Harassment Subtypes for Black and White Women: Double Jeopardy, the Jezebel, and the Cult of True Womanhood." *Psychology of Women Quarterly* 32, no. 4: 347–61.

Burk, James, and Evelyn Espinoza. 2012. "Race Relations within the U.S. Military." *Annual Review of Sociology* 38: 401–22.

Burke, Carol. 1996. "Pernicious Cohesion." In *It's Our Military Too: Women and the U.S. Military,* edited by J. Stiehm, 205–19. Philadelphia: Temple University Press.

Butler, Judith P. 1990. *Gender Trouble: Feminism and the Subversion of Identity.* New York: Routledge.

Byron, Reginald A., and Vincent J. Roscigno. 2014. "Relational Power, Legitimation, and Pregnancy Discrimination." *Gender & Society* 28, no. 3: 435–62.

Callahan, Jamie. 2009. "Manifestations of Power and Control: Training as the Catalyst for Scandal at the United States Air Force Academy." *Violence against Women* 15, no. 10: 1149–68.

Campbell, Rebecca. 2002. *Emotionally Involved: The Impact of Researching Rape.* New York: Routledge.

Campbell, Rebecca, and Adrienne Adams. 2009. "Why Do Rape Survivors Volunteer for Face-to-Face Interviews?" *Journal of Interpersonal Violence* 24, 395–405.

Caproni, Paula, and Joycelyn Finley. 1994. "Crisis of Moral Awareness in Organizations: The Tailhook Case." *Academy of Management Proceedings* 1994, no. 1. https://journals.aom.org/doi/pdf/10.5465/ambpp.1994.10345886.

Cast, Alicia. 2003. "Power and the Ability to Define the Situation." *Social Psychology Quarterly* 66, no. 3: 185–201.

Chappell, Allison, and Lonn Lanza-Kaduce. 2010. "Police Academy Socialization: Understanding the Lessons Learned in a Paramilitary-Bureaucratic Organization." *Journal of Contemporary Ethnography* 39, no. 2: 187–214.

Charmaz, Kathy. 2000. "Constructivist and Objectivist Grounded Theory." In *Handbook of Qualitative Research*, edited by Norman Denzin and Yvonna Lincoln, 509–35. Thousand Oaks, CA: Sage.

Chesney-Lind, Meda and Nikki Jones. 2010. *Fighting for Girls: New Perspectives on Gender and Violence.* 1 ed. Albany: State University of New York Press.

Citroën, Linda. 2018. "Why Veterans Must Relearn the Concept of Trust." https://www.military.com/veteran-jobs/career-advice/military-transition/why-veteransmust-relearn-the-concept-of-trust.html.

Clark, James. 2016. "The Crucible Is Where Marines Are Made, And Here's How." *Task & Purpose*, May 3. https://taskandpurpose.com/news/crucible-marines-made-heres/#:~:text=It's%20a%20prized%20possession.%E2%80%9D,our%20broth ers%2C%E2%80%9D%20says%20Phillips.

Coffey, Amanda, and Paul Atkinson. 1996. *Making Sense of Qualitative Data: Complementary Research Strategies.* Thousand Oaks, CA: Sage.

Cogan, Alison M., Christine E. Haines, and Maria D. Devore. 2021. "Intersections of US Military Culture, Hegemonic Masculinity, and Health Care among Injured Male Servicemembers." *Men and Masculinities* 24, no. 3: 468–82.

Collins, Patricia Hill. 2000. *Black Feminist Thought: Knowledge, Consciousness, and the Politics of Empowerment*, 2nd ed. New York: Routledge.

Collins, Patricia Hill. 2004. *Black Sexual Politics: African Americans, Gender, and the New Racism.* New York: Routledge.

Connell, Raewyn W. 1987. *Gender and Power.* Sydney, Australia: Allen and Unwin.

Connell, Raewyn W. 1995. *Masculinities.* Berkeley: University of California Press.

Connell, Raewyn W. 2005. "The Social Organization of Masculinity." In *Masculinities*, 2nd ed., edited by R. Connell 67–81. Berkeley: University of California Press.

Connell, Raewyn W., and James W. Messerschmidt. 2005. "Hegemonic Masculinity: Rethinking the Concept." *Gender & Society* 19, no. 6: 829–59.

Copp, Tara. 2018. "Here's Mattis' Full Response to VMI Cadets on Women in Infantry." *Military Times*, September 26. https://www.militarytimes.com/news/your-military/2018/09/26/heres-mattis-full-response-to-vmi-cadets-on-women-in-infantry/.

Cortina, Lilia M., and Maira A. Areguin. 2021. "Putting People Down and Pushing Them Out: Sexual Harassment in the Workplace." *Annual Review of Organizational Psychology and Organizational Behavior* 8: 285–309.

Crowley, Kacy, and Michelle Sandhoff. 2017. "Just a Girl in the Army: U.S. Iraq War Veterans Negotiating Femininity in a Culture of Masculinity." *Armed Forces & Society* 43, no. 2: 221–37.

Curtis, James. 2021. "Every Marine a Rifleman." *Marine Corps Gazette*. https://mca-marines.org/wp-content/uploads/0521-Every-Marine-a-Rifleman.pdf.

Darcey, Patrick. 2012. "Special—Officers Eat First." *U.S. Naval Institute*. https://www.usni.org/magazines/proceedings/2012/may/special-officers-eat-first.

Davis, Angela Y. 1981. *Women, Race, and Class*. New York: Random House.

Dean, Donna, Myrna Estep, Francine D'Amico, Jan Whiteley, and Lance Janda. 1997. *Warriors Without Weapons: The Victimization of Military Women*. Pasadena, MD: Minerva Center.

Denissen, Amy M., and Abigail C. Saguy. 2014. "Gendered Homophobia and the Contradictions of Workplace Discrimination for Women in the Building Trades." *Gender & Society* 28, no. 3: 381–403.

Department of the Air Force. 2022. Department of the Air Force Guidance Memorandum to the Department of the Air Force Instruction 36-2406. https://www.sapr.mil/sites/default/files/public/docs/reports/AR/DOD_Annual_Report_on_Sexual_Assault_in_the_Military_FY2021.pdf.

Department of Defense. 2015. Department of Defense Strategy for Suicide Prevention. http://www.dspo.mil/Portals/113/Documents/TAB%20B%20-%20DSSP_FINAL%20USD%20PR%20SIGNED.PDF.

Department of Defense. 2021a. "Department of Defense Annual Report on Sexual Assault in the Military Fiscal Year 2020." https://www.sapr.mil/sites/default/files/4_Appendix_C_Metrics_and_Non-Metrics_on_Sexual_Assault.pdf.

Department of Defense. 2021b. "2021 Demographics Profile Marine Corps Active Duty Members." https://download.militaryonesource.mil/12038/MOS/Infographic/2021-demographics-active-duty-marine-corps-members.pdf

Department of Defense. 2022. "Military Life: Housing." *Today's Military* https://www.todaysmilitary.com/military-life/housing

Department of Defense. 2023. "Military Compensation: Hardship Duty Pay (HDP)." https://militarypay.defense.gov/Pay/Special-and-Incentive-Pays/HDP/#:~:text=HDP%2DL%20is%20intended%20to,hardship%20in%20a%20given%20area.

Department of Defense (Office of the Inspector General). 1992. "Report of Investigation: Tailhook 91: Part 1: Review of the Navy Investigations." http://ncisahistory.org/wp-content/uploads/2017/07/DoDIG-Report-of-Investigation-Tailhook-91-Review-of-the-Navy-Investigations.pdf.

Department of the Navy. No Date. Navy Civilian Attire Policy. http://www.cusnc.navy. mil/Civilian-Attire-Policy.

Desai, Sujata, Ileana Arias, Martie Thompson, and Kathleen Basile. 2002. "Childhood Victimization and Subsequent Adult Revictimization Assessed in a Nationally Representative Sample of Women." *Violence and Victims* 17, no. 6: 639–53.

Deutsch, Francine. 2007. "Undoing Gender." *Gender & Society* 21, no. 1: 106–27.

Diaz, Johnny, Maria Cramer, and Christina Morales. 2022. "What to Know about the Death of Vanessa Guillen." *New York Times*, November 30. https://www.nytimes. com/article/vanessa-guillen-fort-hood.html.

Draper, Deborah. 2011. "Defense Health Care: Status of Efforts to Address Lack of Compliance with Personality Disorder Separation Requirements. Personality Disorder Discharges: Impact on Veterans' Benefits Hearing." Testimony before the Committee on Veterans' Affairs, House of Representatives. https://www.gao.gov/ass ets/gao-10-1013t.pdf.

Duncanson, Claire. 2013. *Forces for Good? Military Masculinities and Peacebuilding in Afghanistan and Iraq.* London: Palgrave Macmillan.

Dunivin, Karen. 1994. "Military Culture: Change and Continuity." *Armed Forces & Society* 20: 531–47.

Eagan, Daniel. 2012. "Documenting Sexual Assault in the Invisible War." *Smithsonian*, June 22. https://www.smithsonianmag.com/arts-culture/documenting-sexual-assa ult-in-the-invisible-war-135440379/.

Emerson, Robert. 2001. *Contemporary Field Research: Perspectives and Formulations.* Prospect Heights, IL: Waveland Press.

Emerson, Robert M., Rachel I. Fretz, and Linda L. Shaw. 1995. *Writing Ethnographic Fieldnotes.* Chicago: University of Chicago Press.

Enloe, Cynthia H. 2000. *Maneuvers: The International Politics of Militarizing Women's Lives.* Berkeley: University of California Press.

Esterberg, Kristin G. 2002. *Qualitative Methods in Social Research.* Boston: McGraw-Hill.

Fine, Michelle, Lois Weis, Susan Weseen, and Loonmun Wong. 2000. "For Whom? Qualitative Research Representations and Social Responsibilities." In *Handbook of Qualitative Research,* edited by Norman Denzin and Yvonna Lincoln, 107–32. Thousand Oaks, CA: Sage Publications.

Firestone, Juanita, and Richard Harris. 1999. "Changes in Patterns of Sexual Harassment in the U.S. Military: A Comparison of the 1988 and 1995 DoD Survey." *Armed Forces & Society* 25, no. 4: 613–32.

Firestone, Juanita, and Richard Harris. 2009. "Sexual Harassment in the U.S. Military Reserve Component." *Armed Forces & Society* 36, no. 1: 86–102.

Flores, Jerry. 2016. Caught Up *Girls, Surveillance, and Wraparound Incarceration.* Oakland, CA: University of California Press.

Fontana, Andrea, and James H. Frey. 1994. "Interviewing: The Art of Science." In *Handbook of Qualitative Research*, edited by Norman Denzin and Yvonna Lincoln, 361–76. Thousand Oaks, CA: Sage.

Furia, Stacie R. and Denise D. Bielby. 2009. "Bombshells on Film: Women, Military Films, and Hegemonic Gender Ideologies." *Popular Communication* 7, no. 4: 208–24.

García-López, Gladys. 2008. "'Nunca Te Toman en Cuenta [They Never Take You into Account]': The Challenges of Inclusion and Strategies for Success of Chicana attorneys." *Gender & Society* 22, no. 5: 590–612.

Glaser, Barney G., and Anselm L. Strauss. 1967. *The Discovery of Grounded Theory.* Chicago: Aldine.

Glass, Christy, and Éva Fodor. 2011. "Public Maternalism Goes to Market: Recruitment, Hiring, and Promotion in Postsocialist Hungary." *Gender & Society* 25, no. 1: 5–26.

Greene-Shortridge, Tiffany Thomas Britt, and Carl Castro. 2007. "The Stigma of Mental Health Problems in the Military." *Military Medicine* 172, no. 2: 157–61.

Guthrie, Doug, and Louise Roth. 1999. "The State, Courts, and Equal Opportunities for Female CEOs in U.S. Organizations: Specifying Institutional Mechanisms." *Social Forces* 78, no. 2: 511–42.

Goffman, Erving. 1961. *Asylums.* London: Penguin.

Hale, Hannah C. 2008. "The Development of British Military Masculinities through Symbolic Resources." *Culture and Psychology* 14, no. 3: 305–32.

Hale, Hannah C. 2012. "The Role of Practice in the Development of Military Masculinities." *Gender, Work & Organization* 19, no. 6: 699–722.

Hall, Lynn. 2017. *Caged Eyes: An Air Force Cadet's Story of Rape and Resilience.* Boston: Beacon Press.

Halvorson, Angela. 2010. "Understanding the Military: The Institution, the Culture, and the People." Substance Abuse and Mental Health Services Administration. https://www.samhsa.gov/sites/default/files/military_white_paper_final.pdf.

Hamilton, Laura T., Elizabeth A. Armstrong, J. Lotus Seeley, and Elizabeth M. Armstrong. 2019. "Hegemonic Femininities and Intersectional Domination." *Sociological Theory* 37, no. 4: 315–41.

Harkins, Gina. 2019. "Marine Commandant Responds to Backlash over Lack of Women in Birthday Video." *Military Times.* https://www.military.com/daily-news/2019/11/07/marine-commandant-responds-backlash-over-lack-women-birthday-video.html.

Harrison, Deborah. 2003. "Violence in the Military Community." In *Military Masculinities: Identity and the State,* edited by Paul Higate, 71–90. Westport, CT: Praeger Publishers.

Hart, Chloe G. 2021. "Trajectory Guarding: Managing Unwanted, Ambiguously Sexual Interactions at Work." *American Sociological Review* 86, no. 2: 256–78.

Haynie, Jeannette. 1998. "Being a WUBA: How Words Shape Power." U.S. Naval Academy Alumni Association. https://women.usnagroups.net/2018/12/26/being-a-wuba-how-words-shape-power/.

Hennen, Peter. 2001. "Powder, Pomp, Power: Toward a Typology and Genealogy of Effeminacies." *Social Thought and Research* 24, no. 1&2: 121–44.

Higate, Paul R. 2002. "Traditional Gendered Identities: National Service and the All-Volunteer Force." In *The Comparative Study of Conscription in the Armed Forces,* Vol. 20, *Comparative Social Research,* edited by L. Mjøset and S. van Holde, 229–35. Bingley, UK: Emerald Group Publishing.

Higate, Paul R. 2007. "Peacekeepers, Masculinities, and Sexual Exploitation." *Men and Masculinities* 10, no. 1: 99–119.

Higate, Paul R., and Alisa Cameron. 2006. "Reflexivity and Researching the Military." *Armed Forces & Society* 32, no. 2: 219–33.

Hinojosa, Ramon. 2010. "Doing Hegemony: Military, Men, and Constructing a Hegemonic Masculinity." *Journal of Men's Studies* 18, no. 2: 179–94.

Hirsch, Jennifer, and Shamus Khan. 2020. *Sexual Citizens: A Landmark Study of Sex, Power, and Assault on Campus.* New York: W.W. Norton & Company.

Hlavka, Heather. 2014. "Normalizing Sexual Violence: Young Women Account for Harassment and Abuse." *Gender & Society* 28: 337–58.

Hockey, John. 2003. "No More Heroes: Masculinity in the Infantry." In *Military Masculinities: Identity and the State*, edited by Paul Higate, 15–25. Westport, CT: Praeger Publishers.

Holstein, James and Jaber Gubrium. 1995a. "Deprivatization and the construction of domestic life." *Journal of Marriage and the Family* 57, no. 4: 894–908.

Holstein, James and Jaber Gubrium. 1999. "What is family?" *Marriage and Family Review* 28, no. 3–4: 3–20.

Höpfl, Heather J. 2003. "Becoming a (Virile) Member: Women and the Military Body." *Body and Society* 9, no. 4: 13–30.

Hoskin, Rhea A. 2017. "Femme Theory: Refocusing the Intersectional Lens." *Atlantis: Critical Studies in Gender, Culture & Social Justice* 38, no. 1: 95–109.

Hoskin, Rhea A. 2019. "Femmephobia: The Role of Anti-Femininity and Gender Policing in LGBTQ+ People's Experiences of Discrimination." *Sex Roles* 81: 686–703.

Hoskin, Rhea A. 2020. "'Femininity? It's the Aesthetic of Subordination': Examining Femmephobia, the Gender Binary, and Experiences of Oppression among Sexual and Gender Minorities." *Archives of Sexual Behavior* 49: 2319–39.

Irwin, Anne. 2012. "'There Will Be a Lot of Old Young Men Going Home': Combat and Becoming a Man in Afghanistan." In *Young Men In Uncertain Times,* edited by Vered Amit and Noel Dyck, 59–78. New York: Berghahn Books.

Jeffrey, Nicole K., & Barata, Paula C. 2017. "'He Didn't Necessarily Force Himself upon Me, but . . .': Women's Lived Experiences of Sexual Coercion in Intimate Relationships with Men." *Violence Against Women* 23, no. 8: 911–33.

Jeffreys, Shelia. 2007. "Double Jeopardy: Women, the U.S. Military and the War in Iraq." *Women's Studies International Forum* 30, no. 1: 16–25.

Kandiyoti, Deniz. 1988. "Bargaining with Patriarchy." *Gender & Society* 2, no. 3: 274–90.

Kanter, Rosabeth. 1977. *Men and Women of the Corporation.* New York: Basic Books.

Ken, Ivy, and Allison S. Helmuth. 2021. "Not Additive, Not Defined: Mutual Constitution in Feminist Intersectional Studies." *Feminist Theory* 22, no. 4: 575–604.

King, Anthony. 2015. "Women Warriors: Female Accession to Ground Combat." *Armed Forces & Society* 41, no. 2: 379–87.

King, Anthony. 2016. "The Female Combat Soldier." *European Journal of International Relations* 22, no. 1: 122–43.

Knight, Bernie. 2013. "Combating Alcohol and Substance Abuse." *Arctic Warrior* 4, no. 2: A2. https://static.dvidshub.net/media/pubs/pdf_11446.pdf.

Koeszegi, Sabine, Eva Zedlacher, and Rene Hudribusch. 2014. "The War Against the Female Soldier? The Effects of Masculine Culture on Workplace Aggression." *Armed Forces & Society* 40, no. 2: 226–51.

Kors, Joshua. 2018. "Suffering from a 'Personality Disorder': How My Promising Military Career Was Cut Short by a Dubious Diagnosis." *Huffington Post*, January 6. https://www.huffpost.com/entry/suffering-from-a-personality-disorder-how-my-promising_b_5a5108bbe4b0cd114bdb33b5.

Lancaster, John. 1992. "Navy Harassment Probe Stymied." *Washington Post*, May 1. https://www.washingtonpost.com/archive/politics/1992/05/01/navy-harassment-probe-stymied/b7dbd49a-f3ab-4de5-b7e3-51da64c5dedb/.

Letherby, Gayle. 2003. *Feminist Research in Theory and Practice*. Philadelphia: Open University Press.

Lofland, John, David A. Snow, Leon Anderson, and Lyn H. Lofland. 2006. *Analyzing Social Settings: A Guide to Qualitative Observation and Analysis*. Australia: Thomson Wadsworth.

Lopez, Vera. 2017. *Complicated Lives: Girls, Parents, Drugs, and Juvenile Justice*. New Brunswick, Rutgers University Press.

Losey, Stephan. 2020. "'Be a Bro': How a Commander's Sexism Derailed this Pilot Training Class—and Brought Down AETC Leaders." *Air Force Times*, August 3. https://www.airforcetimes.com/news/your-air-force/2020/08/03/be-a-bro-how-a-commanders-sexism-derailed-this-pilot-training-class-and-brought-down-aetc-leaders/.

MacLeish, Kenneth. 2013. "Armor and Anesthesia: Exposure, Feeling, and the Soldier's Body." *Medical Anthropology Quarterly* 26, no. 1: 49–68.

Mackinnon, Catharine. 1979. *Sexual Harassment of Working Women*. New Haven, CT: Yale University Press.

Martin, Marilyn. 2002. *Saving Our Last Nerve: The Black Woman's Path to Mental Health*. Roscoe, IL: Hilton.

Martin, Patricia Yancey. 2001. "Mobilizing Masculinities: Women's Experiences of Men at Work." *Organization* 8, no. 4: 587–618.

Martin, Patricia Yancey. 2004. "Gender as Social Institution." *Social Forces* 82, no. 4: 1249–73.

Martin, Susan Ehrlich, and Nancy Jurik. 2007. *Doing Justice, Doing Gender: Women in Legal and Criminal Justice Occupations*, 2nd ed. Thousand Oaks, CA: Sage Publications.

McClain, Natalie, Kathryn Laughon, Richard Steeves, and Barbara Parker. 2007. "Balancing the Needs of the Scientist and the Subject in Trauma Research." *Western Journal of Nursing Research* 29, no. 1: 121–28.

McCoyd, Judith, and Corey Shdaimah. 2007. "Revisiting the Benefits Debate: Does Qualitative Social Work Research Produce Salubrious Effects?" *Social Work* 52, no. 4: 340–49.

McDaniels-Wilson, Cathy, and Joanne Belknap. 2008. "The Extensive Sexual Violation and Sexual Abuse Histories of Incarcerated Women." *Violence against Women* 14, no. 10: 1090–127.

McFarlane, Megan D. 2021. *Militarized Maternity: Experiencing Pregnancy in the U.S. Armed Forces*. Oakland: University of California Press.

McKinney, Kathleen. 1992. "Contrapower Sexual Harassment: The Effects of Student Sex and Type of Behavior on Faculty Perceptions." *Sex Roles* 27, no. 11–12: 627–43.

Messerschmidt, James W. 2018. *Hegemonic Masculinity: Formulation, Reformulation, and Amplification*. Lanham, MD: Rowman & Littlefield.

Miller, Jody, and Rod Brunson. 2000. "Gender Dynamics in Youth Gangs: A Comparison of Males' and Females' Accounts." *Justice Quarterly* 17, no. 3: 419–48.

Miller, Laura L. 1997. "Not Just Weapons of the Weak: Gender Harassment as a Form of Protest for Army Men." *Social Psychology Quarterly* 60, no. 1: 32–52.

Miller-Perrin, Cindy, Robin Perrin, and Claire Renzetti. 2018. *Violence and Maltreatment in Intimate Relationships*. Thousand Oaks, CA: Sage Publications.

Mitra Nishi. 2013. "Intimate Violence, Family, and Femininity: Women's NARRATIVES on their construction of Violence and Self." *Violence Against Women* 19, no. 10: 1282–301.

Moore, Brenda L. 1991. "African American Women in the U.S. Military." *Armed Forces & Society* 17, no. 3: 363–84.

Moore, Brenda L. 2002. "The Propensity of Junior-Enlisted Personnel to Remain in Today's Military." *Armed Forces and Society* 28, no. 2: 257–78.

Muraco, Anna. 2006. "Intentional Families: Fictive Kin Ties Between Cross-Gender, Different Sexual Orientation Friends." *Journal of Marriage and Family* 68, no. 5: 1313–25.

Navy JAG. 2022. "Administrative Reassignment of Alleged Victims & Accused." https://www.jag.navy.mil/legal_services/documents/Reassignment_Alleged_Victims_and_Accused.pdf.

Navy Personnel Command. 2020. "Chapter Two: Grooming Standards." https://dacowits.defense.gov/LinkClick.aspx?fileticket=Gm7Fsualdaw%3D&portalid=48.

Noaks, Lesley, and Emma Wincup. 2004. *Criminological Research: Understanding Qualitative Methods*. Thousand Oaks, CA: Sage.

O'Neill, William. 1998. "Sex Scandals in the Gender-Integrated Military." *Gender Issues* 16, no. 1–2: 64–85.

Payne, Elizabethe. 2010. "'Sluts: Heteronormative Policing in the Stories of Lesbian Youth." *Educational Studies* 46, no. 3: 317–36.

Pessin, Hayley, Michele Galietta, Christian Nelson, Robert Brescia, Barry Rosenfeld, and William Breitbart. 2008. "Burden and Benefit of Psychosocial Research at the End of Life." *Journal of Palliative Medicine* 11, no. 4: 627–32.

PBS.org. 2019. *Frontline: Party Favors*. https://www.pbs.org/wgbh/pages/frontline/shows/navy/tailhook/favors.html.

PBS.org. 2019. *She Rocked the Pentagon*. Produced by Karen M. Sughrue. PBS Retro Report. https://www.retroreport.org/video/the-legacy-of-tailhook/.

Pershing, Jana L. 2006. "Men and Women's Experiences with Hazing in a Male-Dominated Elite Military Institution." *Men and Masculinities* 8, no. 4: 470–92.

Powers, Rob. 2018. "US Military Housing, Barracks, and Housing Allowance: What the Recruiter Never Told You about Military Housing." *The Balance Careers*, February 5. https://www.thebalance.com/what-the-recruiter-never-told-you-3332705.

Prokos, Anastasia, and Irene Padavic. 2002. "'There Oughta Be a Law against Bitches': Masculinity Lessons in Police Academy Training." *Gender, Work and Organization* 9, no. 4: 439–59.

Pyke, Karen. 1996. "Class-Based Masculinities: The Interdependence of Gender, Class, and Interpersonal Power." *Gender & Society* 10, no. 5: 527–49.

Ray, Rashawn. 2020. "Bad Apples Come from Rotten Trees in Policing." *The Brookings Institute*, May 30. https://www.brookings.edu/articles/bad-apples-come-from-rot ten-trees-in-policing/.

Ray, Victor E. 2019. "A Theory of Racialized Organizations." *American Sociological Review* 84, no. 1: 26–53.

Reddy, Madhavi, Matthew Fleming, Nicolette Howells, Mandy Rabenhorst, R. Mitch Casselman, and Alan Rosenbaum. 2006. "Effect of method on participants and disclosure rates in research on sensitive topics." *Violence and Victims* 21, no. 4: 499–506.

Reskin, Barbara. 2000. "Getting It Right: Sex and Race Inequality in Work Organizations." *Annual Review of Sociology* 26: 707–9.

Ricks, Thomas. 2006. *Fiasco: The American Military Adventure in Iraq.* New York: Penguin Press.

Ridgeway, Cecilia L. 1997. "Interaction and the Conservation of Gender Inequality: Considering Employment." *American Sociological Review* 62, no. 2: 218–35.

Ridgeway, Cecelia, and Shelley Correll. 2004. "Motherhood as a Status Characteristic." *Journal of Social Issues* 60, no. 4: 683–700.

Ridgeway, Cecelia, and Shelley Correll. 2000. "Unpacking the Gender System: A Theoretical Perspective on Gender Beliefs and Social Relations." *Gender & Society* 18, no. 4: 510–31.

Risman, Barbara. 2004. "Gender as a Social Structure: Theory Wrestling with Activism." *Gender & Society* 18, no. 4: 429–450.

Rohall, David, Morten Ender, and Michael Matthews. 2006. "The Effects of Military Affiliations, Gender and the Political Ideology on Attitudes toward the Wars in Afghanistan and Iraq." *Armed Forces & Society* 33, no. 1: 59–77.

Rosen, Leora, and Lee Martin. 1997. "Sexual Harassment, Cohesion, and Combat Readiness in U.S. Army Support Units." *Armed Forces & Society* 24, no. 2: 221–44.

Rosenbaum Alan, Mandy Rabenhorst, Madhavi Reddy, Matthew Fleming, Nicolette Howells. 2006. "A comparison of methods for collecting self-report data on sensitive topics." *Violence and Victims* 21, no. 4: 461–71.

Rospenda, Kathleen, Judith Richman, and Stephanie Nawyn. 1998. "Doing Power: The Confluence of Gender, Race, and Class, in Contrapower Sexual Harassment." *Gender & Society* 12, no. 1: 40–60.

Rubin, Herbert J., and Irene S. Rubin. 2012. *Qualitative Interviewing: The Art of Hearing Data*, 3rd ed. Thousand Oaks, CA: Sage Publications.

Russell, Diana. 1984. *Sexual Exploitation: Rape, Child Sexual Abuse, and Workplace Harassment.* Beverly Hills: CA, Sage Publications.

Sadler, Anne G., Brenda M. Booth, Brian L. Cook, and Bradley N. Doebbeling. 2003. "Factors Associated with Women's Risk of Rape in the Military Environment." *American Journal of Industrial Medicine* 43, no. 3: 262–73.

Sasson-Levy, Orna. 2003. "Military, Masculinity and Citizenship: Tensions and Contradictions in the Experience of Blue-Collar Soldiers' Identities." *Global Studies in Culture and Power* 10, no. 3: 319–45.

Sasson-Levy, Orna. 2011. "The Military in a Globalized Environment: Perpetuating an 'Extremely Gendered' Organization." In *Handbook of Gender, Work and Organization*, edited by Emma Jeanes, David Knights, and Patricia Yancey Martin. Malden, 391–411. MA: Wiley-Blackwell Publishing.

Scheirs, Veerle, and An Nuytiens. 2013. "Ethnography and Emotions: The Myth of the Cold and Objective Scientist." In *The Pains of Doing Criminological Research*, edited by Kristel Beyens, Jenneke Christiaens, Bart Claes, Steven De Ridder, Hanne Tournel, and Hilde Tubex, 141–60. Brussels: VUB Press.

Schippers, Mimi. 2007. "Recovering the Feminine Others: Masculinity, Femininity, and Gender Hegemony." *Theory and Society* 36, no. 1: 85–102.

Schogol, Jeff. 2022. " 'Sidewalk,' 'Terminally Stupid,' and 'Meatloaf'—How Military Pilots Get Their Call Signs." *Task and Purpose*, January 21. https://taskandpurpose.com/news/military-pilots-call-signs/.

Schrock, Douglas, and Michael Schwalbe. 2009. "Men, Masculinity, and Manhood Acts." *Annual Review of Sociology* 35, no. 1: 277–95.

Schwerdtfeger, Kami L. 2009. "The Appraisal of Quantitative and Qualitative Trauma-Focused Research Procedures among Pregnant Participants." *Journal of Empirical Research on Human Research Ethics* 4, no. 4: 39–51.

Schwerdtfeger, Kami, and Briana Goff. 2008. "The Effects of Trauma-Focused Research on Pregnant Female Participants." *Journal of Empirical Research on Human Research Ethics* 3, no. 1: 59–67.

Seck, Hope. 2018. "The Navy Is Changing Its Pilot Call Sign Approval Process after African-American Aviators Complained of Racist Designations." *Task and Purpose*, May 21. https://taskandpurpose.com/news/navy-racist-call-sign-protocol.

Sedlak, Andrea, Jane Mettenburg, Monica Basena, Ian Petta, Karla McPherson, Angela Greene, and Spencer Li. 2010. *Fourth National Incidence Study of Child Abuse and Neglect (NIS–4): Report to Congress*. Washington, DC: U.S. Department of Health and Human Services, Administration for Children and Families.

Shanker, Thom. 2008. " 'Don't Ask, Don't Tell' Hits Women Much More." *The New York Times*, 23 June. https://www.nytimes.com/2008/06/23/washington/23pentagon.html

Sharp, Marie-Louise, Nicola Fear, Roberto Rona, Simon Wessely, Neil Greenberg, Norman Jones, and Laura Goodwin. 2015. "Stigma as a Barrier to Seeking Health Care among Military Personnel with Mental Health Problems." *Epidemiologic Review* 37, no. 1: 144–62.

Shields, Duncan, David Kuhl, and Marvin Westwood. 2017. "Abject Masculinity and the Military: Articulating a Fulcrum of Struggle and Change." *Psychology of Men & Masculinity* 18, no. 3: 215–25.

Shields, Chris, Michele Kavanagh, and Kate Russo. 2017. "A Qualitative Systematic Review of the Bereavement Process Following Suicide." *OMEGA Journal of Death and Dying* 74, no. 4: 426–54.

Steidl, Christina R., and Aislinn R. Brookshire. 2018. "'Just One of the Guys until Shower Time': How Symbolic Embodiment Threatens Women's Inclusion in the US Military." *Gender, Work, and Organization* 25, no. 5: 1–18.

Stets, Jan. 2005. "Examining Emotions in Identity Theory." *Social Psychology Quarterly* 68, no. 1: 39–56.

Stets, Jan, and Peter Burke. 2005. "Identity Verification, Control, and Aggression in Marriage." *Social Psychology Quarterly* 68, no. 2: 160–78.

Stickles, Brendan. 2018. "How the U.S. Military Became the Exception to America's Wage Stagnation Problem." Brookings Institute, November 29. https://www.brooki ngs.edu/blog/order-from-chaos/2018/11/29/how-the-u-s-military-became-the-ex-ception-to-americas-wage-stagnation-problem/

Strauss, Anselm, and Juliet Corbin. 1998. *Basics of Qualitative Research: Techniques and Procedures for Developing Grounded Theory*. Thousand Oaks, CA: Sage.

Stryker, Sheldon. 1980. *Symbolic Interactionism: A Social Structural Version*. Palo Alto, CA: Benjamin/Cummings.

Stryker, Sheldon, and Peter Burke. 2000. "The Past, Present and Future of an Identity Theory." *Social Psychology Quarterly* 63, no. 4: 284–97.

Taber, Nancy. 2011. "'You Better Not Get Pregnant while You're Here': Tensions between Masculinities and Femininities in Military Communities of Practice." *International Journal of Lifelong Education* 30, no. 3: 331–48.

Tester, Griff. 2008. "An Intersectional Analysis of Sexual Harassment in Housing." *Gender & Society* 22, no. 3: 349–66.

Texeira, Mary. 2002. "'Who Protects and Serves Me?': A Case Study of Sexual Harassment of African American Women in One U.S. Law Enforcement Agency." *Gender & Society* 16, no. 4: 524–45.

Thompson, Mark. 2010. "Navy Man Claims Aviator Call Signs Get Too Personal." *Time*, August 17. https://content.time.com/time/nation/article/0,8599,2011189,00.html.

Tillman, Shaquita, Thema Bryant-Davis, Kimberly Smith, and Alison Marks. 2010. "Shattering Silence: Exploring Barriers to Disclosure for African American Sexual Assault Survivors." *Trauma, Violence, & Abuse* 11, no. 2: 59–70.

Tjaden, Patricia, and Nancy Thoennes. 2000. "Full Report of the Prevalence, Incidence, and Consequences of Intimate Partner Violence against Women: Findings from the National Violence Against Women Survey." National Institute of Justice, NCJ 183781. https://nij.ojp.gov/library/publications/full-report-prevalence-incidence-and-conse quences-violence-against-women.

Tozer, Jessica. 2011. "Know the Facts—The Military Protective Order." *DoD Live*. http:// www.dodlive.mil/index.php/2011/10/know-the-facts-themilitary-protective-order/.

Turchik, Jessica A., and Susan M. Wilson. 2010. "Sexual Assault in the U.S. Military: A Review of the Literature and Recommendations for the Future." *Aggression and Violent Behavior* 15, no. 4: 267–77.

Tzeng, Wen-Chii, Pi-Yu Su, Hsien-Hsien Chiang, Ping-Yin Kuan, and Jia-Fu Lee. 2010. "The Invisible Family: A Qualitative Study of Suicide Survivors in Taiwan." *Western Journal of Nursing Research* 32, no. 2: 185–98.

Ullman, Sarah. 2010. *Talking about Sexual Assault: Society's Response to Survivors*. Washington D.C.: American Psychological Association.

Uniform Code of Military Justice. 2018. "Article 34." https://www.sapr.mil/public/docs/ ucmj/UCMJ_Article134_General_Article.pdf.

U.S. Marine Corps. 2012. "USMC Fitness Report." https://dmna.ny.gov/forms/naval/NAVMC_10835__EF__5334.pdf.

U.S. Marine Corps. 2018. "Marine Corps Uniform Regulations." https://www.marines.mil/portals/1/Publications/MCO%201020.34H%20v2.pdf?ver=2018-06-26-094038-137.

U.S. Marine Corps. 2020. "Battalion Order 1601.2D." Headquarters Battalion Training and Education Command. https://www.tecom.marines.mil/Portals/90/HQBN/Directives/Unaccompanied%20Housing%20Duty%20NonCommissioned%20Officer%20And%20Assistant%20Duty%20NonCommissioned%20Officer%20Instructions.pdf.

U.S. Marine Corps. 2022a. "Marine Corps History 1st Battalion 6th Marines." https://www.6thmarines.marines.mil/Units/1st-Battalion/History/.

U.S. Marine Corps. 2022b. "Who Are the Marines?" https://www.marines.com/about-the-marine-corps/who-are-the-marines.html.

Verweij, Desiree. 2007. "Comrades or Friends? On Friendship in the Armed Forces." *Journal of Military Ethics* 6, no. 4: 280–91.

Vogt, Dawne, Tamara Bruce, Amy Street, and Jane Stafford. 2007. "Attitudes toward Women and Tolerance for Sexual Harassment among Reservists." *Violence against Women* 13, no. 9: 879–900.

Weber, Max. 1947. *The Theory of Social and Economic Organizations.* London: Collier Macmillan.

Weiss, Karen G. 2009. "'Boys Will Be Boys' and Other Gendered Accounts: An Exploration of Victims Excuses and Justifications for Unwanted Sexual Contact and Coercion." *Violence against Women* 15: 810–34.

Welsh, Sandy. 1999. "Gender and Sexual Harassment." *Annual Review of Sociology* 25: 169–90.

Whitley, Leila, and Tiffany Page. 2015. "Sexism at the Centre: Locating the Problem of Sexual Harassment." *New Formations* 86: 34–53.

Winslow, Donna, and Jason Dunn. 2002. "Women in the Canadian Forces: Between Legal and Social Integration." *Current Sociology* 50, no. 5: 641–67.

Woodward, Rachel, and K. Neil Jenkings. 2011. "Military Identities in the Situated Accounts of British Military Personnel." *Sociology* 45, no. 2: 252–68.

Woodward, Rachel, and Patricia Winter. 2004. "Discourses of Gender in the Contemporary British Army." *Armed Forces and Society* 30, no. 2: 279–301.

Wounded Warrior Project. 2022. "Who We Are." https://www.woundedwarriorproject.org/mission.

Zussman, Robert. 2004. "People in Places." *Qualitative Sociology* 27, no. 4: 351–63.

For the benefit of digital users, indexed terms that span two pages (e.g., 52–53) may, on occasion, appear on only one of those pages.

Note: Page numbers followed by t indicate tables.

downplaying, 83–84, 158–63, 170 (*see also* cases: Angela)
  excusing, 83–84, 159
harassment experiences, types of, 199*t*
hardship duty, 23, 174, 193–94
  defined, 23
  use of the term, 174
hegemonic masculinity, 16–18, 54, 56
  defined, 16
  emphasized femininity and, 16–17, 19–20, 42–43
  "slut" discourse and, 40–41, 42–43
heterosexuality, 42, 55, 103–4
  displays of, 39–40, 42, 46–47
  and elevated sexual harassment and assault, 35–40, 55–56, 176–77
  femininity and, 35, 40–41, 176–77 (*see also* femininity anchor(s))
heterosexual privilege, 17–18, 55, 176–77
heterosexual relationships, 35–36, 39–40, 41, 54–56, 176–77
hierarchy, 12–13, 56, 63–64, 79–80. *See also specific topics*
  of femininities, 16–17, 25, 51–52
  gendered, 16, 26–27, 30–31, 161
  of masculinities, 167–68
  race, power, and, 51–52, 91–93
hierarchy organizations and bureaucratic harassment, 87–88, 181–82
high year tenure, 210n.8
Hirsch, Jennifer, 62–63
homophobia, 58–59, 124
homosexuality. *See* Don't Ask, Don't Tell Repeal Act of 2010
"honorary man" status, 31, 55–56, 161, 166, 167. *See also* "one of the guys"
  and harassment, 158, 160, 161, 167–68, 170, 173, 179–80
  warrior masculinity and, 167–68, 173, 179–80
hyper-masculine culture, 26–27, 150–51, 158, 159, 177. *See also* masculine culture
  femininity and, 18–19, 35, 40
  gendered space and, 177–78
  and harassment, 30, 40, 43

  policy and, 186, 190
  "slut label" and, 43
hyper-masculine jokes, 59–60
hyper-sexual imagery, 61, 190. *See also* pornography
hyper-sexualization of Latina women, 47
hyper-sexual jokes, 59–60
hyper-visibility of servicewomen, 46–47, 69

identity work, masculine
  men's, 16
  women's, 16, 31, 54–55, 167–68, 175–76
Indigenous women, 93, 156
insider status, 145, 204–5. *See also* outsider status
  deployment and, 22, 52, 170
  gender and, 22, 23, 30–31, 54, 125, 161, 188–89
  sexual harassment and, 168–69, 170
internal enemies
  fear of, 192–93
  women who report harassment seen as, 95–96

jokes, 148–49
  about women Marines (WMs), 44, 48
  hyper-sexual and hyper-masculine, 59–60

Khan, Shamus, 62–63
kissing without consent, 3, 38
Knight, Bernie, 120

language. *See* masculine terminology; military abbreviations
Latina women
  harassment of, 47, 50, 90, 91–93, 156
  hyper-sexualization of, 47
lesbian, gay, and bisexual (LGB), 196*t*, *See also* Don't Ask, Don't Tell Repeal Act of 2010
lesbian women, 39–40, 130, 196*t*
Lioness Program, 163–64, 166. *See also* Female Engagement Teams

living in close quarters and sexual
    harassment, 72–73
loyalty, 132. *See also* "no soldier left
    behind"; trust

makeup, wearing, 32–33, 34, 156–57
male privilege, 16, 83–84, 151–52, 184–85.
    See also masculinity: privileging
Marine Corps, 57–58, 60. *See also*
    brotherhood; Officer Candidate
    School; trust; *specific topics*
  The Basic School (TBS), 24–28
  boot camp, 29–30, 118, 130–31, 139
  clothing in, 12–13, 99–100, 140
  "crucible" (exercise), 118–19
  as "Devil Dogs," 95–96
  "every Marine is a rifleman," 60–61, 150–51
  gender-neutral language, 185
  jokes about female Marines, 44
  masculinity and, 60–61, 185
  "No Marine gets left behind unless
      you're a female," 139, 147–48 (*see also*
      "no soldier left behind")
  "problem Marines," 101–2
Marine Corps Commissioning Program
    (MCP), 44–45
Marine on duty, 140–41
Marines, women, 18–19, 24–25, 26–27, 44,
    60–63, 168–71, 187, 196*t*, *See also*
    work, personal, and social spaces;
    specific topics
  jokes about, 44, 48
  men's attitudes toward, 30, 45 (*see also*
      brotherhood)
  pregnant, 48–50, 52–53
marriage, 40
  and elevated harassment, 35, 39–40,
      103–4
  to servicemen, 41, 43–44, 103–5, 155–56
masculine appearance and downplaying
    femininity markers, 32–33, 158
masculine culture, 107–8, 157. *See also*
    hyper-masculine culture
masculine-defined work environments,
    11–12

masculine identity work. *See* identity work
masculine space. *See also* men's
    domination and control of space
  challenging the, 78–83
masculine terminology, 60–61, 185. *See
    also* military abbreviations
masculine warrior, 18–19, 32. *See also*
    warrior masculinity
masculinity. *See also* hierarchy: of
    masculinities; "honorary man"
    status
  privileging, 16, 104–5 (*see also* male
      privilege)
  and sexual harassment, 55–56, 160,
      162–63, 167–68, 180
masculinity insurance, 167–68, 173, 180
  victim identity and, 167–68, 171–72,
      179–80
maternity uniforms, 54
Mattis, James, 111, 150–51
medical discharge, 32, 82
medical problems resulting from sexual
    assault, 80–81, 82, *See also* cases:
    Marie
medical separation, 107–8
men's domination and control of space,
    60–63, 74–78, 83–84, 136, 177–78.
    See also gendered space
  challenging the masculine space, 78–83
  and sexual harassment, 18–19, 69,
      72–73, 79–80, 83–84, 136, 157, 172–73,
      177–78
mental health. *See* personality disorder;
    suicide
#MeToo, 11–12
military. *See also specific topics*
  impact on civilian world, 108
  nature of the, 13–15, 150–51
  reasons for joining the, 116, 174–75
military abbreviations, corruption of, 44,
    208n.8
military-as-family narrative, 127, 136–37,
    145–46, 178, 187–88
  brotherhood and, 116–17, 119–20, 123–
      24, 136–37, 138, 141, 145–46